Bride's
Honeymoon
Travel
Guide

Also by the Editors of *Bride's* Magazine

Bride's Book of Etiquette
Bride's Shortcuts and Strategies for a Beautiful Wedding

Bride's Honeymoon Travel Guide

by the Editors of *Bride's* Magazine

with

Sally Kilbridge

A Perigee Book

Perigee Books
are published by
The Putnam Publishing Group
200 Madison Avenue
New York, NY 10016

Copyright © 1988 by Condé Nast Publications, Inc.
All rights reserved. This book, or parts thereof,
may not be reproduced in any form without permission.
Published simultaneously in Canada

Library of Congress Cataloging-in-Publication Data

Bride's honeymoon travel guide / by the editors of Bride's magazine
with Sally Kilbridge.

    p. cm.
  ISBN 0-399-51457-0
  1. Travel. 2. Honeymoon.   I. Kilbridge, Sally.   II. Bride's
(Condé Nast Publications, inc.)   III. Title: Honeymoon travel guide.
G151.B75   1988   87-29638 CIP
910'.2'02—dc19

BOOK DESIGN BY ARLENE GOLDBERG

Printed in the United States of America
    2   3   4   5   6   7   8   9   10

Acknowledgments

The travel editors and writers of *Bride's* magazine, who comb the planet looking for romance, have some of the happiest jobs in the world. On behalf of *Bride's,* I would like to thank Susan Farewell and Cynthia Penney for their contributions, and Joshua David, a talented young travel writer whose work on this book has been unflaggingly enthusiastic.

Contents

Introduction

When you're in love, any place in the world can be romantic. Your backyard. A shopping mall. Poughkeepsie.

But when you're in love and you happen to be sipping on a piña colada, staring hard at a purple Pacific sunset, and listening to the tradewinds rustle through the palms, romance takes on a whole new dimension.

Even if it's just a business trip or a long drive in the country, traveling with someone you love is wonderful. You feel close (after all, it *is* just the two of you) and excited, seeing new things together. But a honeymoon should be more than just wonderful. It should be sexy and sensual. It should make you feel extra, extra special. It should be the most beautiful trip of your lives.

Planning something that major while you're also working on a wedding (or just plain working) may sound like a chore. This book makes it easy. Part One gives you the facts you need on everything from packing for a week in the Caribbean sun to deciphering the fine print on a hotel brochure. You'll find a quiz you can take together to uncover your travel personalities. You'll find packing lists and driving tips and the lowdown on what a travel agent can do for you. You'll find the inside scoop on package plans (they sound great, but are they your kind of travel?) and on getting married in foreign lands. Even if you've never signed a rental-car agreement, never made a hotel reservation, Part One will turn you into world-class honeymooners.

Part Two is full of places meant for lovers. Lots of them are classic honeymoon havens, islands and beaches and cities that newlywed couples especially love. Others may not be major dots on the honeymoon map yet, but are so impossibly romantic we know they'll send you rushing into each other's arms. Even for non-honeymooners, they're ideal settings for being in love.

We all wish you a marvelous wedding and the most beautiful honeymoon ever.

Sally Kilbridge
Travel Editor
Bride's Magazine

Part One
PLANNING YOUR HONEYMOON

1
A WORLD FULL OF ROMANCE

You don't have to be a globe-trotter to know that the world is filled with honeymoon possibilities. They can all sound wonderful—a sun-bleached Caribbean beach, the canals of Venice, a resort in Colorado's Rocky Mountains. With so many places and so little time, picking the ideal spot could appear daunting. But take it step by step, and it becomes fun—and easy.

In some ways, planning a honeymoon is just like planning any other trip. The additional, all-important consideration is romance. A honeymoon wouldn't be a honeymoon without it. For lots of couples, nothing could be more romantic than basking on a balmy beach with a cool rum punch. For others, Europe holds the monopoly on romance. The grand resort hotel that seems quintessentially romantic to one couple might appear too formal to another. The little bed & breakfast that seems the epitome of romance to some newlyweds could seem too rustic for others. So before starting your planning, determine what each of you thinks is romantic. The bargain ticket to that bustling city is really no bargain if you want an away-from-it-all experience. The tempting package deal to that tropical island is no deal if Europe's really what you want.

Perhaps you've gotten so caught up in wedding preparations that you can only think of the practical considerations—"How much will it cost, how will we get there, will we be able to find any familiar-looking food to eat?" Turn off the practical side of your brain for a moment. Your honeymoon should be the trip of your dreams. So start with your dreams. Then figure out how to make them come true.

DEFINING YOUR DREAMS ℘

If you've ever daydreamed about running off with a lover to an impossibly romantic setting, now's the time to call those images back to the front of your mind. Put reality aside and dive head first into fantasy. Perhaps a movie you saw recently had you in the clouds for weeks afterward. Maybe an eloquent passage in a book made you forget all about the story and left you wishing you were in that exact café drinking that very same bottle of red wine. Let your mind run free, and imagine yourself anywhere in the world. Do you keep seeing a silky-sand beach backed by swaying palms? Maybe an ancient pyramid dominates the scene. Or an open market, the air sweet with spice. When the background is in place, try to picture what you're doing there. Are you lazing in a hammock or rafting down a roaring river? Are you dining in elegant restaurants or picnicking in a flower-filled meadow? And determine whether it's fancy or just plain fun. (Are you wearing designer clothes or practically no clothes at all?) These musings are the seeds of your dream honeymoon. With some planning and imagination, they can become reality.

TWO DREAMS MEET ℘

You are two people, so it's only natural that you might have different ideas about what would make the ideal honeymoon. And it's better to know sooner than later what your other half actually wants. That Hawaiian beach is only romantic if both of you think it's romantic. Springtime in Paris might just as well be winter in Pittsburgh if one of you had your heart set on a mountain view. So set aside some time to sit down and hash it out. Ramble a bit, and don't be afraid to throw out new ideas; what seems silly to begin with might just turn out to be the ideal wedding trip for both of you. You might flip through an atlas or travel magazines and tell each other what seems appealing. Listen to each other. This is not an argument to be won or lost, but a decision-making process that should make both of you happy. If one of you wants to lie around on the beach, for example, and the other wants big-city thrills, places like Waikiki, Rio de Janeiro, and Miami Beach might fulfill both of your dreams. If one of you has been thinking cruises, and the other pining for adventure, maybe the answer is to charter a boat of your own for a few days. There's always a beautiful answer.

ASKING AROUND ℘

Everyone likes to chip in their two cents about both weddings and honeymoons, so play it for what it's worth. Ask people whose opinions you value where they honeymooned and what they liked (and didn't like) about their choice. Even if you end up sitting through Aunt Nancy's three-hour slide show, you'll come out with a better idea of what you want (and don't want) for your honeymoon. Maybe Aunt Nancy has a wonderful idea that you haven't thought of.

HITTING THE BOOKS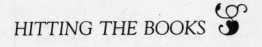

The world remains vast, but it's no longer uncharted. You can find a wide variety of books and magazines devoted to travel. Use them to check up on a fantasy destination (to make sure that it matches your vision) or as a source for new ideas. Magazines will present a wide variety of possibilities, emphasizing how it actually feels to visit certain places. Guidebooks are best for getting the nitty-gritty (how to get there, where to stay, how much it will cost). And the home-video boom has made a third resource available for prospective honeymooners: the travel video. Ask at your local video emporium for travelogue videotapes, which are just starting to become available for a larger number of destinations.

A Quiz to Take Together

The choices seem infinite: Europe, the Caribbean, Mexico . . . the list goes on and on. And you keep changing your mind, first sifting through brochures for Greece, then reading everything there is to read about Guadeloupe. Which is the right spot for your dream honeymoon? If the vision is still blurry, focus in on your day-to-day preferences to better define the image.

1. It's a gorgeous day; you both want to get out and enjoy it. You plan:
   a. an afternoon of tennis.
   b. a hike in the woods.
   c. a trip to the amusement park.

2. It's your first anniversary. You choose to celebrate it with:
   a. a candlelit dinner for two.
   b. a big party, inviting co-workers, family, and lots of friends.
   c. a casual get-together with just your best friends.

3. You're looking for your dream home. You tell the real estate agent that you're most interested in:

a. a neat home in an established residential area, with a bustling town and sports-filled country club nearby.

b. a downtown apartment, with shopping, restaurants, health clubs, and nightlife within walking distance.

c. a handyman's special, oozing with charm in an emerging neighborhood.

4. You're in the market for a car, and money's no object. You buy a:
a. Cadillac.
b. Jeep Cherokee.
c. BMW.

5. You decide to take an adult education class together. You enroll in:
a. Art History of the Renaissance.
b. Photographing Flowers.
c. Beating the Odds: How to Win Big at the Casino.

6. There are three movies left at the video rental shop. You go home with:
a. *A Room with a View.*
b. *Crocodile Dundee.*
c. *Baby Boom.*

7. If you could trade places with one of the three following couples, you'd choose to be:
a. Jane Fonda and Tom Hayden.
b. Mick Jagger and Jerry Hall.
c. Mia Farrow and Woody Allen.

8. On a rainy afternoon, you'd probably:
a. go bowling.
b. go to the art museum.
c. curl up with a book by the fire.

9. You're at a boisterous party with people from all walks of life, but you don't know anyone. You probably:
a. go home and play Scrabble.

b. stand back and immerse yourself in people-watching, then hang out in the kitchen and get to know one or two people fairly well.
c. join the group of revelers who are first on the dance floor.

10. Your idea of dressing up is putting on:
a. a tux or evening gown.
b. an elegant dress or suit.
c. a clean pair of jeans.

Scoring:
Circle the numbers that correspond to your answers. Then tally up your score.

1. a. 2	2. a. 1	3. a. 2	4. a. 3	5. a. 2
b. 1	b. 3	b. 3	b. 1	b. 1
c. 3	c. 2	c. 1	c. 2	c. 3
6. a. 1	7. a. 2	8. a. 3	9. a. 1	10. a. 3
b. 3	b. 3	b. 1	b. 2	b. 2
c. 2	c. 1	c. 2	c. 3	c. 1

Quizzes don't work for everybody, but your score should reveal something about the kind of place that's right for your honeymoon. Below, you'll find an abbreviated listing of the types of destinations you should consider. If your score is right on the border between two categories, either group would probably suit you equally well.

If you scored between 10 and 16, you're probably quiet, down-to-earth people, preferring simple pleasures like solitude and natural beauty to man-made glitter and excitement. There are hundreds of honeymoon options open to you, but there's a good chance that you'd be happy at the following places: the Caribbean's British Virgin Islands, Cayman Islands, Nevis, St. Lucia, U.S. Virgin Islands; the Bahama Family Islands; Mexico's Cozumel or Los Cabos; Hawaii's Kauai, Big Island (Hawaii), or Molokai; French Polynesia's Huahiné; Canada's Nova Scotia or Rocky Mountains; European rural areas like France's Provence, Britain's Cotswolds, or the Italian Riviera, or someplace in the U.S. like coastal Maine, Cape Cod, Block Island, the Rocky Mountains, or the Oregon coast.

If you scored between 17 and 23, you'd probably like a bit of everything on your honeymoon—natural beauty, top-notch sporting facilities, historically minded sight-seeing, and fine dining. A comfortable resort with a good sports setup would work well for you, and you'd probably be happy at one of the following areas: the Caribbean's Antigua, Barbados, Guadeloupe, Jamaica, Martinique, or St. Martin/St. Maarten; Mexico's Ixtapa or Manzanillo; Hawaii's Maui; French Polynesia's Bora Bora; pretty European towns and their surrounding countryside, or playful resort areas in the U.S. like the Florida Keys, Georgia's Golden Isles, or Carmel or Monterey in California.

If you scored between 24 and 30, you're the type of couple that loves parties, action, and excitement. Sure you want a beautiful location, but you've got to have something to *do* there. You'd probably be happy in one of the following places: the Caribbean's Aruba, Puerto Rico, St. Thomas, or Trinidad; the Bahamas' New Providence or Grand Bahama; Mexico's Acapulco, Cancún, or Puerto Vallarta; Hawaii's Oahu; Canada's Vancouver; European hubs like Paris, London, or Rome; or happening spots in the U.S. like New York City, Florida's Gold Coast, or San Francisco.

HONEYMOON HISTORY

The honeymoon tradition evolved from age-old beliefs about the moon and the power it possessed. The moon had connotations of impermanence, reminding couples that within a month—as the phases of the moon changed—things could alter and diminish. Weddings would be unlucky if they occurred during the waning of the moon.

The *honey* part of *honeymoon* refers to the drink of fermented honey called mead, or metheglin. Early Germanic tribesmen, who captured their brides from neighboring villages, enjoyed the intoxicating effects of this brew. Consumed by the bride and groom for thirty days of the moon's cycle, it had the effect of keeping the world at bay for the young couple during the month of changes. Mead or no mead, a period of seclusion following the wedding—to hide from the fickle moon and to strengthen the husband-wife bond—became a tradition which is the basis of the modern-day honeymoon.

The ancients were also wary of evil spirits, and they went to great lengths to protect the pure bride from their influence. Moroccan bridegrooms placed a dagger between the sheets of the marriage bed to ward off evil spirits, and Hungarians danced nine times around the newlyweds' house to keep spirits at bay. The traditional honeymoon practice of carrying the bride over the threshold has its origins here: by being lifted through the doorway, the bride avoided tracking evil spirits in on the soles of her feet.

A number of rituals developed around the wedding-night consummation.

Medieval wedding guests unabashedly accompanied newlyweds into their bedchamber and loosened the knots of the bridal garments, symbolically making the loss of virginity easier. And the marriage bed became the focus of various ceremonial precautions against the dangers that lurked (evil spirits, infertility, or the possibility that the bride might not be a virgin). Beds were hung with red paper by the Chinese, dressed in red satin sheets by the Greeks and Romans, decorated with chili peppers by Peruvians, and graced with a baguette tucked in the sheets by the French.

In the nineteenth century, going away for a few days of seclusion expanded into the "bridal tour," and soon the honeymoon as post-wedding travel became popular. Wealthy newlyweds elaborated, turning the honeymoon into a glamorous wedding tour, as lavish as a six-month cruise or travels throughout Europe. At the very least, well-to-do couples spent several days at a fine hotel in the nearest big city.

Over the years, "in" honeymoon spots became popular. In the thirties newlyweds boarded Pullman sleepers bound for Niagara Falls. Or they lashed their bags to the car and headed for Atlantic City, whose boardwalk lights and hurly-burly beckoned honeymooners like Mary Pickford and George Jessel. With the advent of luxury liners like the *Queen Mary*, wealthier couples set sail for extended tours of Europe. And even before F. Scott and Zelda Fitzgerald had their infamous champagne bath during their Biltmore Hotel honeymoon, New York was a place where honeymooners could find constant excitement. The Plaza, the Waldorf-Astoria, the St. Regis, and other fine hotels gave honeymooners—royalty and commoners alike—the red carpet treatment.

In the forties, honeymooners cruised to Bermuda via the Furness Withy line and stayed at the Princess, one of the old Bermudiana hotels. Hawaii-bound travelers sailed on the Matson Line for the Royal Hawaiian Hotel. Grand hotels in the U.S., built in lovely settings or near therapeutic spas, were places where every need could be attended to. Honeymooners stayed at the Cloister (the "Shangri-la of the South"), in Sea Island, Georgia; the Homestead, in Hot Springs, Virginia; and the Greenbrier, in White Sulphur Springs, West Virginia. In the Catskills, big resorts such as Grossinger's or the Concord rivaled each other with spectacular feasts, shows, and sporting events. And in the Poconos, now the extravagant "honeymoon capital of the world," things began quite simply with the opening of Rudolph von Hoevenberg's Farm on the Hill in 1945. Couples applied for the privilege of "practicing for life ahead" by making beds, keeping house, and waiting tables with other young marrieds.

During the fifties, tropical paradises, once open only in season (December to April), became available all year around. Honeymoon pairs headed south to Miami Beach or cruised to the Caribbean; Jamaica was popular first, then

Puerto Rico, and gradually other Caribbean islands. Las Vegas, just a hop away from Los Angeles, drew a host of entertainers—Elvis Presley, Judy Garland, Ann Miller, Mickey Rooney—for quick, easy weddings.

In the sixties, the West Coast beckoned. Palm Springs, where Clark Gable and Carole Lombard had honeymooned, became the genteel alternative to Las Vegas. Acapulco, the original Mexican resort, attracted bright Hollywood and political personalities (such as the John F. Kennedys) to its exotic beaches, paving the way for newer Mexican resorts like Ixtapa and Cancún.

Air travel, firmly established in the sixties, changed honeymoon travel completely. Even short trips to Europe, or to any place in the world, became reasonable choices, offering excitement, history, and a wealth of enchanting places to stay. And with today's competitively priced fares, package deals, and planes that go just about anywhere on earth, newlyweds find that with money and time, the whole world is their honeymoon oyster.

2
BUDGETING DAYS AND DOLLARS

Oh, no! You finally decided that you really wanted a monthlong cruise through the Greek islands. Now you see that you only can muster up ten days of vacation and $2,000. Reality rears its ugly head.

But take heart. There are ways to get more money and ways to stretch the money that you already have. There are ways to get more time, as well as ways to pare down a dream itinerary to a shorter but equally romantic journey. Be flexible. The trip you end up taking may not be exactly what you started with, but with some careful planning and imagination, it can encompass the same romantic elements of your dream.

TIME FRAMES

The length of your honeymoon will depend on a number of factors: where you want to go; how long you can realistically be away from work and home; and how much money you have to spend. Some couples take several weeks or months for their wedding trip, but most couples today opt for about eight days; it's usually not too hard to get a week off from work, and it keeps costs from running too high. But there is no set length for a honeymoon. A weekend wedding trip can be just as romantic as a monthlong voyage.

TIME STRETCHING

Sometimes outside events can seem to stop your dream honeymoon in its tracks. The boss who has said, "Of course you can take two weeks off," may think differently if he sees that there's an important meeting with a client during the same period. Or maybe signing papers on a new house throw your plans out of whack. Here are some suggestions that may help you still take that dream honeymoon, even if you can't manage a week right after the wedding.

The long weekend honeymoon. Sometimes less is more. As people find they can take less and less time away from high-pressured jobs and two-career households, the long weekend travel market has grown. You'll find that there are a large number of romantic, long weekend honeymoon options. Whether you choose a nearby country inn, an elegant suite in town, or a beachfront resort that's not too far from home, everyone welcomes newlyweds. Even if it's just for a few days.

The postponed honeymoon. Maybe you just can't bear to miss your little sister's graduation. Or that big conference is coming up and you *have* to be there. Consider an all-out splurge on your wedding night, postponing your longer honeymoon to a more convenient time. You'll have a chance to recover from all the wedding-day activity and embark on your dream trip with plenty of energy. And you'll have time to keep your honeymoon bank account growing. A variation: the pre-wedding honeymoon. Yes, people actually do it. If the idea of doing things out of order doesn't upset you, honeymooning before the wedding can often solve scheduling dilemmas. And you'll have the fun of being able to share your honeymoon pictures at your wedding.

The honeymoon as sabbatical. Perhaps one of you will be finishing school within a few months. Or maybe you're quitting your jobs and moving to a new town. If there's an open chunk of time a bit further down the line, you might want to consider putting the honeymoon off until then. With more time come more honeymoon possibilities. There's no such thing as a honeymoon that's too long.

The wedding away from home. This is a wedding-honeymoon combination. Planning a big, hometown wedding often means taking a week off just to finalize all the arrangements, with little time left for a honeymoon. So more and more couples have begun to marry at their honeymoon destination. This means a much simpler, smaller ceremony, but for some, that's just right.

Marrying Away From Home

There are all sorts of reasons for marrying away from home. Perhaps you want to avoid the hassle of a big church wedding. Or maybe you're trying to cut costs (combining your wedding and honeymoon can save literally thousands of dollars). Or it could be that you're marrying for the second time.

The three most important things to know: some countries will not allow foreign marriages; the rules for getting married will be different from those of your home town; and the application process may take a while. If overseas mail and phone calls are involved, delays increase. So allow at least six weeks (two months would be better) to plan a wedding away from home. Each country and state has different regulations, but if you follow these steps, your out-of-town wedding should be as simple as saying "I do."

☐ Contact the consulate or tourist board of the country you've chosen or the license bureau of the state where you'll be married. They will be able to tell you how to obtain a marriage license, what documents are required, and how long the whole process will take. Although rules vary, be prepared to provide at least one—a combination is more likely—of these items: proof of birth; proof of citizenship; written consent from parents or guardian if you're under 21; blood tests and medical records; letter from a priest, minister, or rabbi; and proof of divorce if you've been married before. With some mailing back and forth, some notarizing, and a waiting period, the road should be paved to the altar.

☐ Decide who to invite. If you marry in your honeymoon destination, it would be quite expensive, not to mention awkward, to have lots of guests. Maybe it should be just the two of you. Or you could just invite immediate family—the transport and hotel costs will still be less than an elaborate home wedding. But whomever you choose to invite, consider throwing a party when you get home so all of your friends can share in your joy.

☐ See who can help. When making hotel reservations, ask if there's someone on staff who can act as your agent—finding an officiant, locating a singer or musicians, and ordering flowers. Some resorts offer complete wedding packages; others will recommend a professional wedding planner nearby. Your travel agent can steer you to people who can help.

☐ Pick a simple, easy-to-pack wedding ensemble. When shopping for your outfits, keep your destination (and getting there) in mind. Long trains don't make much sense if you're getting married on a mountaintop; high necks and tight sleeves look out of place (and keep you sweating) in the tropical sun. Think about fabrics that travel well—cotton and organza are good bets. Your hotel's florist can help you with a bouquet. For grooms, simple suits and dinner jackets are always handsome.

☐ Among the exotic places that make it *very* simple for Americans to be married are Barbados, the British Virgin Islands, the Cayman Islands, and Jamaica (all in the Caribbean), Nassau (the Bahamas), Hawaii, and some parts of Mexico.

MONEY MATTERS

The honeymoon you ultimately take will depend on what you can afford. The average couple today spends about $3,000 for their honeymoon. But supremely romantic wedding trips can be arranged for less. And some couples may decide to spend more than that on the trip of a lifetime. Parents of the groom will sometimes offer to pay for the honeymoon. View this as a generous gesture on their part rather than a traditional obligation. If they do offer to pay for a honeymoon, be plentiful with your thanks, and make sure that they understand that you want to plan your own special trip even if they foot the bill.

DOLLAR STRETCHING

You've got your hearts set on two weeks in the Caribbean, but the hotel price alone would put you over budget. Or maybe a driving tour of France is tops on your list, but you hadn't figured on such high rental car rates. Don't despair. There are ways to achieve your honeymoon goals at a price you can afford. It may take some juggling; with these hints, honeymoon dollars will go further than you thought possible.

Get an early start. Put your honeymoon wheels in motion as soon as possible after setting your wedding date. Advance planning can often cut transportation costs. Advance-purchase airline tickets, for example, offer substantial savings over regular coach fare; buying cruise tickets several months in advance can often bring along a sizable discount. And the best of everything, from airline seats to hotel rooms to cruise cabins, is usually the first to go. So the earlier you make your reservations, the better chance you have of getting that ocean-view hotel room or the right flight at the right time on the right day. And you'll save yourself some money.

Research ways to save. As soon as you've narrowed the field to a few places, look into the on-location costs. Supplement the price guidelines you can find in guidebooks by writing to national tourist offices, state travel departments, and city convention and visitors bureaus (they'll send you lots of fact-packed booklets—free). And talk to the professionals who know about cutting travel costs: ask at airline tour desks about land packages you might be entitled to with your round-trip tickets; ask in tourist offices about any special programs they might sponsor; talk to travel agents about packages that combine room, meals, and other extras at a price that can often beat the standard room rate. In the course of this research, certain truths will surface.

* *Cities are more expensive than countryside. So if your hearts are set on France but Parisian hotel rates send your heads spinning, you might consider Alsace or Provence—still impossibly romantic, but more possible financially.*

* *Settling in one area and exploring it thoroughly is far less costly than hopscotching from point to point. The cost of transit is the single most expensive part of most trips. And even if you're nomads at heart, simplifying transportation will make for a smoother honeymoon all around.*

* *Traveling off-season can dramatically cut costs. Almost every destination has a more expensive season and a less expensive one: the luxurious Caribbean hotel room that costs $200 per day in February can cost half that from mid-April to mid-December; Europe in May or October is not only less expensive but less crowded than in July. In the so-called off-season, many hotels and resorts also offer bargain packages (including meals, sightseeing excursions, maybe even a rental car) that simply aren't available in prime tourist time.*

Weigh your options. If you only have a certain amount of money to spend, you should spend it on the things that are most important to you. The money left after subtracting the basics—major transportation, hotel, meals—from your honeymoon fund is yours to spend for such fun activities as sightseeing tours, sporting activities, and nightclub rounds, as well as on local miscellaneous expenses. So think it over. How much do you care about style? Would you rather spend five money-is-no-object days in a posh resort or two stretched-out weeks in a casual beachfront motel? Would you prefer the convenience of taking meals at your hotel, or would you rather forgo the somewhat costly meal plan to explore local (and quite possibly cheaper) local eateries? The variables are almost endless, but each one makes your trip exactly what you want it to be.

3
HONEYMOON HELPERS

What began as a dreamy vision has been researched and refined. You've discovered the dot on the map that seems to fit your honeymoon ideals. Whether you've opted for palm trees or mountains or a star-studded city, arranging all the details might be confusing. Every element of the journey offers up choices: airfares to compare, packages to consider, hotels to evaluate. But don't let the bounty of options overwhelm you. So many choices mean that somewhere out there waits an airfare, a hotel room, or a package plan that can help you realize your honeymoon goals.

YOUR TRAVEL AGENT

Your first big question: to use a travel agent or not. Since travel is their business, travel agents can simplify most honeymoon arrangements. If you've never planned a big trip before, their services can be invaluable. But there may be some types of honeymoon planning that are better to do on your own. What can a travel agent do for you? They should be able to reserve and, if you wish, prepay:

* Airline tickets
* Cruise tickets
* Accommodations
* Car rental
* Sightseeing tours
* Package deals (including honeymoon packages)

Travel agents can save you time and money. If you wanted to track down the cheapest airfare to Hawaii, you'd have to call every airline that flies there. By the time you finished, you'd have reams of paper listing flights, fares, and advance-purchase requirements (and you'd spend enough time on hold to know the Muzak version of "Raindrops Keep Falling on My Head" by heart). But you still might not know which plane to take.

Travel agents can call up flight information for any given destination on computers in seconds. And they can tell you what each advance-purchase fare will save you, as well as any restrictions or penalties those fares might carry. They will also be able to present you with a selection of packages that combine airfare, hotel—maybe even meals and a rental car—that are less expensive than purchasing the same items separately (see "Packages: Deal or No Deal," page 41).

The advice and services of a travel agent usually won't cost you a penny. Travel agents are paid commissions by hotels and airlines for the tickets and rooms that they sell, so the price of their expertise, the phone calls they make, and the time they save you doesn't come out of your honeymoon budget (except in the case of smaller, non-commission-paying hotels; these you must either book yourself or pay your agent a booking fee).

How do you find a trustworthy travel agent? Like members of any service profession, some travel agents are great, others are not so great. And since you're buying a product that you can't see until later, it's sometimes difficult to know what you're getting. Here are some things to consider when choosing a travel agent:

* *Your best bet is to get a personal referral. Ask a friend, family member, or an associate if they know of a good travel agent. Some better travel agents in larger cities will only see new customers by referral.*

* *Look for credentials and affiliations with travel agency organizations. Membership in organizations like ASTA (American Society of Travel Agents) can indicate a high level of professionalism. Your agent's name followed by C.T.C. on his business card indicates that he is a Certified Travel Counselor who has completed an extensive training program and has been in the business for at least five years.*

* *Ask your agent if he has recently been to the area you're considering for your honeymoon. Established travel agents have traveled through much of the world. One who's been there will give you much more helpful information. Does this hotel look like it does in the brochure? Is the two-day excursion to that historic site really worthwhile? An agent who has been there can help you decide.*

* *Let the travel agent you choose know what you want. Do some homework before you go to the agency. It will help your agent swiftly execute your plans. It will also prevent you from being sold a honeymoon you don't actually want. If you want*

the deserted island experience, speak up. If you want to be close to town, let your travel agent know.

* *If you don't feel comfortable with one travel agent, look for another. Nothing binds you to the first travel agent you meet with. Remember: this is the trip of your dreams. You're better off spending a few more hours picking the right agent than settling for inferior services.*

Some travel arrangements are better to set up independently. That adorable little bed & breakfast that your best friend stayed in probably doesn't pay travel agents a commission. Most likely, you'd be charged by the travel agent for booking it, or you might even be dissuaded from going there in favor of a larger, commission-paying hotel. The same goes for many driving tours. If you're planning a roundabout route through Italy, staying at intimate *pensiones* along the way, perhaps you should buy some books, comb over the maps, and write letters to (or phone) the places you'd like to stay. Of course, your travel agent would still be able to steer you to the best airfare and car rental deals.

MORE HONEYMOON HELPERS

Travel agents aren't the only source for travel information. As the travel industry becomes increasingly competitive, new and innovative services develop to help make honeymoons happy. A few that you might consult:

Tourist boards. Virtually any destination you choose will have a national, state, or local tourist board that can provide you with information. Look for these boards in travel guides or big-city phone books. They can send you fact-packed pamphlets about hotels, sightseeing excursions, and government-sponsored packages and promotions that could be just right for you.

Airline travel desks. Many airlines have associated travel services available for their passengers. They can tell you about special car rental rates, hotel prices, or complete packages that are offered in conjunction with your airfare purchase. When you call for reservations, simply ask for the airline's tour desk. See what they have to offer.

Bed & breakfast organizations. Staying in a bed & breakfast (a room plus breakfast in a private home specially set up to receive guests) has become increasingly popular; they can lower honeymoon costs and offer a smaller, more personal environment. With a little research, you'll find both national and local B&B organizations that can provide you with listings in the area of your choice. Since most B&B organizations are regional, you're best off looking for listings in B&B guidebooks. One national organization: **Bed & Breakfast Registry**, P.O. Box 8174, St. Paul, MN 55108-0174. (612) 646-4238.

Car rental agencies. In recent years, car rental concerns have also taken up the travel-planning business. Some larger American companies, like Avis and Hertz, that rent cars in Europe can offer computerized driving tours, with complete information on towns, sights, and hotels along the way. And many car rental agencies have links to hotel chains that could end up saving you money.

Whether you decide to put your honeymoon planning in the hands of a travel specialist or you choose to set it up yourself, it's wise to know as much as possible about your travel options. Acapulco or Ipanema, Hawaii or Hong Kong, every dream honeymoon can be put together in a number of ways. In the following two chapters, we'll outline the variables.

4
TRANSPORT FOR TWO

Choosing a mode of transportation to your honeymoon destination should be a simple decision. The destination itself usually makes the decision for you; you can hardly drive to Hawaii or take a train to the Caribbean. But even when you know that you want to fly, sail, drive, or take a train, finding the best fare for your honeymoon needs can become complex.

UP, UP, AND AWAY: TRAVEL BY AIR

Today's air-travel cliché is that three people in a row on the same plane may have paid dramatically different prices for identical seats. First-time trip planners will do best with an experienced travel agent as their guide through the airfare jungle. That $99 fare advertised in the paper may have all sorts of hidden loopholes. The plain facts of the plane fare game are that there are five primary fare classes on major commercial airlines today:

First class is the ultimate, and the most expensive, way to fly. First-class air travel means wide, comfy seats, multi-course meals, and plenty of personal pampering (champagne before takeoff, gift packs with toiletries, slippers, and lots of pillow fluffing). If you can comfortably afford to travel first class (not many people can), by all means do; there's no better way to get a honeymoon off to a flying start. Budget-conscious honeymooners will find that they could probably purchase an entire honeymoon (hotel, airfare, meals—the works) for the price of first-class air tickets.

Business class occupies the notch directly below first class, and offers many of the same pleasures, although seats tend to be a bit smaller and meals less lavish. Business class is less expensive than first class, but is by no means cheap. Nonetheless, if you're going to be in the air for seven or more hours, the comfort can be well worth the cost.

Economy class is the section of the plane where most travelers sit. An economy fare buys you a seat to where you want to go (plus a meal and a moist towelette) with very few restrictions; you can usually change your plans without penalty until moments before departure. But economy class is definitely not the least expensive way to fly.

APEX fares can take you to your honeymoon destination for a lot less money than regular economy fares. APEX stands for Advance Purchase Excursion. "Advance purchase" means that you must reserve and pay for your seat between 2 and 30 days before departure—the length of time differs from airline to airline. "Excursion" means round trip—there's no such thing as a one-way APEX fare. Although APEX saves money, restrictions usually apply—travel is allowed only on specified days, and there may be penalties for changing your plans. APEX is the only way to go for many honeymooners, but be sure your plans are firm before purchasing your tickets.

Super Saver fares are virtually the same as APEX fares, except they apply to domestic travel (within the U.S.), whereas APEX fares are designated for international travel. The same advance-purchase, round-trip, and possible restriction policies outlined for APEX tickets usually apply to Super Savers as well.

A ROUTE POINT: WHERE ELSE DOES YOUR PLANE GO?

You will save yourself from aggravating surprises by knowing the differences between these three routing methods:

Nonstop flights. A nonstop flight takes you exactly where you want to go: one takeoff, one landing, and you're there. Nonstop is the ideal you should aim for.

Direct flights. Direct flights are often mistaken for nonstop flights. In fact, a direct flight usually takes several hours longer than a nonstop because it may land at one or more airports along the way to discharge and pick up passengers, refuel, or change crews.

Flights with connections. These flights involve changing planes midway through your journey—an experience to avoid whenever possible. Both you and your luggage must go from one plane to another. This may also mean waiting in the terminal until the second plane arrives, unloads its passengers, refuels, and reboards. Traditionally, the longest delays come with changing planes. You may find that changing planes is the only way to get from your home to that perfect, palmy isle. But don't write a plane change into your flight plan unless it's the only way to do it.

Charters

Say Rio is tops on your list, but there's no way you can cough up the $1,500 per ticket price to get there and back home. You looked in the paper and saw charter flights to Rio advertised for $599 apiece. Why so cheap, and what's the hitch?

☐ What is a charter? Charter operators rent entire planes from airlines and sell the seats at a lower price. Look at a hypothetical flight: Airline X offers daily service to Rome. Some days people don't travel, so seats go empty. They must calculate on having empty seats, which raises their price. A charter operator, however, can rent the whole plane, offer just one flight a week, pack the plane by advertising low prices, and still turn a profit. The happy honeymooners ride on a packed plane for a very low price.

☐ The pros: Just one pro, really, but it may prove enticing—charters can be a bargain. When even the lowest regular airline fares seem way past your budget, charters sometimes close the gap. Getting to Europe, South America, the Caribbean—all over—suddenly becomes accessible. Charters can even tack on hotel accommodations, making the whole thing a complete package, and still undersell the airlines.

But there are risks . . .

☐ The cons: First, charters don't make a profit on an empty plane. If enough tickets aren't sold, planes are combined, and passengers are juggled around, sometimes even bumped (eek!), all of which can reduce your time in honeymoon dream land and increase your time in the airport. If time is tight, don't do it. Also, charters have been known to go broke. If your charter goes broke while you're in Rome, someone is theoretically responsible for getting you back. But who? You've got a problem.

☐ The bottom line: Charters can be great. But be careful when purchasing them, especially if you don't have time to spare. Ask what would happen in every conceivable situation, ask how long they've been in business, consult with your travel agent, get their office number at your destination (do they have an office where you're going? Do they answer the phone? Find out). You might get a great deal.

CASTING OFF: TRAVEL BY SEA ᘓ

With the exception of transatlantic crossings, travel by ship has become a vacation in itself rather than just a way of getting where you want to go. So when you choose a ship, you are also choosing your honeymoon destinations, your hotel room, restaurants, and activities. Some points to consider:

Ports of call. Does your ship visit a new port almost every day, or are there more uninterrupted days at sea? Which would you prefer? Days at sea are generally more leisurely, with time devoted to scheduled activities, reading, eating, eating, and more eating. Days in port give you the opportunity to go off and explore.

Your fellow passengers. Some cruises attract families, some attract singles, others attract senior citizens. Singles cruises can be loud and raucous affairs; cruises with senior citizens can be much more subdued. Who would you like to see across from you at the dinner table?

Cabin choice. Wide-angle lenses make cruise-ship cabins look spacious in brochure photographs. In fact, they are quite small. And you will be faced with several options—an outside cabin (with a porthole) or an inside cabin (no porthole). It's nice to be able to look out and see the waves bobbing by, but you'll be able to count the times you look out the porthole on one hand; most shipboard time is spent on deck or asleep. Maybe the lower-priced, inside cabin would suit you fine. What are the sleeping arrangements? On some ships, lowest-priced cabins would put you in bunk beds. Generally, the newer the ship, the more double beds available. Also keep in mind that cabins toward the middle of the ship bounce around less in rough waters.

Cruise fares. The number of fares, discounts, and package arrangements that cruise lines offer could fill a book of their own. Many bargain cruise prices you'll encounter are last-minute, fill-the-ship incentives. But there are also incentives for booking early that can knock hundreds of dollars off your total cruise costs. In addition, some cruises offer air-sea packages, which include the price of airfare to the port of departure.

Remember, you get what you pay for. Unlike hotels, which you can switch if you're not satisfied, once you set sail you're on the cruise for the duration of the trip. A travel agent who specializes in cruises will help you find the best cruise for your honeymoon needs at the best possible price.

ALL ABOARD: TRAVEL BY TRAIN ᘓ

Railroads offer honeymooners a third, distinctly romantic travel option. The miles traveled become an integral part of the whole honeymoon experience; it's not just getting there that counts but also what you see along the way. Whether you'd like to have mountains, castles, vineyards, or farms whipping by the train window, these pointers will keep you on the right track:

American trains. Compared to air travel or cruises, booking a train trip is fairly simple. Fares remain stable, and there's really only one carrier to deal with for longer trips: Amtrak. When buying your ticket, however, you should be aware of two fares that could work to your advantage:

* *Family fare: Now that you're a family of two, you can take advantage of this special fare. One honeymooner pays full fare; the other gets a discount of up to 50 percent.*

* *All Aboard America fare: For the price of round-trip tickets, you can stop off at several places along the way. One honeymoon can become three. Amtrak divides the country into thirds—east, middle, and west—and your fare will depend on whether you travel in just one third, two, or three.*

For more information on Amtrak fares, call **1-800-USA-RAIL**.

Trains in Europe. Once you've made it over the ocean, traveling by train is often the best (sometimes the only) way to go. Europe's rail system is far more extensive than our own; prices are often lower, transit time from city to city (even from country to country) can be shorter than you'd think, and you're bound to meet lots of friendly people along the way.

If you'll be doing a substantial amount of train travel, consider buying a Eurailpass. Basically, Eurailpasses are tickets for unlimited train travel within a set time period (one, two, or three months). Their cost-effectiveness depends on how many miles you cover. If you plan to visit a number of countries and explore them extensively, they're a good buy. If you plan to take just a few rail excursions, buying regular tickets at the station is usually less expensive. And if you plan only to travel in one country, you can usually purchase passes for unlimited train travel within the borders of that country for quite a bit less than the Eurailpass price.

Eurailpasses must be purchased before you get to Europe, so sit down and evaluate just how much train travel you think you'll do. Whether you purchase passes for a one-, two-, or three-month period, the meter starts ticking as soon as you board your first train (the pass must be validated at the train station). If you're under 26, you can purchase a substantially less expensive Eurail Youthpass, good for second-class train travel (second-class trains are fine in most European countries). If you're over 26, you'll purchase a regular Eurailpass, which entitles you to first-class trains, as well as berths for overnight rides. And from October through April, the Eurail Saver Pass, which usually cuts costs for three people traveling together, applies to two people traveling together. For more information, write **Trains, P.O. Box M, Staten Island, NY 10305.**

HITTING THE ROAD: TRAVEL BY CAR

Driving can be the most economical way to approach honeymoon travel, and it certainly offers the greatest freedom. When you hear about a charming restaurant tucked back in the woods or a spectacular beach up the road, you can simply take a quick detour and be there. No timetables, no complicated fares—the sheer spontaneity can be incredibly romantic. Here, some points to consider before starting your engines:

If you'll be using your own car, is it in good mechanical condition? Starting a honeymoon in a car that loves the repair shop could mean trouble. Even if you've never had a breakdown, be sure to take your car to the shop for a once-over: Check the oil, brake and transmission fluids, and tires. Is your car difficult to service? Whether you drive a Jaguar or a Yugo, some foreign cars remain completely foreign to mechanics in remote parts of the country. Be sure to carry a list of mechanics and dealers who are authorized to repair your make of car.

Do you belong to an automobile club like the American Automobile Association (Triple A)? If not, consider joining. Not only will they help you out in emergencies, but they can provide lots of useful travel information like maps, hotel recommendations, and the best and most scenic driving routes.

Will you be happy in your car? Know that you'll be comfortable before you leave. A driving honeymoon in August with no air-conditioning can bake any lovebirds. A ski honeymoon in a car with poor traction can turn mountain roads into black diamond slalom slopes. And although travel on the open road can be extremely romantic, cars may be natural breeding grounds for marital spats. If you don't think your car will be comfortable, consider renting.

Car Rentals

Maybe you don't own a car. Perhaps your car simply isn't suitable for honeymoon touring. Or you plan to fly somewhere and then explore the roads. If you fit into any of these categories, you're bound to find yourself at the car rental desk somewhere along the line. Here are a few ways to make sure that your car rental is a happy experience.

☐ Reserve early. To get that cute little convertible instead of the four-door behemoth, make dibs as soon as possible. Renting in Europe? If you can only drive an automatic shift, be sure to specify that fact. You'll only get one if you ask and reserve early.

☐ Look for hidden costs. The bargain $99-per-week rate may have extra expenses. Car rental concerns usually add on charges for mileage, insurance, tax, and one-way rentals, so calculate on paying out extra dollars when making your honeymoon budget.

☐ Consider splurging for a tape deck. Many car rental companies offer cars with cassette players, and nothing is more romantic than whizzing down the freeway playing "your song."

☐ Check that everything is in working order before you drive your rental car out of the lot. Test the horn, turn signals, headlights, and radio to ensure smooth driving along the way. Check the trunk for the spare tire and jack. Also, make sure you know the number to call should you encounter any mechanical problems on the road.

☐ Do you know how to get out of the airport? Your route may look simple on the map, but airport roads are a maze of their own, especially when the signs are in a foreign language. Ask before you go.

☐ Do you know how to drive the car you've rented? Sit in the seat for a moment before starting off and orient yourself. Where is the gas gauge? Where is the horn? If you've rented a car with a stick shift, go through the gears and find reverse.

☐ Fill her up before returning. Returning a car with a near-empty tank means you'll pay an expensive refueling charge. And while it's not required, it's common courtesy to clear wrappers, cans, and other miscellaneous garbage out of the car before returning.

5
SUITE DREAMS: YOUR HOTEL

The fantasy: checking into the honeymoon suite of your dreams. The reality: securing that dream honeymoon hotel room means you'll have to comb over brochures, look at the books, choose a room, and make careful, clear reservations. No one knows more about pampering than the staff of a fine hotel. But the secret of a happy honeymoon stay is knowing what you're going to get before you get it, knowing who can help you, and knowing how to help them help you.

Look beyond the brochures. To make sure that the hotel that looks so beautiful in the brochure really is beautiful, check its rating in recent travel publications and ask your travel agent for his or her opinion. Is there any construction under way? Hotels are constantly renovating and refurbishing these days—a boon to honeymooners as long as the work is completed before you arrive.

Know the room categories. A deluxe room sounds lovely, but in some hotels deluxe rooms occupy the lower end of the scale, with the nicest rooms in super-deluxe and super-duper-deluxe categories. So determine what each hotel's terminology actually means: which rooms are largest; which have the best views. An ocean-view room and a beach-front room may be two different things altogether (beach-front actually overlooks the beach; ocean-view means that you can see the sea, but perhaps the parking lot, too). If you reserve by phone, drop a letter to the reservations manager with specific questions or needs.

When you call or write for reservations, let the hotel know you're honeymooners. The old "keep it secret" strategy can rob you of the fine treatment many hotels reserve for newlywed guests. For example, if they have the rooms available, many hotel reservations managers make a practice of "upgrading" honeymooners—assigning a room that would normally cost more than the rate requested—at no extra charge. At the very least, they'll see that you get the best accommodations available in your price range.

Mention any special details you'd like to have attended to in advance. Often the manager makes a point of sending honeymooners a bouquet or a basket of fruit or wine with his compliments. Or the honeymoon package that you've chosen may include champagne and flowers. But to make sure that everything will be taken care of, put it in writing. The reservations manager will route your request to the proper department, and all will be as you like on the day you arrive.

Send a deposit for the first night of your stay, or give a credit card number. To the hotel's reservations department, this means you're "more than just interested," and they'll honor your requests immediately with a serious assignment of the best room available in your price range.

When you check in, you're allowed to see the room before signing the register. But since hotels take extra care with honeymoon reservations, you'll rarely be disappointed. If you don't find the room satisfactory even after you've registered, you can call the front desk and ask to be moved.

Villa and Condo Rentals

They sound super: resort-sited villas and condominiums you can rent for maybe half what you'd pay at a hotel just down the beach or up the mountain. And they've got lots going for them: good looks (they're furnished with rent-appeal in mind); space (they've got kitchens, baths, living rooms, and—often as not—more bedrooms than you need); luxury extras like balconies, patios, swimming pools, servants (some villas are staffed with cooks, maids, and gardeners); plus complete do-as-you-please privacy. And recent package plans covering villa and condominium stays mean you can now save on airfare as well as lodging. All of which could mean the answer to your honeymoon prayer for luxury at lower prices. But they are different from hotels. So before you commit yourselves to honeymooning in someone else's home away from home, ask yourselves these questions:

☐ Where exactly will you be? A brochure's "nearby" may mean a few steps or a country mile. Ask to see a scaled map and calculate distances to essential support sites—beach or pool or chairlift, marina, grocery, hotel, restaurants, nightlife.

☐ How will you get around? Is public transportation enough or will you need a car? Some villa packages include a rental car as part of the deal. Does yours?

☐ What does it look like? Try not to take anything for granted. Ask for views *of* the grounds, the porch, the interior, rather than *from* them. Precisely what is provided? There should be linens, cooking utensils, china, silver, maid (cleanup) service, and ideally you should be able to arrange for at least one order of groceries (breakfast things, plus staples) to be delivered in advance. Even in paradise, an empty fridge is cold comfort.

☐ Do you like to cook? If not, are there any restaurants handy? Or someone who'll do meals? And will he/she do the marketing too? Incidentally, are you easy with the thought of planning menus and giving directions?

☐ Will you miss the crowd? It may sound silly, but even for honeymooners, mixing and meeting people can be an important part of the fun. A dream cottage too far away from it all could turn out to be too quiet. Privacy is precious; loneliness may be a drag.

☐ Where can you find out more? From any number of specialists: **Creative Leisure**, 1280 Columbus Avenue, San Francisco, CA 94133, for condominiums and luxury villas in Mexico and Hawaii; **J.A.V.A.**, 200 Park Avenue, New York, NY 10017, for Jamaica villas; **Caribbean Home Rentals**, 28 Highwood Avenue, Tenafly, NJ 07670, for other island homes; **Villas International Ltd.**, 71 West 23rd Street, New York, NY 10010, for villas in Europe and the islands. As always, your best bet could be to ask your travel agent.

PACKAGES: DEAL OR NO DEAL 𝄢

When you go to a travel agent, chances are he'll ask if you'd like to buy a package. Packages come in an infinite array of shapes and sizes. Some are complete, all-inclusive affairs (airfare, hotel, meals, entertainment, and sightseeing—all for one price). Others just combine two or more of the above.

When looking at packages, you will also come across package tours. They, too, include airfare, hotel, meals, and sightseeing, but they're dependent on you traveling in a large group of people from one spot to another. "Luxury motor coaches"—read buses—are the focal point of many package tours. We recommend that you steer away from any package tour that forces you to stick with the herds. Being part of a busload of tourists probably isn't the most romantic way to spend your honeymoon. As for the other types of packages—and there are thousands—here are some points to consider:

Packages can save you money. Since package organizers buy airplane seats and hotel rooms in bulk, they can pass savings along to you and still make a profit. If you are planning to fly to a popular destination, stay in an established hotel, and rent a car, it's almost certain that you can purchase a package that would combine these features at a better price than purchasing them separately.

Read the fine print. Any package brochure will wax poetic about the "experience" of that particular package. Go straight to the part that tells you exactly what's included. Is there an unbelievably low price with an asterisk next to it? Dig down to the fine print and find out what the asterisk stipulates; the low price might hold true only for specific time periods, or depend on another purchase. And try to estimate what each item on the list of included features actually is worth. "Welcome Cocktail," "His 'n Her T-Shirts," and "Special Surprise Gift" are all lovely things to have, but they don't really add that much to the dollar value of the package.

If your hotel room is part of the package, do some quick research on the hotels themselves. A package might offer "choice of deluxe hotels," but your concept of deluxe could be very different from the package operator's. The same goes for your room: Be sure that you know what class of hotel room you are eligible for; even the poshest of hotels can have rooms overlooking the driveway.

A Selection of the Most Romantic Honeymoon Hotels

Naming the most romantic hotels is a difficult task. For every hostelry we've listed here, any of a dozen others could be singled out in its place. For most areas, we've tried to pick one hotel in a populous, excitement-filled area (a bustling city or active resort area), as well as a secluded getaway, where sitting back and soaking up the beauty fills your honeymoon days. Our choices are subjective; some are world-renowned, five-star properties that are listed in many "Best of the Best" columns; others are personal favorites that endear with quiet devotion to comfort and pleasure. We've made selections based on our own travel experience, the beauty of each property and its surroundings, and the standards of its service. They're places that need only your love (and since none are cheap, a good bit of money, too) to be ideal honeymoon hotels.

CONTINENTAL UNITED STATES

Northeast
Stanhope Hotel, New York, NY: Newly renovated, with sumptuous suites overlooking the Metropolitan Museum of Art, it's our favorite hideaway in a city full of luxurious, romantic hotels.

The Point, Saranac Lake, NY: A former Rockefeller Great Camp settled into the Adirondacks, it mixes nostalgia, lakeside natural splendor, and soft luxury in a thoroughly romantic blend.

Southeast
Grand Bay, Coconut Grove, FL: Ciga's recent addition to the Miami hotel scene, its contemporary styling, first-class comforts, and elegant aura have set new romantic standards for this city in the sun.

Ritz-Carlton, Naples, FL: This grand, Mediterranean-style hotel on Florida's Gulf coast shows how pairing old-world sophistication and Florida's balmy beauty can make for a dazzling honeymoon combination.

Midwest
The Tremont, Chicago, IL: The intimate feel of this polished, clubby hotel makes a dreamy retreat in a pulsing metropolis.

The Grand Hotel, Mackinac Island, MI: Rocking away afternoons on the Grand's sprawling porch can make you feel like you've traveled back in time.

Rocky Mountains
The Brown Palace, Denver, CO: Century-old grandeur and dramatic comforts make it a romantic favorite in this Colorado hub.

Tall Timber, Durango, CO: Seductively isolated in the San Juan National Forest, the drama of the surrounding peaks and the decadence of the food and service set a beautiful scene for love.

Southwest
Arizona Inn, Tucson, AZ: Its beautiful gardens, sophisticated colors, and loving service make it a patch of honeymoon heaven.
Rancho Encantado, Santa Fe, NM: Set into the Tesuque hills, with adobe buildings, bright accents, and gracious attention to comfort, it's a romantic standout on the Santa Fe scene.
Southern Pacific Coast
Bel-Air, Los Angeles, CA: People who stay in this flower-filled, mission-style hotel come back raving, wishing all of life could be so pampering, so romantic, so perfect.
Ventana Inn, Big Sur, CA: The rugged Big Sur setting and luxury-laden rooms make viewing the Pacific panorama a hypnotic, soul-settling, and completely comforting experience.

Northern Pacific Coast
Alexis Hotel, Seattle, WA: Service reigns at this intimate hotel, making it Seattle's romantic favorite.
Salishan Lodge, Gleneden Beach, OR: Lush forest, wave-washed shores, well-cushioned suites in Pacific-coast colors, and dining that turns Oregon's natural bounty into gourmet feasts make Salishan a quintessential honeymoon hideaway.

THE CARIBBEAN

Trident Villas, Port Antonio, Jamaica: The unique elegance of each room, the glorious shoreline setting, the fine attention to detail make you instantly fall in love with the place.
Peter Island Resort and Yacht Harbour, British Virgin Islands: For people who fantasize about a perfect suite on the beach, the Beach Houses at this secluded resort island can make the dream come true.

MEXICO

Las Brisas, Acapulco: A complex of villas set on a mountain overlooking the Pacific, Las Brisas courts couples with private pools, flowery terraces, and a sensual, exclusive aura.

Hotel Palmilla, San José del Cabo: The fountains, the towers, and the serene beachside setting of this white hacienda induces an extraordinary feeling of peace and well-being.

HAWAII

Halekulani, Waikiki: Its dreamy comforts, sunset views, and elegant island style make it an oasis of romance in Honolulu.

Hana-Maui, Maui: The sweetness of a stay at this comforting, secluded retreat lingers for months afterwards. It's a true Hawaiian beauty.

CANADA

Le Château Frontenac, Québec City: This landmark 1892 hotel, overlooking the St. Lawrence River, wins over hearts with grand French Renaissance styling and railroad-era grandeur.

Jasper Park Lodge, Jasper, Alberta: Suites overlooking the shimmering green of Lac Beauvert are honeymoon nests that you'll never want to leave.

EUROPE

Crillon, Paris, France: In a city where just buying a loaf of bread can be romantic, the Crillon gleams amid shiny neighbors with a luxurious glow that's unique to Paris.

Ritz, London, England: More personable than some London *grandes dames*, the Ritz is certain to charm; after refurbishing, its opulent accents gleam anew.

Dromoland Castle, Newmarket-on-Fergus, Ireland: The paneled glow, the oil paintings, the silk-and-crystal-clad dining room, and—most of all—the view of deep green out the windows, let you know that you're seeing Ireland at its best.

Villa d'Este, Lake Como, Italy: All marble and silk and crystal, this glorious villa is four centuries old, and the combination of Renaissance luxury and the lakeside beauty will sweep you off your feet.

Pousada de Rainha Santa Isabel, Estremoz, Portugal: Once a medieval palace, now it's a very romantic hotel with canopied beds in a sweet, hilltop village.

6
SPECIAL HONEYMOON CONSIDERATIONS

As newlyweds, you fall into a select group of travelers with unique needs. You want to take advantage of everything that your resort, island, city, or countryside has to offer, but you're ultimately concerned with the romantic quality of your time together. Since not all travel offerings are designed with the needs of honeymooners in mind, you should familiarize yourself with some ways to make your wedding trip exactly what you want it to be.

FIRST NIGHT OPTIONS

Wedding-day travel is not a requirement. You might consider checking into a nearby hotel for your wedding night, then starting travel bright and fresh the next morning. That way, you won't have to rush out of your reception, and you won't be nearly as tired on your first married night together. In fact, some travel plans leave no choice; if you live far from the airport, or if flights for your destination leave only in the morning (it does happen), you won't be able to fit both wedding and travel into the same day.

You could head into town and check into the honeymoon suite of your favorite hotel. Or consider an airport hotel; they're getting nicer and nicer (some are becoming resorts all their own), and you can practically roll out of bed and onto the plane. If your new home (or gussied-up old home) is ready, consider spending your wedding night there. After all, what could be more romantic than spending your first married night in your first married home? Just be sure to make it a special occasion—flowers, champagne—the works.

MATTRESS MATTERS

If you're like most newlyweds, the sight of a pair of single beds in your honeymoon hotel room could be pretty depressing. Some hotels—especially in Europe—still have a large number of Lucy-and-Ricky–style boudoirs, so make it very clear when reserving that you need a queen- or king-sized bed. And although two twins pushed together are better than having a built-in bureau between you, the crack where they join can become an irritant or even a chasm to fall through. Specify a one-piece mattress or turn the pushed-together mattresses horizontally. The best way to ensure that you get the comfortable bed-for-two that you want is to tell the hotel that you're honeymooners. Don't be bashful.

BATHROOMS TOO

Most American hotel rooms have private baths attached. The only exception may be bed-and-breakfast accommodations, which often have rooms that share common bathrooms. Europe-bound honeymooners should be especially aware of the bathroom issue. Many smaller hostelries have bathroomless rooms, although you will always find a sink in your room. Be sure to specify in writing that you'll need your own private bath.

FLAUNT IT

Some newlyweds conceal the fact that they're honeymooners, and by doing so they miss out on some pampering service. Let your travel agent know (and tell him to pass the word), let your hotel know—in short, don't keep the secret from anyone. By saying you're honeymooners, you'll be first in line for that extra-special room, that restaurant table with a view, and the best of anything else available.

How to Say Honeymoon In Ten Languages

Most people will take one look at the stars in your eyes and *know* you're newlyweds. But just in case, here are some translations for the word *honeymoon* that might match up with where you're going. Worried about pronunciation? Say it with a smile!

French: Lune de miel (loon de myel)

Spanish: Luna de miel (loo-na deh myel)

Italian: Luna di miele (loo-na dee mye-le)

Irish: Mi na meala (mee nah mal-ah)

Czech: Libanky (lee-bahn-key)

Dutch: Wittebroodsdagen (viter-broad-dahghen)

Flemish: Huwelijksreis (hu-ve-luks-rice)

German: Flitterwochen (fli-ter-vo-khen)

Swedish: Smekmånad (smeck-moe-nod)

Danish: Bryllupsrejse (bruh-loops-rye-suh)

CROWD CONTROL 🍌

Some hotels and resorts design their facilities, services, and marketing to attract families or singles. Carefully consider the honeymoon implications before reserving a room in either type of resort. The cute little tykes at family resorts may splash and scream at the pool, and wake in the wee hours of the morning, raring to go. The proposals either one of you might get at a singles resort could be flattering, but they could also be intrusive. Brochures can tip you off; if a resort lists extensive activity plans for children, or meet-your-mate parties, as primary attractions, you know who'll be there. Also, ask your travel agent to see if there are any conventions or college groups who've booked large numbers of rooms. Always remember that the people you're surrounded by will have a large effect on your overall honeymoon experience.

Celebrity Honeymoons

George & Martha Washington . . . . Williamsburg, VA

John F. & Jacqueline Kennedy . . . . Acapulco

Ronald & Nancy Reagan . . . . Phoenix, AZ

Elizabeth Taylor & Conrad Hilton, Jr. . . . . Paris

Elizabeth Taylor & Mike Todd . . . . World tour

Debbie Reynolds & Eddie Fisher . . . . Greenbrier, WV

Elizabeth Taylor & Eddie Fisher . . . . Los Angeles, CA

Elizabeth Taylor & John Warner	Blue Ridge Mountains, WV
F. Scott & Zelda Fitzgerald	New York, NY
Clark Gable & Carole Lombard	Palm Springs, CA
Marilyn Monroe & Joe DiMaggio	Japan
Jane Russell & John Peoples	Catalina Island, CA
Lucille Ball & Desi Arnaz	Cross-country train trip
Maria Shriver & Arnold Schwarzenegger	Antigua
Prince Andrew & Sarah Ferguson	The Azores
Caroline Kennedy & Edwin Schlossberg	Hawaii
Diana Ross & Arne Naess, Jr.	Tiano, French Polynesia

7
PASSPORTS, PAPERS, AND PACKING

Even with your reservations made, it may seem that the planning has just begun. Sure, you know where you're going, how you'll get there, and where to stay. But what about the rest? There are still papers, shots, luggage, packing, and cameras to worry about—and that's just to start. If it sounds like a lot, don't panic. If you follow this outline, no last-minute anything can be forgotten. We'll take you from three months before your wedding day to the moment your dream trip begins, step by step.

Preparation Chart

THREE MONTHS BEFORE

☐ Be happy with the choice you've made
☐ Check on passports
☐ Check on visas
☐ Apply for credit
☐ Get shots
☐ Look into languages
☐ Read up on your destination

☐ ONE MONTH BEFORE

☐ Purchase luggage
☐ Review your wardrobe
☐ Check your camera
☐ Refill prescriptions

ONE WEEK BEFORE

☐ Begin packing
☐ Double-check travel arrangements
☐ Buy travelers checks
☐ Purchase foreign currency
☐ Arrange rides from reception to hotel, hotel to airport

THE DAY BEFORE

☐ Confirm reservations
☐ Finish packing
☐ Pass around your itinerary
☐ Go down the lists

THREE MONTHS BEFORE

Be happy with your choice. By now you've considered your honeymoon possibilities, consulted a travel agent, and the wheels are in motion. Do your plans excite you? If something doesn't seem right—the hotel too remote, the itinerary over-packed—now's the time to speak up. You should both be happy with the decision you've made. There's still time to change it.

Check on passports. If you plan to travel outside of the United States, you must have a passport to cross into the foreign country and for return to the United States. Even through most of Mexico, the Caribbean, and Canada, where a birth certificate or naturalization papers are considered acceptable documents for entry, nothing gets the point across clearer—and quicker—

than a passport. And it's the best piece of general identification you can have for banks, hotels, and airlines.

If you've never had a passport, you must go to the passport office in person to apply. If you're renewing an old passport, mail in the out-of-date passport with an application, fee, and photos, and a new one will be mailed back. Allow at least six weeks for the process. For information on passport applications and renewals, write to the **Department of State, Passport Correspondence Branch, Room 386, 1425 K Street N.W., Washington, DC 20524.**

Check on visas. Some international travel requires a visa (a stamp in your passport issued by the country in question, which specifies when, and for how long, you can visit). Most countries in Western Europe don't require visas, but it's wise to double-check with a consulate or tourist board. France, for example, has introduced a visa requirement. Like getting a passport, obtaining a visa will take you through rolls of red tape, so start now. Passport offices, tourist offices, and consulates will tell you if you need one.

Consider major bank credit cards. They can be your best friends—besides one another—while you're on the road. You can pay for almost anything with credit cards (meals, hotel, and transportation) and you can even get cash in crunch situations. So if you don't already have a credit card, seriously consider applying. If finances are still a bit wobbly, you might be able to get a satellite card on your parents' account. Plastic-packing pairs should make sure that previous bills are paid before leaving home, especially if airline tickets have been charged (credit cards won't buy anything if they're charged to their limit).

Get any necessary shots. While there's no need for inoculations for domestic travel and most foreign travel, double-check with the tourist boards and consulates of the countries you plan to visit. They'll also be able to tell you about other health considerations, such as taking malaria-preventing medication in some tropical destinations. Set up an appointment with your doctor well in advance for any shots or prescriptions that you need.

Brush up on foreign languages. Do you know how to say please and thank you? Make an effort to at least know the rudiments. Just being able to say words like "Hello," "Could you please tell me something?" and "This is beautiful," will make you feel more comfortable. And everyone you meet will appreciate your efforts. So check your bookstore for the basic language learning tools—tapes and books—or consider the fun of taking an evening class together. The time you spend learning now will make you love your honeymoon even more.

Learn a bit about where you're going. It will prevent culture shock. Familiarize yourself with the climate—both physical and social—of your honeymoon destination. If you're going to Italy, for instance, you'll want to know that shops and banks are closed for several hours at midday. Caribbean-bound

couples should be aware that the standard of living on some islands may be
very different from our own. By scanning a book or two on the history of
the area you're visiting and keeping an eye out for relevant articles in the
newspaper, you'll be ready to adapt to different customs, weather, and life-
styles.

ONE MONTH BEFORE ℘

Purchase luggage. It doesn't have to be beautiful (in fact, fancy luggage is
more prone to theft). But your honeymoon luggage should be sturdy, practical, and as lightweight as possible. Don't plan on bringing more than you
can comfortably carry yourselves.

Luggage

You've chosen the perfect place and filled out your wardrobes.
Now to complete the picture, you need luggage to boot—ideally
cases that will not only get you neatly from here to your honeymoon
destination, but carry you through lots of weekends and vacations to
come. With so many shapes, sizes, and materials, how do you pick?

☐ Evaluate your needs. Where are you going? Cold climates mean
   packing sweaters and coats—bulky items that take up more room.
   Sunny skies let you take easy-to-pack lightweight items like shorts
   and bathing suits. Will you need fancy-dress? Make sure you have
   luggage that keeps things wrinkle-free; suit- and dress-bags that
   can hang will keep clothes neat. Are you flying? Checked-in luggage takes a beating going on and off the plane; carry-on luggage
   must fit beneath the seat or in the overhead bin, so keep carry-ons
   23 inches high and 9 inches wide, at most.

☐ Plan to carry it. Even if you think you'll pay porters every step of
   the way, you should be able to haul it all, just in case. Solid-con-
   struction suitcases (hard frame and solid sides of molded plastic or
   metal) protect breakables and take abuse well, but they can be
   very heavy, even empty. Built-in wheels can make heavy luggage

---

more mobile. Soft-construction luggage (fabric sides, some have frames, others do not) weighs less, but clothing may shift and wrinkle, and breakage can occur.

☐ Make room for purchases. You'll pick up things along the way, so make sure you have space to carry them. Maybe buy a case slightly larger than you need. Or stow away an empty soft-sided bag (they fold up to take very little space) that you can use just for souvenirs.

☐ Test thoroughly before buying. Lift the bag. Does the handle feel comfortable, secure? Is it centered so the bag balances? How much does it weigh? Check the closures. Do the zippers work smoothly? Are there any hanging threads? Do hooks and buckles fit snugly, align well? Do the locks work smoothly? Stand the bag up. Is it steady? Are there "feet" to prevent wear? Look inside. Is the lining wrinkle-free, stain resistant? Are all the pockets and straps sewn firmly? And look outside. Will the surface wipe clean? Does the styling or the color make it easy to see in a crowd?

☐ When all's said and done, you should have these items: carry-on bags for both of you, to stuff with enroute essentials and all valuables; a combination of bags to carry the bulk of your wardrobe (perhaps two full-sized cases, or one case and a foldover hang-up bag to share); and any extras you need for purchases along the way, sports equipment, and camera (a well-designed camera bag can be a photographer's best friend). Your home address and destination should be clearly written on waterproof name tags and attached to all your bags—even carry-ons.

Review your wardrobe. If you're heading to the tropics with lots of wool blazers but no cotton tops, it's time to fill in the gaps. Know your chosen destination's climate—even if it's steamy at noon, it could be chilly at night—so be prepared for it. Don't feel that you need to buy a whole trousseau, because it's generally best to rely on tried and true favorites—clothes you know you love. Comfortable walking shoes, bathing suits, and dressing for dinner (as well as for comfort) are all things to think about. Make a list of what you'll need (or use one of ours), then consult your closet. Every item you bring should work with two or three others. Try to make everything function in several ways.

Check your camera. If the camera from your college photo class is gathering dust, bring it out for a cleaning, checkup, and a practice roll of film. Couples without cameras might think about buying one; new 35-millimeter automatics make it easy to take fine photos. Even an old Instamatic will give you honeymoon snaps you'll treasure. Remember to buy all film and accessories *before* departure.

Refill prescriptions. You should be well supplied with any regular medication that you take. It's easier to refill them here and now, than there and then.

Photography Checklist

Sharing honeymoon snapshots with friends and family can be almost as much fun as the trip itself. And you'll want to have an attractive set of wedding-trip shots to look back on in the years to come. Since buying photography supplies can be tricky (and expensive) in some tourist spots, leave home with a well-stocked camera bag, containing these items.

For the Novice

☐ Automatic 35-mm camera with built-in flash; or Instamatic camera
☐ Protective case
☐ Selection of film—64 ASA or Instamatic cartridges
☐ Lens-cleaning paper
☐ Fresh batteries for camera

For Advanced Photographers

☐ 35-mm camera with both automatic and manual light settings
☐ Extra lenses (wide angle, telephoto, macro)
☐ Filters
☐ Extra lens cap
☐ Protective case and shoulder strap
☐ Lens-cleaning paper
☐ Flash
☐ Fresh batteries for both camera and flash
☐ Selection of film—100 ASA for bright beaches, 400 ASA for dark days
☐ X-ray–proof film bag (or ask airport security to check film manually)
☐ Padded, compartmentalized camera bag

Also stock up on over-the-counter medications, health supplies, and birth control apparatus before you go. Avoid starting any new medications when you're about to leave.

ONE WEEK BEFORE ℘

Begin packing. Start now, working with the lists you made (or with one of ours). Save the things you'll need last before leaving (toothbrush, makeup, hairbrush) and the things you'll need first on arrival (bathing suit, nightgown, birth control) to go in a separate tote or carry-on bag.

Packing can be one of life's great anxiety-producing experiences. How many pairs of underwear to take? How will other people be dressed? Will you be able to buy anything over there? What if you forget your bathing suit? Well, relax. Even people who lose their suitcases and don't have a thing to wear still have wonderful honeymoons.

Start by thinking about the weather and what you'll be doing. Then list everything you'll need for those activities. Make selections carefully; if you calculate on four shirts, don't pick the four fanciest, wildly-patterned silk tops. Take the four that are comfortable, easy to care for, and can go from casual to fancy just by adding jewelry or a tie. Skip the sequined nightclub outfit in favor of something styled simply that looks great anywhere. Remember: You can rinse things in the sink, send out laundry, and purchase forgotten items.

Once everything is laid out on the bed, try to subtract all less-than-vital items. In short, pack light.

Here are basic outlines for him and her, with variables added for sunny skies and colder climates. They're designed with a one-week all-around honeymoon in mind, so modify if your wedding trip will be longer or shorter, or will revolve around a specific activity, like skiing, safari, tennis, or scuba diving.

Packing Lists

FOR HIM

☐ 7 pairs underwear
☐ 7 pairs socks

- [ ] 1 pair jeans
- [ ] 1 pair khakis
- [ ] 1 pair dress pants (neutral color)
- [ ] 4 washable T-shirts, button-downs, or polos
- [ ] 3 dress shirts
- [ ] 2 ties
- [ ] 1 blazer
- [ ] 1 pair walking shoes or sneakers
- [ ] 1 pair dress shoes
- [ ] 1 belt
- [ ] 1 mid-weight sweater
- [ ] 1 all-weather jacket
- [ ] Pajamas (if desired)

For sunny skies, add:

- [ ] 2 or 3 swim suits
- [ ] 2 pairs shorts
- [ ] 1 pair sandals

For colder climates, add:

- [ ] 1 sweater-vest
- [ ] 1 pair loafers
- [ ] 2 long-sleeved jerseys or turtlenecks
- [ ] 1 pair gloves
- [ ] 1 scarf
- [ ] 1 pair boots

HIS TOILETRIES

- [ ] Toothbrush
- [ ] Toothpaste
- [ ] Shampoo
- [ ] Razor (with adapter, if needed)
- [ ] Shave cream

☐ Hair brush
☐ Styling gel
☐ Cologne
☐ Moisturizer
☐ Suntan lotion
☐ Aspirin
☐ Deodorant
☐ Contact lenses and solution
☐ Prescription medicine
☐ Contraceptives

FOR HER

☐ 7 sets underwear
☐ 3 pairs pantyhose (if needed)
☐ 3 pairs socks
☐ 2 pairs casual pants/skirts
☐ 1 pair dress slacks/skirt
☐ 2 belts
☐ 4 washable tops
☐ 2 blouses
☐ 1 mid-weight sweater
☐ 1 jacket
☐ 2 evening outfits
☐ 1 slip (if needed)
☐ 1 pair walking shoes
☐ 1 pair dress shoes
☐ 1 nightgown
☐ 1 evening purse
☐ 1 travel robe

For sunny skies, add:

☐ 2 or 3 bathing suits
☐ 2 pairs shorts

☐ 1 pair sandals
☐ 1 beach cover-up

For colder climates, add:

☐ 2 wool tops
☐ 1 wool skirt
☐ 1 heavy sweater
☐ 1 pair gloves
☐ 1 scarf
☐ 1 wrap or shawl
☐ 1 folding umbrella
☐ 1 pair boots

HER TOILETRIES

☐ Makeup
   —Foundation
   —Blusher
   —Powder
   —Under-eye cover-up
   —Eye shadow
   —Mascara
   —Eyeliner
   —Lipstick or gloss
☐ Moisturizers
☐ Toner or astringent
☐ Shampoo and conditioner
☐ Blow dryer (if needed)
☐ Hairclips or bobby pins
☐ Hairbrush or comb
☐ Nail brush
☐ Body powder
☐ Deodorant
☐ Razor or depilatory
☐ Toothbrush and paste

☐ Emery boards
☐
☐ Nail polish and remover
☐ Nail clippers
☐ Perfume or eau de toilette
☐ Tweezers
☐ Prescription medicine
☐ Aspirin
☐ Contraceptives
☐ Contact lenses and solution
☐ Tampons or sanitary napkins
☐ Suntan lotion
☐ Needle and thread
☐ Safety pins

What Not to Pack

Keep your honeymoon baggage as light as possible. Anything you might use, or will only use once, should be left at home in favor of multi-purpose items. Below, a list of items commonly, but needlessly, lugged thousands of miles to honeymoon destinations.

☐ Ski equipment: Almost all downhill honeymooners are happier traveling light, then renting equipment once they reach the slopes.

☐ Golf clubs: It's your honeymoon. Leave them at home this time; you can rent clubs when you need them.

☐ Video equipment: Sit back, relax, and enjoy the moment. You'll have plenty of other vacations to videotape.

☐ Hardcover books: You'll be happier if you leave heavy volumes at home.

☐ Beach towels: If you're going to a resort hotel, they'll have beach towels for you.

☐ Snorkel and scuba equipment: If you're visiting a place where the underwater sights are an attraction, there'll be plenty of places to rent equipment. If you're particularly attached to your own mask or respirator, bring it, but definitely leave the flippers and tanks behind.

☐ Second pair of dress shoes: Try to make do with one pair. The same goes for bulky sweaters.

☐ Excess toiletries: Jam-packed toiletry bags can become ball-and-chain suitcases. Bring small, travel-sized containers of whatever you need, and leave the econo-size creme rinse at home.

☐ Iron: Pack wrinkle-resistant clothes and you won't need a travel iron. Garments that do bunch up can always be sent down for pressing or hung in the shower and steamed.

☐ Groceries: Just because Mrs. Donald Trump travels with a pantry in her purse doesn't mean you have to. Sure, bring some chocolates, nuts, or cookies. Leave the six-packs and cans of tuna at home.

☐ Office work: People tend to bring work with them ("Oh just this one five-hundred-page report, honey,") and then barely touch it. Think twice before taking a portable office on your honeymoon.

☐ Drugs: Watch *Midnight Express* if you don't know why.

Double-check travel arrangements—more to get them fixed in your mind than to unearth agency errors (although if there are any of those, you've still got time to mend them).

Buy traveler's checks. Plan to carry as little cash as possible, and be ready to pay for meals, shopping, and hotel with travelers checks, converting them to cash or foreign currency as you need them. If there's a limit on your credit cards, you'll want to keep your credit line free for emergencies and deposits on rental cars and hotel rooms.

Purchase foreign currency. Be prepared for closed banks—especially if you'll be arriving on a Sunday—or long lines on arrival. Have enough currency exchanged at home ($100, perhaps) to pay for taxi, tips, and that first cappuccino or rum punch.

Arrange rides. Know how you're getting to the airport, train station, or docks. Whether you're taking a cab or limousine, or your best friend will drive you, firm up the plans. Your driver should know what flight you're

taking, where it departs from, and how long it will take you to get there—
keeping traffic in mind.

THE DAY BEFORE ℰ

Confirm reservations. You don't really need to in many cases. But for your
own sense of security, call and make sure the airline, hotel, or cruise ship
knows that you'll be there.

Finish last-minute packing. You should have one suitcase sitting by the door,
ready to go into the trunk, and one carry-on bag, half-filled, open on a chair
in your room, waiting for those last few items.

Pass around your itinerary. Two different people should know where you
are and how to reach you. Make a couple of copies, and pass them along to
the proper people.

Go down the lists. Everything should be prepared and at your finger tips.
So check your lists and ours, and you'll be neatly arranged and ready to go.

8
DEPARTURE

The day has arrived. With everything all set up for your honeymoon, you can kick back and enjoy your wedding—a day to remember always.

After the vows, after the reception, the time will come to leave. It's only natural to feel that you shouldn't leave; you're surrounded by loved ones, and you've looked forward to this day for so long. But after the guests are greeted, the dances done, the cake cut, it's time to move on. Sneak off and change into your travel clothes, and with a shower of rice (or birdseed), you're off.

WHAT TO WEAR IN TRANSIT

Think of where you're going, rather than what you're leaving, when deciding what to wear on the plane, car, boat, or train. If you're headed for an elegant hotel, you'll want to look your best walking through the door. Tropics-bound duos should consider that blast of hot air when they step off the jet. And take cues from experienced travelers—nothing matters more than comfort. So skip your best silk dress or linen suit in favor of something nice but simple, loose, and wrinkle-resistant. The same goes for shoes; brides who trek through airports in three-inch-high heels are painfully reminded of the fact each time they step onto the dance floor or hike in the hills.

GETTING THERE ON TIME

Choosing the best way to get to the plane, boat, or train is up to you. If you had a limousine hired for your wedding party, consider keeping the car through the reception hours so that you can go in grand style. Or you could drive yourself; airports, train stations, and ship terminals all have long-term parking facilities for passenger convenience. But sometimes the nicest way to go is to have best friends or parents see you off. Just make sure that whoever is driving knows when and where to go ahead of time, and make clock-watching at the reception the driver's responsibility.

Bon voyage!

Part Two
LOVE LANDS
BRIDE'S
FAVORITE
HONEYMOON
LOCATIONS

INTRODUCTION

There is a *lot* of romance out there. Covering the world could fill a hundred honeymoon books that could take you a lifetime to read. To make it easy for you, we've boiled down our discussion to America's wedding-trip favorites: ultraromantic destinations that are accessible—both timewise and financially—to a young couple planning a one- or two-week getaway. Of course, if your heart is set on Africa or the Far East, pursue the dream; the Taj Mahal, the pyramids of Egypt, and the beaches of Bali all beckon honeymooners who seek the exotic and have plenty of time and money to spend. But if you're like most newlyweds, you want an easygoing dream spot: a splendid beach, a city suite, a mountain lodge—anyplace where the air, the landscape, and the people whom you meet work together to create an atmosphere that's both exciting and relaxing, foreign and welcoming. You don't have to go around the world to find romance. In the pages that follow, you'll find enticing invitations to Caribbean and Hawaiian islands, Mexican resorts, Europe's Old World cities and countryside, and a whole lot of places right here in America, plus much, much more. They are places that have earned, over the years, a romantic reputation for setting the scenes for love stories. Some you may have heard about already. Others will be new to you. It's a collection we know you'll love.

9
ISLANDS EAST

Step off the plane and a warm blast of air tells you that idyllic pleasures lie ahead. The Caribbean, the Bahamas, and Bermuda—we call them "Islands East"—may not be far from home, but their flavor is decidedly foreign. No BMWs here; you'll be traveling by Mini-Moke, jalopy cab, maybe on a sleek white sloop. You won't find too many Big Macs either; feast instead on flying fish, conch fritters, spiny lobsters, all washed down with cool rum punch. You might be hard-pressed to find a TV set, but who needs one with calypso and reggae tunes plus limbo and flamenco dances to keep your toes tapping? In just a few hours, you'll be whisked from an American metropolis to a land of jungled hills, castaway beaches, and shimmering aqua sea. In short, you'll be plopped down in paradise.

How to choose an island? You could simply spread the map, close your eyes, and blindly pick with the poke of a finger, because any of these palmy isles would make a splendid honeymoon choice. Each one offers the away-from-it-all aura that you've been searching for. Each one bathes in skin-tanning, mango-ripening, sand-bleaching sun. But if you want some advice on the best basking beaches, the hottest hotels, the most intriguing sights to see, read on. We'll show you just what to expect on these honeymoon-minded islands.

The Caribbean

Sweeping down in a curve from Florida, the Caribbean chain looks like a scorpion's tail, but its sting is pure pleasure. The history of these many and

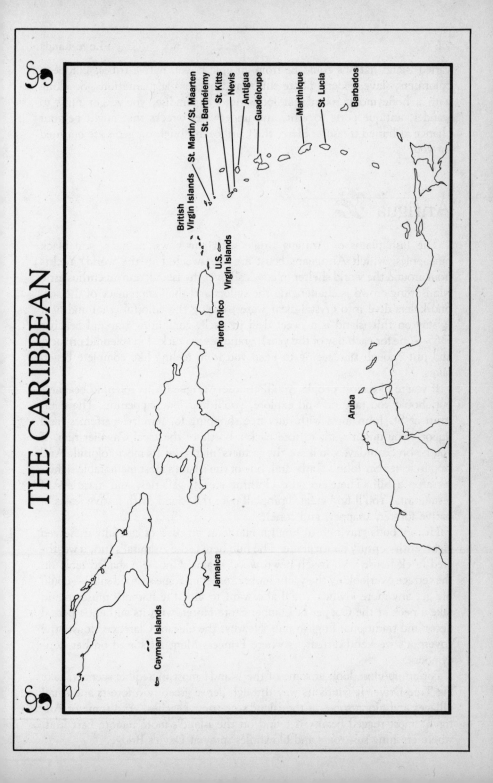

THE CARIBBEAN

British
Virgin Islands

St. Martin/St. Maarten

St. Barthélemy

St. Kitts

Nevis

Antigua

Guadeloupe

Martinique

St. Lucia

Barbados

U.S.
Virgin Islands

Puerto Rico

Aruba

Jamaica

Cayman Islands

varied island nations could be from an epic novel: native tribes, European colonizers, slave traders, pirate ships, and huge sugar plantations. So along with a honeymoon room that looks out on paradise, you've got ruins to wander, antique ports to visit, and underwater wrecks that might be your chance at buried treasure. Here, the Caribbean's brightest gems are outlined for you.

Antigua

The lush plains of Antigua tingle with paw-paws, mangos, and black pineapples, which Antiguans boast are the sweetest in the world. Yachts from around the world shelter in coves all over the island, and an enthusiastic windsurfing crowd is challenging the sailors and their supremacy of the sea. Snorkelers dive into crystal-clear water, eyeing the colorful coral and fish. A stay on this island is a sweet deal in itself, combining tranquil beaches (365—one for each day of the year), grand resorts tucked in splendid privacy, and just enough sightseeing to keep you from feeling like complete beach bums.

If you're like most people, you'll choose Antigua for its splendid beaches, but should you take off and explore, you'll find lots happening. The main town of St. John lures with duty-free shopping for jewelry, perfumes, and liquor—you might want to tote back a bottle of the local Cavalier rum. If you go on Saturday, you'll see the farmers' market at its most colorful. And stop in to see St. John's Cathedral, one of the island's most memorable sights, set atop a hill. There are also clothing stores, galleries, and a variety of restaurants. You'll find great dining all over the island, with festive feasts of native lobster, snapper, and conch.

History buffs gravitate to English Harbour, an oasis of carefully preserved eighteenth-century nautical life. The hub here is the Admiral's Inn, a weathered brick house with rough-hewn wood beams. Choose a shaded table on the terrace overlooking the yacht harbor, order up some seafood salad—could life get any more idyllic? You'll also want to visit the harbor's museum and take a peek at the Copper & Lumber Store Hotel, with its authentic period decor and traditional English pub. Nearby, the elegant Clarence House, the governor's weekend retreat, is where Princess Margaret stayed on her honeymoon.

For an up-close look at some of the island's most incredible scenery, take Fig Tree Drive. It winds its way through dense green rain forests and small villages and along some of the island's prettiest beaches. And some of Antigua's most rugged beauty is found on the island's more remote East End, where crashing surf roars and blowholes spray at Devil's Bridge.

FACTS TO GO ON ℘

- ☐ Getting there: Eastern, American, and BWIA offer direct service to Antigua from either New York or Miami, and cruise ships dock weekly in the deepwater harbor.
- ☐ Entry requirements: Proof of identity is required for U.S. citizens; a passport is best, but birth certificate or voters registration card (plus a photo driver's license) will do. You must have a return or ongoing ticket.
- ☐ Currency: The Eastern Caribbean dollar, with the U.S. dollar widely accepted
- ☐ Language: English
- ☐ *Bride's* Best Beds
- ● *Jumby Bay:* Actually set on a small island of its own, Jumby Bay offers a spectacular palm-backed beach, large, luxurious villa-style rooms, a beautiful main house for elegant dinners, a beach restaurant, tennis courts, bike paths, and a full water-sports menu. Expensive.
- ● *St. James's Club:* The jet-setters' favorite, Mediterranean-looking, with spacious luxury rooms and suites, complete sports facilities (tennis, boating, scuba, fishing, horseback riding), three restaurants, disco, casino, and attitude galore. Expensive.
- ● *Curtain Bluff:* Clubby, with an emphasis on superior service, built on a hill with gorgeous ocean views and breezy rooms. Expensive.
- ● *Half Moon Bay:* Country club meets resort, with nice oceanfront, terraced rooms (especially in the new wing). Full sporting facilities. Expensive.
- ● *Long Bay:* Smaller, simpler than other Antiguan hotels, Long Bay gets stars for its friendly, casual atmosphere, fine beach, and good honeymoon packages. Moderate.

- ☐ For more information, write: Antigua Department of Tourism, 610 Fifth Avenue, New York, NY 10020; or call: (212) 541-4117.

Aruba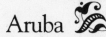

Aruba, a tiny Dutch hideaway just 15 miles off the coast of Venezuela, has all the tropical treats that you'd expect from the Caribbean—including some of the world's most beautiful beaches. And it's got a style all its own: The swaying palms, spectacular sunsets, bustling casinos, and duty-free shopping are all set in an arid and elegant landscape full of cactus and wildly shaped boulders that look like they dropped from the moon.

The best place to unwind is on the beach. And Aruba has plenty of lazable sands, both on the southwest coast, where the hotels are, and on the north, where the rough water is for champion windsurfers only. But even here the sunning is splendid, especially with a picnic lunch. If you can tear yourself away from the beach, you might get as far as the water. It's easy to find Jet-Skis, powerboats, snorkeling and scuba equipment, Sunfishes and windsurf boards (your hotel will arrange lessons and rental).

Aruba is also easy to get to know—the island comes in very manageable bites. All the luxury hotels are strung along a seven-mile stretch called Palm and Eagle beaches. Just a $4 taxi away lies Oranjestad, Aruba's capital. On Nassaustraat, the main shopping street, you'll be overwhelmed with bargains on duty-free items like jewelry, watches, china, crystal, and liquor. There's always a restaurant close at hand, perhaps an open-air café like Coca-Palm that serves local specialties—*pastechi* (meat patties) and *sate* (pork with peanut sauce) along with light American fare.

You might also want to sample some sights around the island. A few minutes' drive takes you out into the *cunucu*, past herds of goats and the occasional sunbathing iguana. You'll see the divi-divi, Aruba's trademark tree, bent at a right angle by the wind. They look like something out of Dr. Seuss. Head south to Savaneta and San Nicolas, towns with the hot colors of Caribbean-style houses and the cool tones of Spanish-style haciendas. Or head northeast to the largest of Aruba's natural bridges—a long slab of coral carved by the pounding surf.

At night you'll enjoy a wide range of dining possibilities: an elegant bistro overlooking the water; a floating barn that serves exotic Indonesian specialties; a seafood place with tableside aquariums; even a restaurant in a windmill. After that, it's casino time at all the hotels, and later on, dancing in discos like Scaramouche and Visage. Cap it off with a stroll on the beach under the light of the moon. Because in Aruba everything comes down to the beaches. Sunning, snorkeling, or snuggling—you're always close to the shining shores.

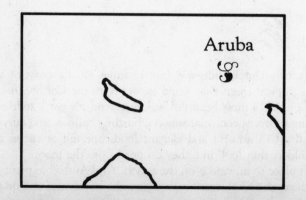

FACTS TO GO ON ℘

☐ Getting there: American Airlines flies nonstop, from New York to Aruba, and Eastern flies direct from Miami. Both airlines have service from major U.S. cities, changing planes in San Juan.

☐ Entry requirements: Proof of citizenship (ideally a passport, or else a birth certificate or voters registration card) and a return or ongoing ticket.

☐ Currency: The U.S. dollar is accepted absolutely everywhere, so you won't need to trade in for Aruban florins, unless you'd enjoy handling the pale green bills.

☐ Language: Dutch, English, and Spanish. The local language is Papiamento.

☐ *Bride's* Best Beds
● *Golden Tulip Aruba Caribbean:* Where H.R.H. Queen Beatrix of The Netherlands stayed on her Aruban visit. Recently renovated, with four restaurants, an open-air bar, health club, and shopping arcade. Expensive.
● *Divi-Divi Beach Hotel:* Long and low, with luxurious rooms that let you walk right out onto the beach. Rooms in their Divi Dos Wing have whirpool bathtubs and big private balconies. Expensive.
● *Holiday Inn:* Recently redone, it bustles with volleyball, bingo, all manner of water sports. Expensive.
● *Manchebo Beach Resort Hotel:* Europeans flock to the comparatively modest rooms, which open smack onto the widest, most dazzling stretch of beach on the island. Expensive.

☐ For more information, write: Aruba Tourist Authority, 1270 Avenue of the Americas, New York, NY 10020; or call: (212) 246-3030.

Barbados 🐚

Think of coral-walled ruins and powder-blue sea; of rippling canefields and fresh summer rain; of gingerbread cottages and child-sized churches and drinks that look like melted sherbet. You're thinking of Barbados, one of the Caribbean's sweetest islands. Surely it's a dream world: Pink beaches, silken waters, and dreamy resorts just don't exist in the nine-to-five scheme of things. But what makes Barbados such a real-life wonder are its practicalities. It's easy to get to, easy to feel at home in, and there's something about the mix of lush tropical looks and proper British accents that works to create an atmosphere of unusual comfort and peace.

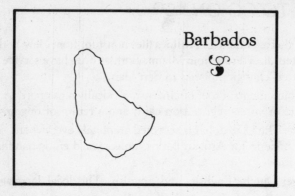

Barbados

This lush, lovely island boasts lots of Edenistic attributes, so days tend to be lazy and languid. If you want lots of sun, you'll find the beaches superlative. Best swimming strands are on the Caribbean side, where the sea spreads out in a rainbow of blues and greens; the east coast is wilder, with thrashing Atlantic waves breaking in prismatic explosions. Boats and beach toys are always close at hand. Most hotels have fins and snorkel masks to lend or rent, and there are a number of scuba outfits up and down the west coast that are set up to teach you, then take you where the best reefs and wrecks are found. Land-based sports may tempt you too. Tennis, golf, and horseback riding are favored at many resorts; more adventurous sorts can sign up with the Outdoor Club for a hike through rippling canefields, palm groves, and rain forests.

If so inclined, you could easily spend as much time sightseeing as sunbathing. Though it's possible to skim the island's sights in one day, splitting the explorations into several chunks is more in keeping with Barbados's mellow tone. Some of the highlights: the Platinum Coast, lined with casual beach bars and manicured compounds (the island's toniest resorts and private estates hide behind neat hedges); Folkestone Underwater Park, where you can snorkel along a special underwater trail; Speightstown, where you'll find Heywoods Beach Resort (its cluster of shops spotlights island crafts, and if you're hungry, there are several terraced restaurants and a beachside café for light eating). Farther afield: the surf-tossed east coast, dune-contoured and studded with giant boulders; the Farley Hill National Park—its many-arched ruin was a set for the movie *Island in the Sun*; Villa Nova, a particularly handsome Great House built in 1834; Harrison's Cave, where an electric tram takes you down to stalactite-filled caverns; and Bathsheba, for the sheer drama of its beach and the lush romance of the Andromeda Gardens. Wherever you head, you're bound to pass through Bridgetown, where day-trippers pour out of cruise ships to admire Trafalgar Square (Lord Nelson's statue is the centerpiece) and to shop in the duty-free stores and open-air crafts markets.

Evenings start off with melting sunsets and island dinners—dine in a plantation's Great House, a gourmet French restaurant, or at a cozy table in an old Barbadian home. Then move on to calypso and disco dancing under star-filled skies. One night you can applaud the colorful production of *1627 and All That Sort of Thing*, a folk-dance extravaganza at the Barbados Museum dinner theater. Another evening, get tickets for a boat trip on the *Jolly Roger* or *Bajan Queen*. And anytime of the night, there's a silver beach and a sky full of stars waiting to inspire you, which, when all's said and done, may be the nicest nightlife of all.

FACTS TO GO ON

☐ Getting there: American, Pan Am, and BWIA all operate nonstops to Barbados from New York. A number of airlines also offer direct service from Miami. Also, cruise ships regularly dock in Bridgetown's harbor.

☐ Entry requirements: U.S. citizens need proof of citizenship, ideally a passport, or else a birth certificate or voters registration card, plus photo ID, and return or ongoing tickets.

☐ Currency: The Barbadian dollar. You can usually pay in U.S. dollars, but you'll probably end up paying less by using local currency.

☐ Language: English

☐ *Bride's* Best Beds

● *Cobbler's Cove:* Both friendly and luxurious, this small, elegant resort offers villa-style rooms with terraces, a fine stretch of beach, and dining on a breezy, ocean-view terrace. Expensive.

● *Coral Reef Club:* Luxurious buildings set amid tropical plantings along a beautiful beach. Full water-sports setup. Expensive.

● *Glitter Bay:* Elegant cluster of condominiums with a Moorish flavor, superb beachviews, and lush tropical plantings. Expensive.

☐ For more information, write Barbados Board of Tourism, 800 Second Avenue, New York, NY 10017; or call: (800) 221-9831, or (212) 986-6516 in New York.

British Virgin Islands

In the case of the British Virgins, pictures almost do say it all. The beaches really are that white, that unspoiled, that luxuriously isolated. The water is as gem-clear and baby-soft as it looks. The skies are as blue, the palms as

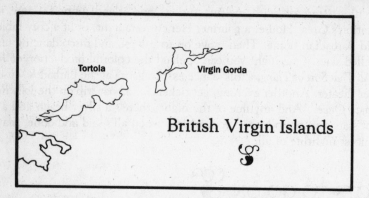

Tortola

Virgin Gorda

British Virgin Islands

shady, the hills as jungled green. But what the photographs here don't show is pretty important too. You don't see any bustling downtowns, any bank-ridden skylines, any neon-shattered nights. There's a conspicuous lack of tooting tour buses and busy store windows. And just try to find a seaside hotel that isn't as beguiling as the sands on which it rests. For small-island lovers of all descriptions (but honeymooners especially), as well as for sailing buffs, the British Virgin Islands are perfection. Period.

Tortola, by far the largest and most civilized island of the group, is also the most explorable. You might start in Road Town, capital of the B.V.I.'s, a child-sized collection of bright-painted stores and open-air snack shops. Then head out for a rather memorable island tour—as notable for the climbing, curling roads you'll traverse as for the staggeringly beautiful beaches you'll discover along the way. Drive west toward Nanny Cay, where you might inspect the shiny marina, the small curve of beach, and the stilt-topping Peg Leg Landing, known for its lobster and West Indian fare. Or if it's still early, keep going past a seascape of diving pelicans and bobbing work boats and around the tip of the island to Little Apple Bay and Long Bay Beach (as long as a holiday weekend, tinted pale pink, and as unpeopled as paradise). Farther up the northwest coast, you'll spot Cane Garden Bay, with a curve of sand as sweet as they come. Within feet of the foam sit Stanley's Beach Bar and neighborly Rhymer's, both famed for their lobster dinners, their late-night limbos, and the yachting crowd that comes to play.

Virgin Gorda, to the east of Tortola, was named by Columbus's men, who thought its hilly silhouette resembled a plump woman. With only 1,000 residents, it's a sublimely unspoiled island, with nearly two dozen delicious beaches and a cacti-covered interior. There's an abandoned copper mine in the south and a boulder-strewn western end where you'll find The Baths, a series of shallow pools, grottoes, and colossal rocks that are wonderful to explore with masks and fins.

Other British Virgins like **Peter Island, Anegada, Mosquito Island, Marina Cay,** and **Jost Van Dyke** lure with secluded resorts—often just one per island—and calm coves for sailboats. From any one island, you're bound to see a handful of others—proximity which makes boating in B.V.I. waters a spontaneous series of hops between islands and their respective beachy coves, fine snorkeling sites, and casual marina tie-ups. Operations like The Moorings will arrange bareboat charters, and Virgin Island Sailing can set up crewed charters on an elegant selection of sloops, ketches, and power cruisers. Rent a boat for a week and skip between a group of islands, or sign up for a day sail on any of a number of special boat excursions.

Below the sailing surface, superlative scuba diving spreads wide and clear in crystal depths. Even if your previous experience is limited to Jacques Cousteau reruns, you can be diving in just half a day with a safety-minded resort course. Once down deep, it's like an aquarium in reverse—you're the one behind the glass. The wreck of the RMS *Rhone* (filmed in *The Deep*) is a popular dive; the sheer wonder of swimming through its coral-crusted skeleton more than makes up for the anxiety of being strapped into tanks and tubes, then pushed backward off the dive boat.

Nights are simple and sweet. Though B.V.I. restaurants probably wouldn't rate too many Michelin stars, their seafood dishes and fruity concoctions are decidedly up to par. There's not much in the way of nightlife—even in Road Town. Sunset is social hour, so make a point of having cocktails by a view. The look of the sky as those great pearly clouds sail across the horizon, turning more velvety with each moment, is as much nightlife as you'll need.

FACTS TO GO ON ৎ

☐ Getting there: The simplest way to go is to fly to San Juan and board an Air BVI, Eastern Metro Express, or American Eagle flight to Beef Island (joined to Tortola by a bridge). If you're not staying on Tortola, you'll take a boat to the island of your choice. There is also boat service from St. Thomas (U.S. Virgin Islands) to Tortola. Starting from New York, you'll use a complete day getting down to the B.V.I.'s.

☐ Entry requirements: For U.S. citizens, a passport (preferred) or a birth certificate or voters registration card—plus an ongoing or return ticket.

☐ Currency: The U.S. dollar

☐ Language: English

☐ *Bride's* Best Beds

- *Peter Island Resort and Yacht Harbour:* With most of an island to itself, splendid new beachhouses (large rooms done in wood, tile, and stone, with spacious oceanview balconies), a full sports menu, and attractively priced off-season packages. Stylish, secluded, and *very* romantic. On Peter Island. Expensive.
- *Little Dix Bay:* A luxurious honeymoon tradition, from the Rockresort people. Comfortable, colorful rooms on the beach, complete sports facilities, and fine food. On Virgin Gorda. Expensive.
- *Bitter End Yacht Club:* A sailors' heaven, offering unlimited use of the hotel's fleet, tropically furnished rooms on a hillside or beach, and lots of nautical fun. On Virgin Gorda. Expensive.
- *Sugar Mill Estate:* Set in hillside ruins of a sugar mill, offering fun food, good prices, and a small patch of beach. On Tortola. Moderate.

☐ For more information, write: B.V.I. Tourist Board, Suite 412, 370 Lexington Avenue, New York, NY 10017; or call: (212) 696-0400.

Cayman Islands

The Cayman Islands aren't famous . . . yet. For years they've been kept top secret by devoted divers and snorkelers. But today this trio of isles is rapidly becoming one of the Caribbean's most luxurious honeymoon destinations. Whichever Cayman Island—or islands—you settle on, you'll always be near water that's as clear as freshly washed windows. And whether you pollywog around in snorkel gear or glide down deep with tanks on your back, you'll see underwater treasures—sea-gardened reefs and barnacled wrecks—that will make your hearts do double somersaults.

Grand Cayman, the largest and most populated of the three, is where you'll find the big hotels, a selection of restaurants, duty-free shops, and

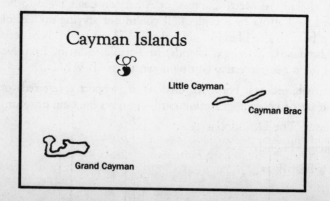

Cayman Islands

Little Cayman

Cayman Brac

Grand Cayman

sparkling nightlife. Though it's tempting to plant yourself on one of the island's sun-splashed beaches and tan yourselves silly (the Seven Mile Beach is the most famous—perhaps the best—though it's really five and a half miles long), be sure to rent a car and explore. Because it's so flat, driving on the left comes easy and it's hard to get lost. If you'd prefer, a host of tour operators or cabdrivers will offer to show you around.

One day, explore the West Bay district, where most of the hotels are based. Stop at the Cayman Turtle Farm where you can see thousands of turtles that range from six ounces to 650 pounds. (When Columbus first came upon the Caymans, he named them "Las Tortugas" because of the turtle-filled seas, but since then they've become endangered species.) Then go to Hell, a hamlet from which you must send a postcard (some say the island's biggest export is the stamp from Hell). One look at the jagged black rock formations tells you how this town got its name. Afterward, have a beer at the Inferno Club, which, coincidentally, is owned by the McDooms. There's lots to see on the rest of the island: the Shipwreck Bar at the Seaview Hotel; snorkel sites off the "ironshore," where coral walls rise straight from the sea; Bodden Town, made for photo-snapping; the island's north side, with some of Grand Cayman's loveliest, and least populated, beaches; and the East End, with superb snorkeling sights and the wreck of the M.V. *Ridgefield* poking up from the reefs.

Allow yourselves at least a morning to shop and stroll around George Town, the Cayman Islands' capital. Good buys include black coral jewelry and duty-free finds like crystal, watches, perfumes, and porcelain—though you may have to push aside some cruise-shippers to get to the register.

The flight over to a smaller island—Cayman Brac—takes less than an hour. And before you know it, you've gone from calm to even calmer. The Brac is a favorite with divers and seclusion seekers. You can rent a pair of mopeds and see it all in a day. For drama, the towering bluffs, caves, rocky beaches, and blowholes on the eastern end of the island are sights to see, as well as the lighthouse at the end of a long, bumpy dirt road. Don't bother looking for a main town—you won't find one. But there is a museum where you can inspect artifacts, old tools, cameras and radios, and information on the hurricane of 1932, which everyone talks about as though it happened yesterday. Cayman Brac isn't as beachy as Grand Cayman, but you'll find a nice stretch of sand at Tiara Beach.

If you want to get even farther away from it all, consider heading over to Little Cayman, the smallest, most remote of the Cayman trio. A few tiny lodges will put you up, leaving you to bask on the beach and explore the spectacular underwater worlds of Bloody Bay and Jackson Point. Forget sightseeing and shopping. The sun and sea are the only action in town (though there is no town). You'll feel a million miles away from the rest of the world.

FACTS TO GO ON ⨏

☐ Getting there: Eastern, Cayman Airways, and Northwest fly from Miami; Cayman Airways also flies from Atlanta, Houston, and Tampa. Shuttle between islands on Cayman Airways.

☐ Entry requirements: U.S. citizens need proof of citizenship (passport, birth certificate, or voters registration card), as well as a return or ongoing ticket.

☐ Currency: You'll pay with Cayman Island dollars.

☐ Language: English

☐ *Bride's* Best Beds

● *Hyatt Regency Grand Cayman:* Newest on the Grand Cayman resort scene, it offers all the luxuries, a dazzling sports scene (golf, tennis, private marina, and a one-third-acre swimming pool), and handsome British Colonial looks. Expensive.

● *Cayman Kai:* At Grand Cayman's Rum Point, a big, attractive complex of sea lodges and beach houses with a central clubhouse and restaurant, water skiing, sailing, tennis, and diving off nearby reefs. Moderate.

● *Tiara Beach Hotel:* Polynesian-flavored, on a sun-bleached stretch of sun-bleached sand. Very big on diving. On Cayman Brac. Moderate.

☐ For more information, write: Cayman Islands Department of Tourism, 420 Lexington Avenue, New York, NY 10017; or call: (212) 682-5582 (they also have offices in Chicago, Coral Gables, Houston, Los Angeles, and Toronto).

Guadeloupe 𝕾

The minute you step off the plane in Guadeloupe, you feel like a privileged member of a select group of travelers. It's one of those special-find places that hasn't sprouted into a major tourist trap, and—thanks to good French manners—probably never will.

Though it looks like one island on the map, it's actually two, connected by a drawbridge. You'll probably settle on Grande-Terre, home to the region's most appealing beaches, many better hotels and resorts, and the commercial capital, Pointe-à-Pitre. The other half of Guadeloupe, Basse-Terre, is wilder and covered with mountains and forests.

Most of Grande-Terre's hotels and resorts huddle around the south-coast towns of Bas du Fort Gosier, Ste. Anne, and St. François, within easy driving distance of Pointe-à-Pitre and most island sights. But one look at the color of the water, and you'll probably see no reason to do anything but sip and

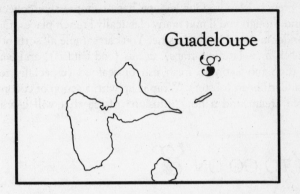

Guadeloupe

swim, then sun and snooze. And if either of you enjoys windsurfing, you'll find some of the best waters in the world for skimming about; everywhere you look, hot-pink and lime sails whip along in water as green as pistachio ice cream.

When you can tear yourselves away from the water, spend a little time poking around Pointe-à-Pitre. It's a fascinating town whose narrow streets teem with Guadeloupeans going about their business. A simple jaunt through the marketplace can turn into an eye-opening lesson in "foods of the world," as you pass stalls piled high with odd-shaped fruits and vegetables. Though the friendly *doudous* are more than eager to help, don't expect their explanations in Creole-accented French to make much sense to you.

Set aside an afternoon to explore Grande-Terre's sights: Fort Fleur d'Epée, a well-preserved eighteenth-century fortress; St. François, a fishing village with several good Creole restaurants; Pointe des Châteaux, the island's easternmost tip, where Atlantic and Caribbean waters meet to create a towering swirl of waves; and Moule, an antique sugar port with an archeological museum.

When you cross over to Basse-Terre, you'll feel as though you've entered another world. Unlike Grande-Terre's low, chalky hills and flat canefields, its mountainous terrain is covered with lush green. If you're up for a little hiking, set out early in the morning so you can get to La Soufrière while the sky is still clear. From the top, you can see Iles des Saintes, Dominica— sometimes even Martinique. Even if you're not rough and rugged types, you can enjoy the natural beauty Basse-Terre has to offer. Just follow the well-paved road through the Parc Naturel and pull over anytime you see an alluring trail. You don't have to walk more than 20 feet, and you can be at the base of waterfalls rushing off cliffsides, spraying tangled vines and blossoms. Other suggested stops include Ste. Marie, the point where Columbus landed in 1493 (there's a statue commemorating the event), and Basse-Terre, the region's capital, a small, neat city with narrow streets.

Like all French islands, Guadeloupe has an impressive collection of restaurants, and though you'll find many classically French places, Guadeloupe's forte is—undeniably—Creole cuisine. You can sample all sorts of spicy starters like *crabes farcis* (stuffed crabs), *accras* (cod fritters), and *boudin* (blood sausages), then move on to fresh fish or seafood (especially red snapper, conch, and Caribbean lobster). Wrap it up with a scoop of coconut, mango, or guava ice cream and a hot "infusion" of tea that will guarantee sweet dreams.

FACTS TO GO ON 🔊

☐ Getting there: American, Eastern, and Air France offer flights to Guadeloupe from New York, Miami, San Juan—most with connections en route.

☐ Entry requirements: To enter Guadeloupe, you'll need a passport (even one that's been valid in the past five years will do) or birth certificate (they're picky—it must have a raised seal), or voters registration. Either way, you'll need a second photo ID, as well as an ongoing or return ticket.

☐ Currency: You'll be paying in French francs.

☐ Language: French

☐ Bride's Best Beds

● *Le Salako, La Créole Beach, Arawak:* Three Gosier hotels grouped in one category because they all provide the same modern guestrooms, inspiring views, and lots of social action. Expensive.

● *Hamak:* Elaborate resort in St. François, with acres of tropical plantings, pleasing villa suites, a bustling marina, golf course, tennis, water sports. Expensive.

● *La Toubana:* A marvelously secluded cluster of bungalows set on top of a hill in Ste. Anne, with a fantastic view of the Caribbean and a small beach. Moderate.

● *Auberge du Grand Large:* Intimate, no-frills beachfront bungalows on an idyllic stretch of sand in Ste. Anne. Moderate.

☐ For more information, write: French West Indies Tourist Board, 610 Fifth Avenue, New York, NY 10020; or call: (212) 757-1125.

Jamaica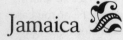

Jamaica doesn't sneak up on you with her charms. It's more of a friendly frontal assault. You're met with jungles of palm trees, jeweled sea (emerald, lapis lazuli, sapphire), music that shakes through your bones and rocks your soul. You see mountains smoldering with memories of the Maroons, who escaped their Spanish captors and still conduct their own courts of law. You float down rivers that run with life—rafters selling beer and boiled peanuts, boys diving for coins, men casting nets for jack, snook, and perch. Even Jamaica's food is intense—jerk pork that sends a shot of fire down your throat, Blue Mountain coffee, bananas sizzling in butter and rum. Where, in all this glory, to base yourselves? For honeymooners, four major resort areas—Montego Bay, Negril, Port Antonio, and Ocho Rios—hold particular appeal.

Montego Bay is vacation land with a capital "V." Jets stream in from cold northern cities. Discos disgorge college kids clutching piña coladas. Beaches are patchworks of volleyball games, tropical bars, and multicolored towels. Can two honeymooners find happiness in the madness of Montego? The answer is an emphatic yes. Tranquility is king on the Martha Brae river, where raftsmen pole you down the shimmer of green. Long-ago days come to life at Rose Hall, where the White Witch murdered husbands and slaves and made quite a name for herself. And while the tanning scene on Doctor's Cave Beach seems more like *Spring Break* than *Swept Away*, most hotels have strands long enough to provide nice pockets of privacy (and enough water-sport options to keep you wet all week).

Negril offers a funkier, laid-back Jamaican experience. If all the beach girls and all the barflies set about creating a bohemian dream retreat, they'd invent Negril. In fact, that's how this barefoot paradise on the West End came to be. The allure? First, there's the so-called Seven Mile Beach, a white stretch where you could walk for an hour or more and never run out of sand. Along the way, hawkers offer hair-braiding sessions, aloe massages, snorkeling lessons, banana bread, Red Stripe beers, and numerous illegal substances. On the other side of Negril, you'll find an unworldly vision: pockmarked limestone cliffs rising from ultramarine sea. They form an entire coast here, and

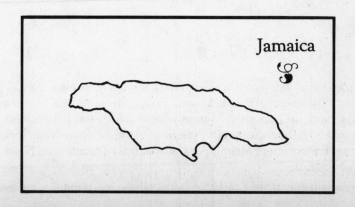

some are topped with thatched cottages, open-air restaurants, and late-night bars. In either area, days pass slowly—you can rent rubber rafts and float around the translucent pools, bike down the "main" road, stopping to shop for T-shirts and snacks, or just laze into a hammock with a book, a drink, and a splendid beach view.

Backed by the hazy Blue Mountains, Port Antonio offers a sophisticated and eclectic honeymoon scene. A late-night hour spent at the Roof Club paints part of the picture; the decor is Day-Glo rain forest, the ceiling a mass of palm fronds and posters, the music a blend of reggae and pop. Or head to the Bonnie View Hotel for a spreading panorama of musty gingerbread buildings, ships in the twin harbors, and lush little Navy Island with its sailing marina. More active Port Antonio pastimes include rafting on the Rio Grande (a sport invented by Errol Flynn); diving into the "bottomless" depths of the Blue Lagoon (the bluest blue since antifreeze); swimming in waterfalls named Somerset and Reach; and sailing to the tumble of palm trees called Princess Island. But most honeymooners never stray far from their resorts—some of the most exclusive on the island.

Ocho Rios's landscape is a marvel: giant waterfalls and generous rivers, trees heavy with salmon-colored ackee, long-tailed hummingbirds as brilliant as a Fabergé egg. Less frenetic than Montego, posher than Negril, and more tourist-oriented than Port Antonio, Ocho Rios seems just the right size. And it boasts a fair amount of actual sights (Firefly, Noel Coward's modest home, Shaw Park Gardens, where a 66-year-old banyan tree shades an entire grove of palms). But first on most itineraries is the slippery climb up Dunn's River Falls, a series of wide, foam-washed ledges scaled daily by hundreds of bathing-suit-clad tourists.

Evenings all over Jamaica are whatever you dream them to be: jacket-and-tie dinners in a formal resort, beach bonfires and barbecues, or sunset dinner cruises, followed up by dazzling nightclubs or rowdier reggae joints. Or, taking another tack, you could retreat to your terrace, lie on your backs, and spend the midnight hour just drinking in the stars.

FACTS TO GO ON 𝔖

☐ Getting there: Air Jamaica offers direct service from New York, Phila-delphia, Baltimore, Atlanta, Miami, Tampa, Toronto, and Los Angeles. Also serving the airports at Montego Bay and Kingston (where most Port Antonio-bound people land): American Airlines, from New York and Boston; Eastern, from Miami; Air Canada, from Toronto; and Northwest from Memphis.

☐ Entry requirements: U.S. and Canadian citizens need proof of citizenship (passport, birth certificate, or voters registration card) and an ongoing or return ticket.

☐ Currency: You'll be paying with Jamaican dollars.

☐ Language: English

☐ *Bride's* Best Beds

● *Half Moon Resort and Club:* For all-indulgence in Montego Bay, this soothing, pastel-shaded complex of villas and suites surrounded by tennis courts, golf course, and a lovely beach is the tops for relaxation. Expensive.

● *Sandals:* A 24-hour party of a place, boasting some of Montego Bay's best water-sporting. Sandals (and Sandals Royal Caribbean, a quieter sister resort) offer all-inclusive packages. They're both couples-only. Duos who like DJs at the pool, costume parties, and an as-much-as-you-can-eat (or drink) honeymoon style, will find Sandals to their liking. Expensive.

● *Rockhouse:* Negril's thatched place on the cliffs, where Tarzan might feel at home. No luxuries (the bungalows have no electricity or phones— you'll use kerosene lamps at night), but truly exotic, with lots of private sunning space and cool coves where *au naturel* is the preferred swimming style. Moderate.

● *Trident Hotel and Villas:* Port Antonio's elegant little covey of white cottages furnished with four-poster beds and plush wing chairs, all with views of the rocks, gazebo, and sea. Expensive.

● *Plantation Inn:* One of Ocho Rios's top-of-the-line places (Jamaica Inn and Sans Souci are both equally luxurious and romantic), set on a private hill and spilling onto two crescents of sandy seclusion. Expensive.

☐ For more information, write: Jamaica Tourist Board, 866 Second Avenue, New York, NY 10017; or call: (212) 688-7659 (there are also offices in Chicago, Coral Gables, Dallas, Los Angeles, Montreal, and Toronto).

Martinique

If you've ever thought that a Caribbean island is all palm trees and sand, Martinique will come as a surprise. It's not very big, but it can fool you into thinking you're in the Alps one minute and the Amazon the next. Its northern half is covered largely by a dense green rain forest; the eerie peak of a live, though dormant, volcano dominates the scene. The south has a drier terrain—even a patch of cacti-studded desert. Along the northwest coast there are miles of volcanic black-sand beach, while the east coast is edged by steep cliffs. All around the island's south: the sloping white sands that are pictured on so many Martinique postcards.

Martinique's man-made centerpiece is Fort-de-France, an intriguing city

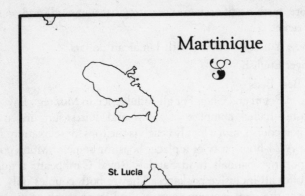

that resembles the Riviera with its waterfront promenade, chic shops, and sun-splashed cafés. Devote a morning to the customary sites (the Prefecture, the Schoelcher Library, and La Savane, a sprawling park with a statue of Napoleon's Josephine), souvenir shopping in the Caribbean Arts Center and the outdoor market, and bargain hunting in the luxury shops.

Rent yourselves a Peugeot or Renault for exploring the rest of the island. The road that winds through the mountains just north of town makes a nice quick afternoon trip, revealing beautiful vistas around every twist and turn. Balata Church seems like a mirage; perched among rich green peaks, it was designed after Paris's Sacré-Coeur. Carry on to the Balata Garden, a warren of tropical groves centered around an old Creole house.

You'll need a full day to explore the north, which some say is the prettiest part of the island. From Fort-de-France, take the road that clings to the western coastline. Along the way, you'll pass fishing villages where you can stop for a cup of strong French coffee and a freshly baked croissant. Linger awhile as men with sun-creased faces stencil names on crayon-colored boats, repair fishing nets, and clean their morning's catch.

In Le Carbet, where Columbus landed in 1502, wander around the small Gauguin Museum, then move on to the jumbled town of St. Pierre. In addition to its modern-day attractions—a lively marketplace, a boat-filled harbor, several shops—you'll see vine-draped stone walls, an old theater, and a dilapidated cathedral—all that's left of the original town wiped out when Mt. Pelée erupted in 1902.

Just north of St. Pierre the road turns inland, taking you through the lushest part of the island and up to its towering heights. Before long, you'll reach Leyritz Plantation, one of Martinique's restored great houses, where you can feast on spicy seafood and stroll the gardened grounds. Check out the main house; it's full of polished antiques and priceless furniture you'll covet for your own home. Walk out the back door and you're hit with a far-reaching view of the island and patterned sea beyond.

Afterward, resume your journey south along the east coast. With the thrashing Atlantic and rugged bluffs on your left, rolling hills and pineapple fields on your right, you won't know which way to look.

You'll find the biggest concentration of shorelining hotels and the longest expanses of white sand beach in the southern part of Martinique. Ask any locals which beach is their favorite and they're sure to say Plage des Salines. Once you take a look at its sloping sands lapped by the silky Caribbean, you'll have to agree.

As in any genuine *département* of France, you'll want to top off every day with a long meal and a good wine. Afterward, you can choose a fashionable nightclub, one of two casinos, or a quiet nightcap in sight of the sea.

FACTS TO GO ON

☐ Getting there: Eastern and Air France offer direct flights from Miami and San Juan, and American Airlines can make fairly simple connections from most U.S. cities to Martinique through its San Juan hub.

☐ Entry requirements: You'll need a passport (either a valid one or one that's been valid within the past five years), or a birth certificate or voters registration card plus photo ID. A visa will be issued to you at the airport on arrival.

☐ Currency: You'll be paying with French francs.

☐ Language: French

☐ *Bride's* Best Beds

● *Bakoua Beach:* Of the larger hotels in Pointe du Bout, Bakoua Beach has the most personality. Lovely views of the beach from some rooms, lots of water sports and tennis. Expensive.

● *Leyritz Plantation:* This eighteenth-century plantation house, surrounded by small stone cottages and lush tropical gardens, offers history and an away-from-it-all aura. Rooms in the main house are nicest. Transport to beach provided, but you'll probably want a car for freedom. Moderate.

☐ For more information, write: French West Indies Tourist Board, 610 Fifth Avenue, New York, NY 10020. Or call: (212) 757-1125.

Puerto Rico

Its Latin spirit sweeps you into island life. You'll find yourselves dancing in the streets alongside marching bands and stepping back into Spanish history on the narrow, cobbled streets of Old San Juan. But Puerto Rico's Spanish influence is just part of the picture. Licked by the milk-soft Caribbean on the southern coast and pounded by Atlantic breakers on the northern, split down the middle by a rugged mountain range and dotted with jungly forests, Puerto Rico is naturally gorgeous. And to top it all off, Puerto Rico is exceptionally easy to get to: American carriers fly direct from several U.S. cities every day of the week.

Start things off in San Juan, the city which is really two; splash and sun admid Condado's high-style beach towers, then dry off and explore Old San Juan. The majority of historical sites are found in this small, seven-block area, founded in 1508 by Ponce de Leon. Cobbled streets are lined with museums, churches, restored mansions smothered with bougainvillaea. Start at San Cristobel, one of two forts that loom above the Atlantic and which have guarded the city for centuries. Stroll along the Calle Norzagaray past the Old San Juan cemetery to El Morro, the more famous of the forts, where you can join a guided tour around the ramparts. Then head to Casa Blanca, set high above the harbor; built as the home for the Ponce de Leon family, it's now a museum of sixteenth- and seventeenth-century island life. Continue down to the San Juan Gate and La Forteleza, the part-citadel, part-palace residence of Puerto Rico's governor. Other old-city sights to see: the Pablo Casals Museum, housing the maestro's cello and manuscripts; La Casa del Libro (a book and bookmaking museum); and the Dominican Convent, with a small museum of Puerto Rican culture, as well as handmade crafts for sale.

Dedicated shoppers in Old San Juan can find bargains on straw bags and hats, ceramics, and hand-carved *santos* (wood statues of favored saints). There are also local paintings and sculpture to consider, as well as potential good buys on gold jewelry. Bottles of Puerto Rican rum are the best bargain of all.

Lots of honeymooners base themselves at a slick Condado beachside hotel in San Juan. Others head for nearby resorts like Dorado or Cerromar to sun on smooth sands and take advantage of extensive sports menus. But the rest of Puerto Rico—known as "Out on the Island"—is full of exploring possi-

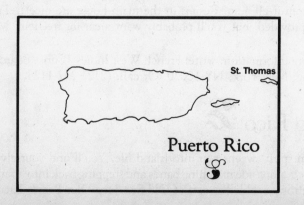

St. Thomas

Puerto Rico

bilities. Easy day-trips from San Juan include El Yunque, a tropical rain forest with giant ferns, spilling waterfalls, and thousands of intensely colored flowers, and Luquillo Beach, a gorgeous stretch of white sand ringed by hundreds of palms. You might also consider a few days completely away from the urban (and suburban) bustle. Head out through splendid countryside to San Germán, which feels like an open-air museum with its picture-postcard plazas and narrow streets; Ponce, for fascinating history (the Plaza's cathedral, a brightly painted firehouse dating to 1883) as well as the beautiful, modern-day Museum of Art; or to an offshore island like Vieques, ringed by lovely beaches, offering a marvelous, away-from-it-all feeling.

In the evenings you'll feast on continental meals in your resort's dining room overlooking a wave-pounded beach. Or head to local restaurants to sample island specialties like black bean soup, *bacalitos* (salt-fish fritters), *tostones* (deep-fried plantain), *arroz con pollo* (chicken with rice), and *jueyes* (land crabs). Then wander into the casino to join (or just watch) fortune-seekers concentrating on cards. More cultural doings include live music in Old San Juan's cafés and flamenco cellars as well as concerts and plays at the newly restored Tapia Theater.

FACTS TO GO ON &

☐ Getting there: American, Delta, Eastern, and TWA schedule nonstop flights from New York. American flies in from Dallas/Fort Worth, Hartford, Raleigh-Durham, Chicago, Baltimore, and Philadelphia. Eastern has daily nonstops from Miami, Atlanta, Baltimore, Boston, Philadelphia, Newark, and Pittsburgh.

☐ Entry requirements: U.S. citizens don't need any proof of citizenship to enter Puerto Rico.

☐ Currency: You'll be paying with U.S. dollars.

☐ Language: Spanish and English

☐ *Bride's* Best Beds

● *Caribe Hilton, Condado Plaza, and El San Juan:* All placed in one category for modern luxury settings on the beach. Expensive.

● *El Convento:* A Carmelite convent turned hotel in the heart of historic Old San Juan. Pleasantly scaled, antique-decorated, with a small pool and sun deck. Expensive.

● *Sands Hotel and Casino:* If you love casinos, this is the place. Newly opened in November 1987, the Sands features the largest casino in the Caribbean and a lot of Atlantic City hoopla on a prime San Juan beach. Moderate.

● *Hyatt Dorado Beach and Cerromar Beach Resorts:* An hour out of San Juan, these sister, sports-happy resorts on the coast continue to please with renovated, waterview rooms, golf and tennis galore, and an idyllic stretch of beach. Cerromar recently added a megafun pool—1,776 feet of waterfalls, slides, and swim-up bars. Expensive.

☐ For more information write: Puerto Rico Tourism Company, 1290 Avenue of the Americas, 22nd Floor, New York, NY 10104; or call: (800) 223-6530, or (212) 541-6630 in New York (there are also offices in Chicago, Dallas, Los Angeles, Miami, and Toronto).

St. Barthélemy

Fashion shoots are a common sight on picture-perfect St. Barts. Major magazines come from around the world to photograph their pages in this little pocket of the Caribbean. They can count on beautiful blue skies, flawless landscapes, and water the color of green apples. St. Barts offers a truly hedonistic combination: French refinement in a balmy, unspoiled hideaway.

Familiar Caribbean colors strike you first—the deep green of small round hills, the pastel blues of lapping waves, bright red tiles on a villa roof. St. Barts is a curvaceous island with wind-combed fields, flower-speckled valleys, coral-sand beaches, and a dollhouse-scaled capital port. It takes about two hours to see it all in a rented Mini-Moke, an open-air jeep that makes VW bugs look huge. From the airport you can reach the popular Baie St. Jean beach area in a few minutes. If it weren't for the scores of windsurfers darting about, you'd think it was a gigantic kiddie pool. Its sandy, sun-bleached shores are home to a couple of small, tastefully designed hotels (all hotels on St. Barts are small and tastefully designed). Take in the scene while you sip something fruity on the deck of the Filao Beach Hotel. From there, cruise along the north road, rising and falling over once-active volcanic hills and

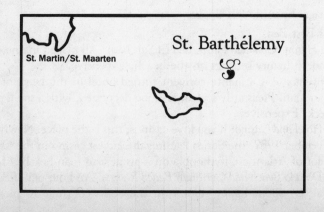

deep green valleys, passing pockets of sandy beach in hidden coves. Go ahead, pull over. You won't be able to take your eyes off the view.

The road curves down around the east coast to the south shore, where rock-hewn beaches are pounded by aggressive waves. The landscape looks like Brittany or Ireland—stone-walled pastures, farms, and tiled roofs built into steep hillsides. Continue inland and head for Corossol, on the western end of the island, where you'll see descendants of the island's earliest French settlers: old ladies in white starched bonnets selling straw hats alongside the road. Then head north to Anse des Flamands, where a hilltopping lookout scans the coast.

Set aside a couple of hours to poke around the French boutiques and duty-free shops of Gustavia. You'll find Parisian fashions, perfumes, and cosmetics, plus imported table and glassware. Then wander around the waterfront where sailboats from around the globe bob in the harbor. Mixed in with Gustavia's French Creole buildings, you'll see traces of the Swedes who owned St. Barts for a century: the Town Hall, the former yacht club, and the old Clock Tower at the foot of Morne Lurin, plus some street names and the name of the town itself (after their King Gustav).

At night, you may want to dine in a Gustavia restaurant, choosing between French, Creole, or seafood specialties. Or drive a bit south of town to Les Castelets, a one-of-a-kind hotel/restaurant perched on a hilltop overlooking the emerald sea. At night, when the moon pours molten on the inky black water, and the island's lights twinkle like stars, it's about as romantic as a place can be.

FACTS TO GO ON ॐ

- [ ] Getting there: Fly to St. Martin, St. Thomas, or Guadeloupe first, then board the 19-seater that flies to St. Barts; Air St. Barthélemy and Windward Island Airways fly from St. Martin, Air Guadeloupe from Guadeloupe and St. Martin, and Virgin Air from St. Thomas.
- [ ] Entry requirements: You'll need a valid or expired passport (no more than five years old), or proof of citizenship (a birth certificate or voters registration card), a photo ID, and a return or ongoing ticket.
- [ ] Currency: You'll be paying with French francs or U.S. dollars.
- [ ] Language: French; English is widely spoken.
- [ ] *Bride's* Best Beds
- *Les Castelets:* Offers ten antique-filled chalets with spectacular views. Expensive.
- *Filao Beach:* A crescent of bungalows right in the heart of the action on Baie St. Jean. Expensive.

● *Hotel Manapany:* Gaining fame for its exquisite restaurant, this posh colony of cottages spreads up the hill from a small, tranquil beach. Expensive.

☐ For more information, write: French West Indies Tourist Board, 610 Fifth Avenue, New York, NY 10020; or call: (212) 757-1125.

St. Kitts and Nevis 🐚

A solitary wind-flapped woman raking dried stalks of sugarcane seems symbolic of the sugar industry on St. Kitts and Nevis. Rickety trains still carry fresh-cut cane from field to factory, but many plantations have let fields lie fallow in favor of tourism. Converted to historic inns, these plantations form the base of a uniquely sophisticated island experience. You'll dine in plantation great houses, take bumpy rides to private beach cabanas, maybe stay in a plantation windmill made over as a honeymoon suite.

The two islands bathe in aqua seas west of Antigua. St. Kitts is larger, more modern, but a small-town feeling prevails. Cows meander on curvy mountain roads, a lonely spotlight runs on its own chugging generator, and in the eighteenth-century British capital town, Basseterre, even the smallest purchase is lovingly wrapped in brown paper, each edge meticulously taped. The island's prettiest beaches include Cockleshell Bay (accessible only by boat) and Frigate Bay on the Caribbean side, and Conaree Beach on the Atlantic side. A complete island tour takes just a day. Pack a picnic for Brimstone Hill Fortress, where stone arches frame a view of perfect blue, and cannons point to sea.

Any day of the week (except Thursday and Sunday) the white and turquoise ferry *Caribe Queen* will take you across the two-mile strait to Nevis, St. Kitts's cloud-crowned sister island, floating just off St. Kitts's southern tip. It'll dock in Charlestown, a port that seems stopped in time. Walk from the pier past

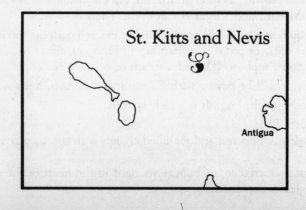

St. Kitts and Nevis

Antigua

a working cotton gin into the town's tiny center. A coffin-shaped square marks the war memorial, Alexander Hamilton House makes a quick historic stop (he was born on Nevis), lines form at the Philatelic Bureau for pretty postage stamps, and shops each display their specialized selections—three hammers, five dresses, a few tempting flavors of island fruit preserve.

To see the rest of Nevis, you'll need a car and lots of patience. It's not uncommon to come across a donkey in the center of the road, or a herd of goats. The island tour (a single road wraps around the island) reveals the ruins of the once-magnificent Bath Hotel, where wealthy Europeans came to take the waters; the New River Estate, Nevis's last operating sugar mill; Pinney's Beach, a three-mile-long palm-fringed strand; and the rambling ruins of Eden Rock Estate, built by a rich planter as a wedding present for his daughter. The grand house fell to ruin when the groom and best man killed each other.

Almost all restaurants are found in the islands' hotels and plantation inns, and the same goes for nightlife, which may amount to a calypso band out by the pool, or just the sounds of the night itself. On St. Kitts there's a disco or two, but evenings on both islands tend to be early-to-bed affairs.

FACTS TO GO ON 🕉

☐ Getting there: Eastern and American offer service from New York to St. Kitts, via San Juan. You can take either the ferry or a small plane to Nevis. If you plan to head to Nevis first, you might find it easier to fly to Antigua (lots of nonstops go there) and take a small plane to Nevis.

☐ Entry requirements: You'll need proof of citizenship (passport, birth certificate, or voters registration card) and a return or ongoing ticket.

☐ Currency: You'll be paying with Eastern Caribbean dollars. U.S. dollars are accepted widely.

☐ Language: English

☐ *Bride's* Best Beds

● *Rawlins Plantation:* St. Kitts's loveliest, most relaxing plantation inn, set high on a hill overlooking splendid gardens and canefield to the spreading blue Caribbean. Splurge and reserve the honeymoon suite, set in the plantation sugar mill—it's as romantic as you can get. You'll find a pool, tennis courts, horseback riding, and you can arrange to do a day or overnight sail with the owners on their 75-foot catamaran. Expensive.

● *Nisbet Plantation:* Of all Nevis plantation inns (and there are a number of beauties), this one gets top billing because it's right on the beach. Stately colonnades of palms are punctuated with cozy guest cottages, and dinner is served in the elegant manor house. Expensive.

● *Cliffdwellers:* Offering a more modern experience, Cliffdwellers sets its guest cottages on a steep slope looking over a spectacular view of Tamarind Bay and St. Kitts. Expensive.

☐ For more information, write: St. Kitts/Nevis Tourist Board, 650 Fifth Avenue, 23rd Floor, New York, NY 10019; or call: (212) 535-1234.

St. Lucia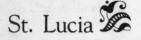

Doctor Doolittle talked to the animals on its shores. Its lone traffic light guides pedestrians across the airport runway. And every Friday night, one of its neighborhoods throws a party that the whole island attends. St. Lucia has a lot of character.

With roosters crowing in the main street and roads that could keep a repair crew busy into the twenty-first century, you might wonder about St. Lucia's charms. Look a bit closer and you'll find a happily natural island, stunningly beautiful at times (think of its mountains, its vines and flamboyant trees clinging like moss to a boulder), a touch sinister at others (think of its hissing volcano, its blessedly rare Fer-de-Lance snake). But always, it is a place unlike home—where twin mountains are wreathed in clouds and the sea is a bolt of navy silk Charmeuse.

Rent a car for at least part of your stay; you'll be able to tour at your own pace. And sharing the twisty mountain roads with cows, bicycles, and overloaded buses is an adventure in itself. Castries is the capital port, with a busy morning market and a backdrop of villa-dotted hills. Wind your way to the top of Morne Fortune for a spreading panorama: To the north, you'll see Pigeon Point, an excellent picnic spot with ruins for wandering and a quiet beach; densely jungled hills to the south open onto wide valleys of banana plantations.

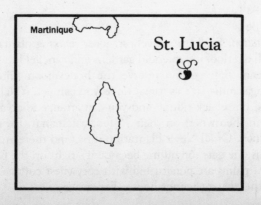

The sleepy fishing port of Soufrière is St. Lucia's second city. The Pitons—two volcanic cones, lushly green, rising from aqua waves to summits half a mile high—loom up beyond lower, verdant hills. Nearby Mt. Soufrière, a dormant volcano, attracts visitors with bubbling yellow pools and steamy hisses spewing from the earth's hot fissures; it's impressively smelly and hot enough to boil an egg. Since it takes you two impossibly bumpy hours to get there, reward yourselves afterward with a lobster lunch at Hummingbird; the rum punch is dusted with nutmeg, and the Pitons make an inspiring backdrop.

Another day, sail off to Marigot Bay, where *Doctor Doolittle* was filmed. Spend an afternoon on the palm-circled water; the world's smallest ferry will take you from a hotel on one shore to a bar on the other.

Finally, do plan a Friday night in Gros Islet, a tiny town that, every week, turns its houses into beer shops and its yards into gambling parlors, while a DJ blasts reggae from a second-story window. The whole island—locals and tourists alike—spends midnight dancing in the streets.

FACTS TO GO ON 🦢

☐ Getting there: Eastern, BWIA, and American Airlines fly into Hewanorra Airport from New York, San Juan, and Miami.

☐ Entry requirements: You'll need proof of citizenship (passport, birth certificate, along with a photo ID), as well as a return or ongoing ticket.

☐ Currency: You'll be paying with Eastern Caribbean dollars or U.S. dollars.

☐ Language: English

☐ *Bride's* Best Beds

● *Cunard's Hotel La Toc and La Toc Suites:* A small, British-accented pocket of privacy, La Toc is undeniably St. Lucia's beachfront luxury leader. If you can, by all means splurge on one of the La Toc suites; you'll have your own plunge pool in addition to two levels of pretty pine furnishings, a wet bar, tile floors, and a VCR. Expensive.

● *Marigot Bay Resort:* Situated on one of the Caribbean's favorite sailing harbors, simple cottages rise up a hill and look to sea. If you want to spend much time sailing, it's a fine, casual base. Moderate.

● *Dasheene:* Perched high on a mountain with jaw-dropping views of the Pitons and sea, these open-air, contemporary apartments offer total seclusion that might be just right for solitude seekers. Expensive.

☐ For more information, write: St. Lucia Tourist Board, 41 East 42nd Street, New York, NY 10017; or call: (212) 867-2950.

St. Martin/St. Maarten

Don't wait till the day before you're cruising down the aisle to make reservations for St. Martin/St. Maarten. Almost year-round, this reliably sunny island is booked solid. It's the kind of place that couples discover on their honeymoon, come back to on their anniversaries, returning later with their children. Ask them what's the appeal and they'll answer, very simply: the beaches, the sea, the sunshine.

It's one island that smiles in two languages—Dutch and French—which is rather surprising. Because even by Caribbean standards, this is a very small island, with only 37 square miles to its two names. Between two such august powers, squeezed onto such a little land dot—the solid Dutch who lay claim to 16 square miles on its southern shores, and the proud French whose tricolor flag flies over the other northern 21—there might be friction anywhere else in the world. Not here. Instead Dutch St. Maarten and French St. Martin share the warmth—they celebrate each other's holidays, sun on each other's beaches, feast in each other's restaurants, and play in the same casinos.

There's no requisite sightseeing, but if you insist on doing something stimulating, you can take a circle tour of the island, stopping at landmark resorts like La Samanna (one of the Caribbean's most luxurious—and expensive—hotels), and meander around the Dutch side, snapping a shot of the obelisk border monument just before you cross over (border crossing is done easily and informally—no guards, no gates, not a sign of a customs officer). But beach-basking and picnicking are what exploring is really about. Least-peopled sands are apt to be those along Long Bay, north of Cupecoy; Plum and Rouge bays, on the French side; and a number of nameless but nonetheless lovely notches along the eastern shoreline.

Shopping is genuinely duty-free here, so there are notable buys on both sides of the border. Each has its specialties: Phillipsburg shops shine with fine jewelry, crystal, and china, as well as Dutch delftware, pipes, cheeses,

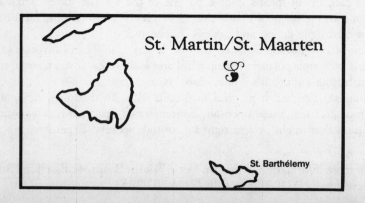

St. Martin/St. Maarten

St. Barthélemy

and chocolates. In the French capital of Marigot, you'll find dozens of chic boutiques displaying the latest Parisian fashions, perfumes, cosmetics, and gourmet treats.

If you prefer to work on your tans and stay within sight of the water, you really don't have to venture far from your hotel. You can swim, snorkel, and sail right from its beach. You'll also find tennis courts, riding stables, and a palm-dotted golf course on the island. When you want a scene change, consider a day trip to St. Barts, Anguilla, Saba, or St. Eustatius.

Sociable evenings start with sundown drinks in an island café, followed by an elegant dinner (wherever you go, be sure to make reservations). Choose one of Marigot's small harborside French spots, or head to Grande Case, a truly unique fishing village lined with one restaurant after another. Then there are Dutch casinos and discos to turn to, or just the pure simplicity of the island's starlit romance.

FACTS TO GO ON ❧

☐ Getting there: Eastern offers daily service from Miami; Pan Am, ALM, and American fly nonstop from New York. American also offers connecting flights from Dallas/Fort Worth and Boston via San Juan. LIAT, ALM, BWIA, and Windward Islands Airways offer interisland flights. Phillipsburg has long been a favored cruise-ship port, and ships are just starting to sail into Marigot.

☐ Entry requirements: You'll need a valid or expired passport (not more than five years old) or proof of citizenship (a voters registration card or birth certificate), and a return or ongoing ticket.

☐ Currency: On the French side you'll be paying with French francs and on the Dutch side you'll pay with Netherland Antilles florins (or guilders), but U.S. dollars widely accepted.

☐ Language: French and Dutch

☐ *Bride's* Best Beds

● *La Samanna:* This posh resort set the standard for luxury hotels in the Caribbean, and it remains a favorite of privileged travelers. Set on St. Martin's loveliest beach, white stucco buildings house large, luxurious rooms with dreamy seaviews. Expensive.

● *L'Habitation:* A brand-new resort tucked away on beautiful Anse Marcel, where everything from the lampposts to the room appointments was imported from France. Expensive.

● *Oyster Pond Yacht Club:* An isolated, Dutch-side resort, offering luxurious accommodations looking to the sea, wonderful dining, and escape from the tourist bustle. Expensive.

☐ For more information, write: St. Maarten Tourist Office, 275 Seventh Avenue, 19th Floor, New York, NY 10001-6708; or call: (212) 989-0000. You can also write: French West Indies Tourist Board, 610 Fifth Avenue, New York, NY 10020; or call: (212) 757-1125.

U.S. Virgin Islands

Three American islands lie anchored in azure sea. The first, St. Thomas, specializes in air-conditioned resorts, bustly beaches, and serious shopping for Rolex watches. The next, St. John, is a shy, almost reclusive place which prefers the simplicity of pure sand, quiet sunsets, and starry nights. The third, St. Croix, has a nostalgic bent, a countryside of haunting sugar mills, a town of sailors' pubs and antique lemon-yellow buildings. All together, they welcome enough honeymooners each year to nearly sink the lot. They boast some of the prettiest beaches and bluest waters (we mean blue—like Paul Newman's eyes) this side of Tahiti. And they're incredibly easy: just four nonstop hours from New York—no need for passports, no customs to clear, and no money-changing lines (U.S. dollars are the way to pay). It just might be your kind of paradise.

If you like romance novels and two-handkerchief movies, St. Croix will delight you; its molded hills and port towns are steeped in nostalgia. St. Croix's real beauty doesn't lie in palm-fringed beaches—though it certainly has its share. Instead, you'll be drawn back time and time again to the antique streets of Christiansted. Down by the water, grand old buildings have been painted canary yellow, trimmed with white. Boats bob in the harbor, waiting to ferry day-trippers to Buck Island. Paintbox sidestreets of shops, cafés, and small hotels make wandering with a camera pure happiness.

When you rent a car and head for the hills, you'll discover abandoned sugar mills scattered across the Scottish-looking landscape; remnants of the

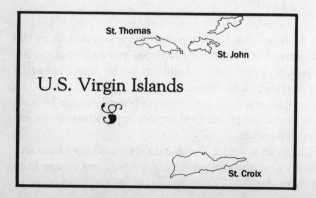

great plantations—named Solitude, Rust Up Twist, Sally's Fancy; and several stops which you really shouldn't miss—St. George Botanical Gardens; the Virgin Islands Rum Distillery; and Whim Great House, which somehow looks more like a church than a house. When you've had enough history, it's time to take the sail to Buck Island Reef; it's a castaway isle fit for Robinson Crusoe himself which boasts the nation's only underwater national monument—a beautiful excuse for a few hours on the water. Half of the boats that make the daily trip dock near the underwater trails of the reef; the other half anchor off what must be the world's most pristine beach. At midday they change places.

The St. Thomas honeymoon story: silvery beaches, endless vistas, and restaurants ensconced in Danish manor houses. It's a world of water sports—you can learn to windsurf, ride giant sea tricycles, and—with masks and fins—open your eyes to a whole new underwater world. And St. Thomas is famous for its wealth of duty-free shops—glittery warehouses that display enough gold watches, precious gems, and electronic gewgaws to outfit a thousand harems.

Mornings here are meant to be lazy, so sleep in, then wake to the world with a splash in the sea. When you're ready to explore Charlotte Amalie, the U.S. Virgins' capital port, outfit yourselves in comfortable shoes and call for a taxi. You might start a tour near the waterfront, keeping an eye peeled for the so-called Grand Hotel, which probably once was, but now houses a Visitors Center; Cardow Jewelers, the first sign of St. Thomas's duty-free shopping district; Fort Christian's dungeons, full of Arawak and Carib Indian artifacts; and Government House, with a collection of paintings by St. Thomas artists (including Camille Pissarro, who was born here).

If it's a major cruise ship day, however, forget about exploring town or any of the bigger beaches. Instead, head for smaller strands like Atlantic-lapped Hull Bay, or take to the hills on Crown Mountain Road, where patches of jungled valley yawn just feet from your car. Another smart option: Run away to sea on a party sail; schooners charge about $100 per couple for a day of pampered yachting, including coffee and Bloody Marys when you set sail, sunning and snorkeling in an inviting glassy cove, and rum punches all the way home.

St. John, the baby U.S. Virgin, is one of the Caribbean's favorite day-trip destinations. Every morning, sailboats and ferries shuttle here from St. Thomas's Red Hook dock, offering vacationers a break from the big-island bustle. Once on St. John, they snorkel in crystalline water, beach-comb on unhurried sands, and take a look at another side of paradise.

If you choose to stay on St. John, your days will take on a very different tempo. You'll wake slowly, stretch, listen to the finches outside your window. Perhaps you'll decide on a swim before breakfast; the sea is just steps from your door, and there's not another body in sight (remarkable, when you consider these are some of the world's finest strands). Over coffee, you can plot your day. Maybe a visit to the island's National Park, which encompasses 20 densely green square miles (two-thirds of the whole island) and 5,000 offshore acres—including the National Park Service Underwater Trail just off Trunk Bay. There, markers steer snorkelers toward huge brain coral and a wealth of fish life—Queen Angelfish, Foureye Butterflyfish—that will knock your flippers off.

You might want to drive to Cruz Bay, to look around and check the bulletin board for any news. Strike up a conversation over a beer, watch the ferry unload, and consider how pleasant life in a backwater town could be. Or perhaps you'll just stay where you are, loafing on the beach until lunch. There's nothing you really have to do on St. John, and that makes it one of the most relaxing isles in this or any sea.

Virgin Island evenings run the gamut. They should start with drinks in a couple of seaside chairs, watching the sky turn to gold. Then dinner, which could be anything from conch fritters to a nouvelle feast of rare lamb and baby vegetables. Afterward, there's probably something happening at your hotel—steel bands, limbo contests, and calypso dancing, or choose from a selection of late-night clubs that buzz all over the islands. But you might just prefer a walk on the beach, a bit of stargazing, and your own private serenade.

FACTS TO GO ON 🎵

☐ Getting there: American Airlines schedules nonstop and one-stop flights from New York to both St. Thomas and St. Croix; from Boston, though the plane stops, you'll reboard almost immediately. Eastern Airlines flies from Miami; if you're traveling from midwest, southern, or western cities, your flight will be routed through their Miami gateway or San Juan's International Airport. Honeymooners headed for St. John land first in St. Thomas, taxi to the Red Hook dock, and catch a ferry for Cruz Bay.

☐ Entry requirements: Though you won't need proof of citizenship to enter the U.S. Virgin Islands, you'll need it to get back home. If you don't have passports, a birth certificate or voters registration card will do.

☐ Currency: You'll pay for everything with American dollars.

☐ Language: English

☐ Bride's Best Beds

● Buccaneer Hotel and Beach Club: On St. Croix, just outside of Christiansted, the Buccaneer sprawls down a hillside, offering golf, tennis, and lots of beaching. It's one of the most extensive resort settings on the island, and the honeymoon packages could be enticing. Expensive.

- *Carambola Beach Resort:* On St. Croix, it's Rockresort's newest luxury entry into the Caribbean resort race. Expensive.
- *Stouffer Grand Beach Resort:* St. Thomas-bound newlyweds looking for the big resort experience might do well here. On Pineapple Beach, it includes a complex of bright rooms, half a dozen tennis courts, and a beachside pool that's a stunner. It's all fresh, airy, and awfully appealing.
- *Frenchman's Reef Beach Resort:* At the mouth of Charlotte Amalie's harbor on St. Thomas, Frenchman's Reef pleases with big, waterview rooms and extensive sporting facilities. Expensive.
- *Caneel Bay Plantation:* On St. John, a serene Rockresort, boasting seven pristine beaches, lavish luncheon buffets (plum-rum soup to bacon burgers), and dressy evenings. The crowd is high-brow preppy, the atmosphere is pure peace and tranquility. Expensive.
- *Virgin Grand Beach Hotel:* The deluxe new entry on St. John's hotel scene. Expensive.
- *Cinnamon Bay and Maho Bay Campgrounds:* For St. John-bound couples who like the idea of roughing it, these two campgrounds are a honeymoon bargain. Whether you're in Cinnamon Bay's one-room cottages or tents by the beach, or in Maho Bay's canvas-sided, wooden "floored" houses with hillside views, the pristine beauty of St. John makes it naturally romantic. Inexpensive.

☐ For more information, write: U.S. Virgin Islands Division of Tourism, 1270 Avenue of the Americas, New York, NY 10020; or call: (212) 582-4520 (there are also offices in Atlanta, Chicago, Los Angeles, Miami, San Juan, Toronto, and Washington, D.C.).

The Bahamas

Just a generous stone's throw from Miami's climate-controlled shopping centers, Straw Market ladies hawk their wares from gingerbread porches. Bobbies in pith helmets direct traffic, and fringe-topped surreys clop-clop along palm-shaded avenues. Miles of spun-sugar beach sweep to the horizon, and a single boat bobs at the end of a ramshackle pier. Incredibly close to the U.S. (you can jet from Miami to Freeport in half an hour), the Bahamas are really nothing like home. Life moves slowly; the sun burns bright. Tongues wrap around a low-pitched island cadence. Tropical fish flirt around coral gardens, and flamingos eyeball cameras with a skittery gaze.

Most tourists visit the two major Bahamian islands—meaning New Prov-

THE BAHAMAS

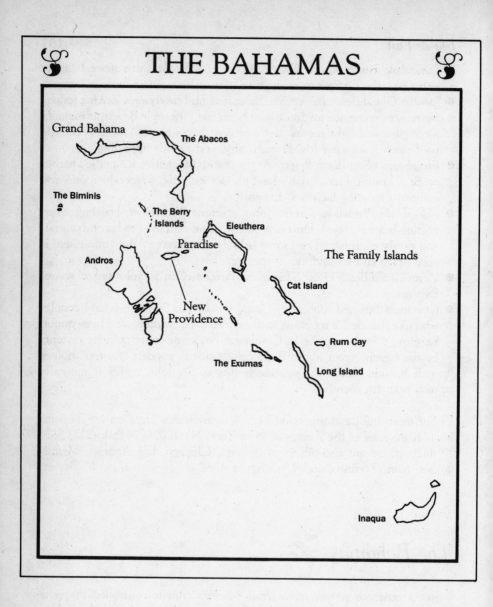

Grand Bahama

The Abacos

The Biminis

The Berry
Islands

Eleuthera

Paradise

The Family Islands

Andros

Cat Island

New
Providence

Rum Cay

The Exumas

Long Island

Inaqua

idence (usually referred to as Nassau, its capital) along with its sister, Paradise Island, and Grand Bahama, home to the resort areas of Freeport and Lucaya. But there are some 698 other Bahamas—many no larger than a beach blanket, others grand and sprawling and flecked with posh cottage compounds. So though you might fall for the casino action and shopping frenzy of the Big Two, do your honeymoon a favor and sample at least one of the Bahamas' smaller, sweeter Family Islands. Here's a rundown on what to expect.

New Providence and Paradise

New Providence is certainly not the Bahamas' largest island (just 21 miles long and 7 miles wide), but it's home to the nation's capital and to some of its greatest attractions. On the northern end, you'll find the historic port of Nassau with its bevy of duty-free shops, mesmerizing Straw Market, and collection of pastel buildings. About five miles to the west lies the stretch of sands known as Cable Beach, a resort area with ultra-luxe hotels and condos, a glittery casino, and some of the island's best restaurants. Paradise Island, just across the harbor from Nassau, can be reached by ferry or bridge. It's known for gleaming hotels, fine restaurants, round-the-clock casinos, and pristine white beaches.

Nassau and Paradise deal in luxury. Days begin slowly with breakfast on a terrace—sweet Eleuthera pineapple, honey rolls, and coffee served to the sounds of a gentle surf. Then it's beach and sun time—with a parasail flight, a water-ski lesson, a concentrated go at windsurfing. Or sail with a Nassau-born skipper in his island-made boat. There's tennis and golf and mopeds to buzz about on, plus downtown Nassau to explore.

The usual starting point for a Nassau tour is palm-shaded Rawson Square, in the heart of downtown. Stroll along Woodes Rogers Walk on the waterfront, aiming for Bay Street, to check out the cluster of colonnaded government buildings on Parliament Square. Then head up any of the sloping narrow lanes, admiring centuries-old churches, pretty pastel houses, and historical mansions surrounded by walled gardens. At the intersection of George and Duke streets, snap a shot of the pink-and-white Government House and its larger-than-life statue of Christopher Columbus (every other Saturday there's a formal changing of the guard ceremony). Then make your way to Elizabeth Avenue and up to the Queen's Staircase. Its 65 steps were carved out of limestone by slaves in the late 1700s. At the summit, inspect the ruins of Fort Fincastle, ride the elevator to the top of the water tower for a sweeping view of the islands, and examine costumes and artifacts in the Junkanoo Art Gallery.

With a healthy dose of history under your belt, it's time to put away the cameras and take out your wallets. Serious shoppers can spend days in Bay

Street emporia, collecting imported British woolens, bone china, French perfumes, crystal, and Swiss watches—usually at 20 to 40 percent less than U.S. prices. If you plan on any really big purchases—like filling out your china pattern—bring a list of prices from home for comparison. And save some money for local crafts; the Straw Market bustles from early morning to late evening seven days a week. Big Bahamian women will slip coral necklaces over your heads, hand you five straw bags at one time, and hold up joyously decorated dresses and smocks. Afterward, treat yourselves to a pub stop (maybe Smugglers, in the Prince George Arcade) before heading for home.

After a few pure beach-basking days, you'll be tempted to explore the rest of the island. Your best bet is to rent a car, a pair of mopeds, or spring for a limousine tour. Whichever way you choose, take along a copy of the Bahamas' *Trailblazer Map*, free at most hotels and tour desks. Start at Fort Charlotte, off West Bay Street. The well-preserved fortification boasts magnificent views. Then move on to the Ardasta Gardens, where you can watch a performance of marching flamingos. Next stop: the Seafloor Aquarium, a showcase of luminous underwater life. As you leave the Fort Charlotte area, you'll pass the Western Esplanade Beach, also known as Lighthouse Beach for the stunning vista across the harbor.

On the eastern end of the island, you'll pass several tony yacht clubs, grand mansions, and impressive private homes including one that's a replica of a lighthouse. Near the intersection of Fox Hill Road and the Eastern Road, a trail leads to Blackbeard's Tower, thought to be the pirate's lookout; the view from the top is spectacular. Farther along, you'll come to the St. Augustine Monastery, where the monks will be happy to show you around (they'll also sell you guava jam). In the prestigious Prospect Ridge Road and Skyline Drive area, you'll pass more sprawling homes on the way to Cable Beach, the snazzy resort stretch which was named in 1892 after the first communications cable was laid from Florida to the Bahamas. Save your sunning for the afternoon and continue on to the Caves, supposed hiding places for seventeenth-century pirates and their booty. If hunger strikes, you'll be right at the Traveller's Rest, a beautifully situated restaurant serving up hearty Bahamian meals and drinks. From there you'll pass through the Pine Barrens, thousands of acres of casuarina pines, palmettos and cycads, and flowering shrubs. Adelaide Village, a settlement of stone, thatched-roof cottages, is a sweet spot to stop for pictures. Then take a look around the Bacardi Rum Distillery.

Just before you're back in town, you'll pass through two "over the hill" towns—Bains Town and Grants Town—small communities of wooden homes literally just over the ridge from Nassau. You'll find some of the best (and cheapest) Bahamian food at small, hole-in-the-wall restaurants in both neighborhoods. Be sure to have peas 'n' rice, fried plantain (like a banana sautéed in butter), maybe some conch salad.

Paradise Island doesn't take long to explore. A wee bit of an island (a narrow two and a half miles), you can tour it in less than an hour. You'll see traces of the island's aristocratic past, when it was a playground for jet-setters, politicians, and European royalty. On the grounds of the Ocean Club stand medieval cloisters that were dismantled and brought stone by stone from France to be reassembled in Versailles Gardens. But today's biggest magnet is the casino and the deluxe hotels and gourmet restaurants that have sprung up around it. Elsewhere on the island you'll find lots of shops and boutiques, white sandy beaches, and a huge variety of sport setups. Athletic-minded visitors will be in their glory on this little island. There's an 18-hole golf course, dozens of tennis courts, riding stables, plus all manner of water sports: Windsurfers, parasailers, sailboats—you name it.

Most nights you'll dine at your hotel—because MAP (Modified American Plan) prices include your room plus breakfast and dinner. But make a point of one or two off-campus evenings. A trio of elegant Nassau choices: gardeny Buena Vista, stylish Graycliff, the mansion-set East Hill Club. Later, roulette wheels spin in Paradise Island's casino while nightclubs stage showgirl revues. Most hotels continue on into the wee hours with calypso bands and starlight dancing. Or hit a local hotspot like Peanuts Taylor's Drumbeat Club, where the rocking is genuinely Bahamian.

FACTS TO GO ON &

☐ Getting there: Eastern, Pan Am, TWA, Delta, and United fly nonstop or direct to Nassau and/or Freeport from several U.S. cities. Bahamasair has flights from Atlanta, Fort Lauderdale, Orlando, Miami, and New York, with connections between the Family Islands. Chalk International offers seaplane trips to Paradise Island, Bimini, and Cat Cay—all from Florida.

☐ Entry requirements: You'll need a passport, birth certificate, or voters registration card.

☐ Currency: The Bahamian dollar (B$), which is on a par and interchangeable with the U.S. dollar. Banking services are limited on the Family Islands, and many places don't take credit cards, so be sure to have enough cash and traveler's checks.

☐ Language: English

☐ *Bride's* Best Beds on New Providence

● *Cable Beach Hotel and Casino:* The newest, the most elaborate, on the Nassau hotel scene, with balconied, oceanfront rooms, multiple restaurants, ten tennis courts, racquetball, squash, golf, waterskiing, parasailing, snorkeling, scuba, swimming pool, splendid sands, and access to a casino complex. Expensive.

- *Royal Bahamian Hotel:* Gorgeously traditional, this Wyndham property offers rooms and lavish villa suites looking over the beach, plus café, lovely dining room, pool, water sports, health spa, and nighttime fun. Expensive.
- *Ocean Club (on Paradise Island):* Resorts International's handsome, recently refurbished luxury landmark, with large, balconied rooms, cushy villas, plenty of sports and prime beach locations. The most elegant Paradise Island option. Expensive.

☐ For more information, write: The Bahamas Tourist Office, 150 East 52nd Street, New York, NY 10022; or call: (212) 758-2777. There are also offices in Atlanta, Boston, Chicago, Dallas, Detroit, Houston, Los Angeles, Miami, Philadelphia, San Francisco, St. Louis, and Washington, D.C.

Grand Bahama 🐚

Grand Bahama Island, the most northerly of the Bahamas, lies just 60 miles off Florida's Palm Beach coast. Freeport, with its wide, palm-lined boulevards, and the gardened suburb of Lucaya are its centerpiece, highlighted by an impressive collection of hotels, a world-famous bazaar, a pair of casinos, and several fine restaurants and nightspots. But more than anything else, Freeport and Lucaya specialize in sport. In addition to 90 challenging holes of golf and some extraordinary diving, you'll find plenty of tennis and a wealth of beaches. Plus Sailfish, Sunfish, and Hobie Cats to rent, horses to ride (check Freeport's Pinetree Stables), and cricket, soccer, and rugby to applaud in season.

Though it's not exactly a sport, you can exercise your credit cards in the International Bazaar, a collection of shops and restaurants displaying treasures from India, Israel, France, Mexico, Denmark, Spain—you name the country, they've got the goods. Double-decker buses that tour Freeport/Lucaya can drop you off there.

Other times, rent motor scooters and chug off to the Rand Memorial Nature Center, a 100-acre park full of subtropical trees and flowers, exotic birds, and waterfalls. Then continue on to the fancifully landscaped Garden of the Groves, a marvelous spot for a picnic among leafy ferns, fountains, and tranquil lagoons. From there explore some of the island's most beautiful sands—Taino Beach is a stunner. If you're certified divers or want to learn, stop by UNEXSO (the Underwater Explorers Society). It'll open your eyes to a submarine world of dreamy beauty.

Rent a car to visit the western end of Grand Bahama, where the world takes on a laid-back perspective. You'll pass through a number of charming villages: Eight Mile Rock, where Fragrance of the Bahamas makes perfume from local hibiscus and frangipani; Seagrape, a sweet hamlet whose bakery turns out some of the island's best bread; and West End (the very western tip), an eccentric seaside village with a couple of churches and about a dozen bars. Stop for a pair of rum punches at the Star, a building that used to be a hotel back in the '40s. Or wait until you're heading back through Eight Mile Rock and stop at Harry's American Bar. If it's sundown, you're in for an unforgettable extravaganza.

At night, you can sup on Bahamian fare at the Fat Man's, Freddy's Place, or New Peace and Plenty. Or dress up for lobster Arawak at the Lucayan Country Club. One night, gamble a few honeymoon dollars at the legendary Princess Casino. Or opt for the risk-free fun of an island disco; your hotel's front desk can clue you in on the current Freeport favorites.

☐ *Bride's* Best Beds on Grand Bahama
● *Bahamas Princess Resort and Casino:* The biggest hotels with a glittery casino, lots of water sports, and a party feel. It offers some enticing honeymoon packages. Expensive.
● *Lucayan Beach Resort and Casino:* Recently redone, with a grand new casino. Expensive.

The Family Islands ॐ

They seduce you with gentle sensations: the softness of the sand, the cellophane sea, the smiles of the people and the scent of flowers, the slow, patterned pace of things. The Bahamas Family Islands:

The Abacos are often referred to simply as Abaco, but are actually a whole string of islands. You can fly into Marsh Harbor (the Abacos's main hub) Walker's Cay (a fishing resort in the extreme south), or Treasure Cay (actually part of the main island) and stay in a sprawling resort complete with golf, tennis, and a lively social scene. Or perhaps you'll choose a secluded spot where the entire island feels like your own. Wherever you settle, you're sure to find plenty of perfect white-sand beach, aquamarine water, and swaying palm trees, plus a pleasing array of water toys. There's also some sightseeing to do. Take the ferry over to Green Turtle Cay and check out the peaceful little town of New Plymouth, which looks like New England (plus palms) with its Colonial houses, white picket fences, and flower gardens. Plan to spend a day strolling its narrow streets, sampling its food, and relaxing on its sun-splashed beaches.

Back on Abaco, spend a little time exploring Marsh Harbor, a meeting place for boaters from around the world. Don't miss the bread at Key's Bakery.

Cynthia's Kitchen, in the center of town, features specialties like curried goat, turtle steak, stuffed crabs, and Cynthia's own johnnycakes. Elbow Cay, easily reached by ferry, is noted for its much-photographed red-and-white lighthouse; you can climb to the top for a 360-degree view.

Andros, the Bahamas' largest—and one of its least developed—islands, is a mecca for scuba divers and snorkelers. The 120-mile-long Tongue of the Ocean reef, second only to Australia's Great Barrier Reef, is less than a mile offshore and boasts some of the world's most exotic marine life. In addition to underwater wonders, there are long stretches of deserted beaches, some picturesque settlements along the eastern coast (Staniard Creek, Nicholls Town, and Morgan's Bluff), a batik-fabric and fashion workshop, and several sporty resorts and hotels for staying.

The Berry Islands, a cluster of tiny cays north of Andros and New Providence, are largely uninhabited. But if you're into diving, the Chub Cay Club offers a full scuba program and all the fishing you could ask for.

The Biminis, just south of Grand Bahama Island, are known mostly for their big-game fishing, but there are also great diving sites and glorious sunning sands. You'll find most of the bars, nightclubs, and shops—including a straw market—around Alice Town (all within walking distance) and the long, winding beaches, rustic resorts, and marinas on the Gulf Stream side. Attractions include the Blue Marlin Cottage, where Ernest Hemingway stayed during his fishing visits, the Hall of Fame (anglers from around the world are pictured with their prize-winning catches), and the Lost Continent, a group of large flat rocks that jut 20 to 30 feet out of the water, which some say is part of the fabled Atlantis.

Cat Island, across the sound from the Exumas, is the ideal island for seclusion seekers, divers, and fishermen. It boasts hundreds of miles of untrodden beaches, the highest point in the Bahamas (Mount Alvernia soars to 206 feet), and a complete refuge from the hustle and bustle of modern-day life. Some of the locals rely on lanternlight, cook outside, and draw water from wells as they did centuries ago.

Eleuthera, the Family Island you may have heard about, is long (110 miles) and never much more than two miles wide. Which means you're never far from the crystal-clear sea. Punctuated with historic villages, posh resorts, distinctive restaurants, and surrounded by endless white-and-pink-sand beaches, it's a quintessential honeymoon island. Take some time off from sunning to explore Harbour Island, just off the northeast coast. Home to the seventeenth-century village of Dunmore Town, it's one of the most beautiful spots in the Bahamas. Spanish Wells is another small island off the northwest end, named for the Spaniards who came ashore to replenish their water supplies.

Eleuthera's other attractions include its sporty resorts (lots of tennis and golf) and underwater discoveries. The Devil's Backbone is a spine of reefs that caused many shipwrecks in the late 1880s; some still lie sunken in their depths.

The Exumas are a chain of islands that stretch from just south of New Providence Island down to Long Island. They say there are 365 of them, one for each day of the year. Sailors, fishermen, and divers are their biggest fans, but the Exumas boast plenty of other attractions for sun-worshiping newlyweds. You'll find miles and miles of unspoiled beaches, a number of pretty villages and weathered plantations, plus lots of activity in the busy capital of George Town. Steeped in history (pirates and plantations), it's an interesting place to get to know. There's also some good shopping (a great straw market) and delectable lunch spots—the Sunrise Café and Eddie's Edgewater both offer delicious Bahamian fare. To tour the settlements north and south of George Town, you'll need a moped, taxi and driver, or rental car. At some point, be sure to get up to the Exuma Land and Sea Park by Sampson Cay. Accessible only by boat, it boasts miles and miles of protected cays, islands and coral formations just below the water's surface.

Inagua, the most southerly of the Bahamian islands, is not exactly the place to go if you crave excitement. One of the most remote Family Islands, it's a haven for nature lovers and wildlife enthusiasts. Its interior Lake Windsor, surrounded by parklands protecting hundreds of tropical bird species, is home to the largest colony of pink flamingos in the world. The only developed area on the island is Matthew Town, where you'll find friendly people, government buildings, and a couple of hotels and restaurants serving island specialties.

Long Island lives up to its name. Just south of the Exumas, its cliff-edged Atlantic shore is pounded by surging sea while the leeward side is a stretch of long, quiet beaches, hidden coves, and the calm surf. The 57-mile highway that runs the length of the island passes through several small settlements like Deadman's Cay and Hard Bargain. There's some history to see—ancient Indian drawings on cave walls, the ruins of Lord Dunmore's plantation—and shopping too (nearly every village has a straw market). Stella Maris Inn is the island's only major resort with tennis, fishing, and diving.

Rum Cay, just to the east of Long Island, got its name in the 1700s when a West Indian ship transporting rum was wrecked on its shore. A tiny place, it's home to fewer than 100 people. There are historic ruins to explore, miles of secluded beach, and an encircling necklace of coral reef that would impress even Jacques Cousteau.

☐ *Bride's Best Beds on the Family Islands*
● *Treasure Cay Beach Hotel and Villas (Abaco):* Offering leisure-class style, good-looking villas, an active sports life (golf, tennis, pools, scuba, sailing), and a perfect curve of beach. Expensive.

- *Bluff House (Abaco):* Perched on its own hilltop on away-from-it-all Green Turtle Cay. Super views. Moderate.
- *Small Hope Bay Lodge (Andros):* On a lovely palm-backed beach, this cheerful resort concentrates on diving, fishing, and cheerful informality. Moderate.
- *Las Palmas Hotel (Andros):* Snorkel-happy resort (masks and fins provided free) with air-conditioned rooms, sailing, and putting green. Moderate.
- *Chub Cay Club (Berry Islands):* The marina provides the focus for this fishing-oriented resort with tennis courts, pool, houseboats, and handsome condominiums. Expensive.
- *Bimini Big Game Fishing Club (Bimini):* A friendly place set up to arrange deep-sea and bonefishing trips, it lives up to its name. Moderate.
- *Fernandez Bay Village (Cat Island):* For the ultimate in sunny seclusion, these well-endowed cottages right on the beach could be perfect. Moderate.
- *Cotton Bay Beach and Golf Club (Eleuthera):* Near Rock Sound, boasting championship golf, tennis, fine fishing, and two miles of glorious white sand beach. Expensive.
- *Windermere Island Club (Eleuthera):* Serenely romantic on a little island of its own, with well-appointed rooms, cottages and suites, formal dining, and a wealthy aura. Charles and Di stayed here. Expensive.
- *Out Island Inn Village (Exumas):* Stretched along a nice beach, with stone cottages looking to sea. All manner of water sports, plus tennis, fishing trips, and enticing packages. Moderate.
- *Hotel Peace and Plenty (Exumas):* In George Town, informal guesthouse atmosphere and soothing views of Stocking Island. Moderate.
- *Ford's Inagua Inn (Inagua):* Airy rooms and delicious island cuisine. Moderate.
- *Stella Maris Inn (Long Island):* A rambling cottage resort with extensive diving plus sailing, fishing, snorkeling, and on-island sporting. Moderate.
- *Rum Cay Club (Rum Cay):* On a limestone bluff above the sea, this resort caters to divers and those who want to learn. Horseback riding, fishing, underwater photography, and nighttime entertainment also on the premises. Expensive.

Bermuda

Anchored about 600 miles due east of North Carolina, the 21-mile-long stretch called Bermuda is actually a chain of seven islands—some so close together you scarcely notice when you cross the bridge from one to the next—as well as another 100-plus scattered atolls. British in manner and subtropical in clime, it doesn't have the razzle-dazzle pizazz of many Caribbean islands. Bermuda prefers things a bit calmer, gentler, and has gone as far as to outlaw neon, banish high-rises, even limit the number of cars on the isle (which, aside from the fun of it, is why so many Bermudians—not just tourists—ride mopeds). From the salt-scented West End to capital Hamilton and St. George's antique alleys, Bermuda invites you to come share. To wiggle your toes on pink beaches and buzz down hibiscus-edged lanes. To sketch its creamy-roofed cottages and sing along in its dark-paneled pubs. Because for islanders, seeing the pleasure you take in their home is part of the joy of Bermuda.

First things first: you'll probably want to hit the beach right away. Chances are that your hotel or cottage colony has a nice beach of its own, but there's a special sense of discovery that comes from finding your own strand. So pack up a picnic (your front desk can help), rent a pair of mopeds (which even bona fide klutzes can master before too long), pick up a copy of *The Bermuda Beach Guide* (Bermuda's Department of Tourism gives them out free), and head off for the sun. The South Shore's pink beaches are the ones you see on most Bermuda travel posters. They're concentrated around the

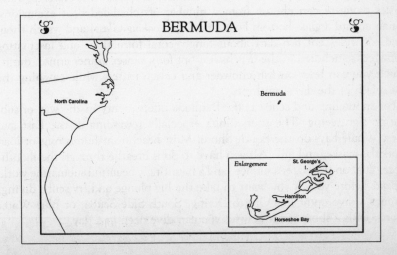

BERMUDA

North Carolina

Bermuda

Enlargement   St. George's I.

Hamilton

Horseshoe Bay

parishes of Southampton, Warwick, and Paget. A special few to make footprints on: Warwick Long Bay, Church Bay, and Horseshoe Bay—a trio of beauties open to the public, free of charge. Horseshoe Bay is astonishingly beautiful, with quiet rocky coves, shallow lime-green water, and lots of hideaway spots where you can stretch towels and have complete privacy. But check when the cruise ships come in. It's a favorite spot for passengers, too. Out toward the eastern end of the island, near Tucker's Town, you'll find the Natural Arches, a beach strewn with enormous rock formations that feels like some remote country on the other side of the world. Other special finds include Jobson's Cove, where you see more Bermudians than tourists, and both East and West Whale Bays—finest for snorkeling.

Bermuda is also famous for the quality of her land sports—golf and tennis, especially (in fact, tennis was introduced to the U.S. by one of the colony's own). Most of the hotels have their own tennis courts. If yours doesn't, you can play at the Government Tennis Stadium, just north of Hamilton (tennis whites a must), or at the Port Royal golf complex. And the golf scene is nonpareil. Not only are the courses gorgeous, with holes surrounded by stunningly blue water and cliffs that drop into frothy sea, but there are plenty of them. You'll find a trio of government-owned 18-hole courses: one in St. George's, one at the Port Royal in Southampton, and one at the Ocean View in Devonshire. You can also arrange to use the courses at the Belmont Hotel and Marriott's Castle Harbour Resort.

Looking toward the sea, you'll find boats brightening every Bermudian cove and bay, a modern reminder of the days when this "Gibraltar of the West" was famed for the quality of her ships and the men who sailed them. It's still true today, and whatever your seagoing skills, you can join the salty fun. There are Sunfish to borrow at most hotels, day-sailers to rent, even shiny, skippered sloops available for charter. Couples who prefer to have others navigate can choose from a number of scheduled boat excursions. Climb aboard a glass-bottom boat (like *The Looking Glass*) and watch thousands of iridescent fish dart about tangly coral formations and fascinating shipwrecks anchored in the depths. Or opt for a sunset dinner cruise, during which you can feast on fish chowder and conch fritters while catching the last splash of the day's sunshine.

For snorkeling and scuba buffs, Bermuda offers plenty in the way of submarine sightseeing. The snorkeling's especially rewarding at the East and West Whale bays on the South Shore. Most beachfront hotels rent or loan snorkels, masks, and fins. All you have to do is breathe through the mouthpiece, float on the water's surface, and a hauntingly beautiful submarine world appears before you. If you want to take the big plunge and try scuba diving, contact a dive outfit like Grotto Diving, South Side Scuba, or Blue Water Sports; with a short resort course, you can dive deep in a day.

After a few days the kinks will work themselves out of your body, and you'll be tanned, relaxed, and ready to head for town. Hamilton's harborfront streets teem with travelers from around the world. There are small bistros and open-air cafés for sipping and people-watching. And the architecture—a rainbow of pinks, light blues, and yellows—is most photogenic. The best way to see Hamilton is on foot—you can do it all in an hour. Park your mopeds or bikes at Albouy's Point, near the policeman's traffic birdcage, then head east on Front Street past the colony's collection of impressive shops. Between May and October there are usually at least two cruise ships docked across the street. Wander around to Parliament and Court streets, where you'll see a cenotaph honoring Bermuda's war dead; in the park behind sits the cabinet building where the Senate meets. Across the street is the Supreme Court, where judges still wear white wigs, British-style. From there, move along to Reid Street, where you'll see the Sessions House and the home of the House of Assembly. On Church Street you'll pass the Gothic Bermuda Cathedral and the City Hall of Hamilton, a restored Victorian stronghold.

But shopping on Front Street is really Hamilton's biggest draw. You'll find phenomenal savings on all sorts of items: British woolens, French perfumes, Italian leather, Swiss watches, jewelry, and liquor. Check out the stock at A. S. Cooper (softly woven winter mufflers in cranberry, teal, and mint; Woods of Windsor talcums and fragrances; aisle after aisle of crystal and china), Trimingham's (woolens, knits, tweeds, an entire minishop of Crabtree & Evelyn goodies, fine nautical antiques), and H. A. & Smith, Ltd., for British sportswear and fine gift items—leather picture frames, Bromley English soaps, and all sorts of porcelain figurines. Afterward, treat yourselves to a fish-and-chips feast at the Hog Penny, a pint of ale at Ye Olde Cock & Feather, or indulge your sweet tooth at the Fourways Pastry Shop (delectable kiwi and strawberry tarts).

If it's history you're after, hop on your mopeds or catch a pink-and-blue Bermudian bus and head toward St. George's, the colony's first capital, founded almost 400 years ago. You'll want to spend a while in St. Peter's (the oldest Anglican church in the hemisphere), inspecting the 1594 "Breeches" Bible, the priceless silver collection, and the churchyard's old tombstones. From there, step through the back gate and walk a few paces to Featherbed Alley, where you can visit the Printery and the Historical Museum with its powder room, once used for touching up gentlemen's wigs. Then down to the square—for a pose in the stock and pillory, a look inside cedar-fitted Town Hall, and a tour of the *Deliverance II*, a copy of the vessel that shipwrecked sailors built in 1610 to take them to Virginia. Wander about narrow alleys and lanes named Old Maid's, Aunt Peggy's, Needle & Thread; get in a bit of shopping if you like (Which Craft sells all sorts of left-handed items and made-in-Bermuda crafts); finish with lunch at the White Horse Tavern or the Pub on the Square, or with something a bit fancier at the Carriage House.

Another day you might grab your camera and bikes and push off for the West End—as much for the wind-in-your-hair, sun-in-your-face pleasure of the ride as for the scenery you'll pass on the way. First stop: Gibbs Hill, where you can climb the world's oldest cast-iron lighthouse for a view of bobbing boats and green islets crowned with houses of lemon, pink, and peach. Then on down past the Port Royal Golf Course and over the smallest drawbridge anywhere (just wide enough for a sailboat's mast) to Fort Scaur, more like a park than a fort (there's a pleasant picnic area). Next, Somerset, a village so small you'll have to look hard not to miss it, and the Maritime Museum out at the Dockyard. Take an hour or two to inspect its nautical exhibits and dim-lit Treasury, displaying silver coins, Spanish jewelry, and bars of gold. Then a walk on the ramparts before catching the ferry back to Hamilton.

Bermuda nights are celestial. Start off one evening with a sunset dinner cruise around the harbor. Or head for a romantic cocktail spot like the Princess's Gazebo Lounge or the terrace of Inverurie, watching Great Sound light up as the sun goes down. Come dinnertime, you've got some very special options. Even if you've opted for a MAP (Modifed American Plan) program— in which breakfasts and dinners are taken at your hotel—do make a point of at least one dinner at a totally indulgent place like Fourways, where the service, the food, the entire spirit of the night tell you this is one of life's rare treasures; Romanoff, full of last-days-of-the Empire elegance; Waterlot, in a restored inn near the water, known for its candlelight-and-flowers Bermudian charm; or Once Upon a Table, in Hamilton, serving nouvelle cuisine.

Afterward, you can raise frothy mugs and watch a darts game in your favorite pub. And there are nightly shows at many of the big hotels, featuring island favorites like the Talbot Brothers and the Fiery Limbo Dancers. At smaller hotels and guest houses, you might listen to a calypso singer or a pianist. For steel band and calypso music, make tracks to the Clay House Inn on North Shore Road in Devonshire. If dance clubs are your thing, line up at exotic Oasis Club and adjoining Bamba Lounge for a late-night jazz session, or at sophisticated The Club. For mellower nightcaps, slow dance at The Touch Club in the Southampton Princess or Cheek to Cheek, Grotto Bay's nightclub, set in a cave. Then call it an evening with a stroll along a moon-washed beach and settle into a night of sweet Bermuda dreams.

FACTS TO GO ON 🜊

☐ Getting there: Eastern, Pan Am, and American make the two-hour flight from New York; American and Delta fly from Boston. There are also direct flights from Atlanta, Philadelphia, Newark, Baltimore, Washington, Tampa, Toronto, as well as from Chicago. A number of cruise ships sail to Bermuda from New York, docking in Hamilton and St. George's.

☐ Entry requirements: You'll need proof of citizenship (valid or expired passport, birth certificate, or voters registration card) and a return or ongoing ticket.

☐ Currency: The official currency in Bermuda is the Bermuda dollar which is on par and interchangeable with the U.S. dollar.

☐ Language: English

☐ *Bride's* Best Beds

● *Elbow Beach Hotel:* A large, Paget-based resort with a lovely stretch of sand in addition to well-tended grounds, glowing nightlife, and all sorts of accommodation possibilities (beachfront lanais, balconied suites, duplex cottages). Expensive.

● *Southampton Princess:* Sister to the Princess in Hamilton, a large luxury hotel that looks over the sea from a hillside. With beach, tennis, golf, dive and snorkel shop, and a selection of restaurants. Both Princesses are known for the loving way they treat newlywed guests. Expensive.

● *Cambridge Beaches:* A cottage colony on a point in Somerset that's entrancingly private, boasting a wealth of private sands, sailing, water sports galore, tennis, and entertainment at night. For seclusion seekers, this is the place. Expensive.

● *Pink Beach Club and Cottages:* Spacious cottages that make you feel luxuriously at home, on a beachfront estate on the South Shore. Expensive.

● *The Reefs:* A spine of attractive buildings, housing rooms with lanais, running along a ridge overlooking a lovely private beach. Moderate.

● *Pompano Beach Club:* Suites, cabanas, and cottages dotted up a hill overlooking a private beach. Moderate.

☐ For more information, write: The Bermuda Department of Tourism, 310 Madison Avenue, New York, NY 10017; or call: (212) 818-9800 (there are also offices in Atlanta, Boston, Chicago, and Toronto).

10
ISLANDS WEST

To wake up on an island—to the soft roar of waves washing the sand, to sunlight filtered through a louvered door, to the scent of flowers in the early air—is a honeymoon dream. On the magical land dots we call Islands West (the gentle curve of the Hawaiian isles and the lagoon-bordered shores of Tahiti and French Polynesia), mornings are especially lovely. Not just because of the sensations themselves, but because mornings promise so much: chunks of sweet pineapple and rich Kona coffee; cool plunges in a silk-watered pool; outrigger rides on curling waves and lazy basking on golden beaches.

Which of these islands would you be happiest on? Perhaps it's Oahu, Hawaii's most rollicking isle, where you can mail coconutgrams and hike Diamond Head. Or maybe you'd want to explore the Big Island, with its hissing lava fields and green valleys. Or perhaps you'd love French Polynesia's Bora Bora, which some people call the most beautiful island on earth. The following Pacific sketches may speed your way.

Hawaii

The islands of Hawaii take hold of you and never really let go. Long after you've returned home, you'll dream of rainbows arching across dewy skies and black lava beds edging toward the sea. You'll smell the green lushness of jungle ferns and hear the whoosh of torch fires flamed by the wind. And you'll remember sunsets when a white-gold flash sent shivers of light rippling on the water, capturing a lone palm in perfect Pacific silhouette. Though it

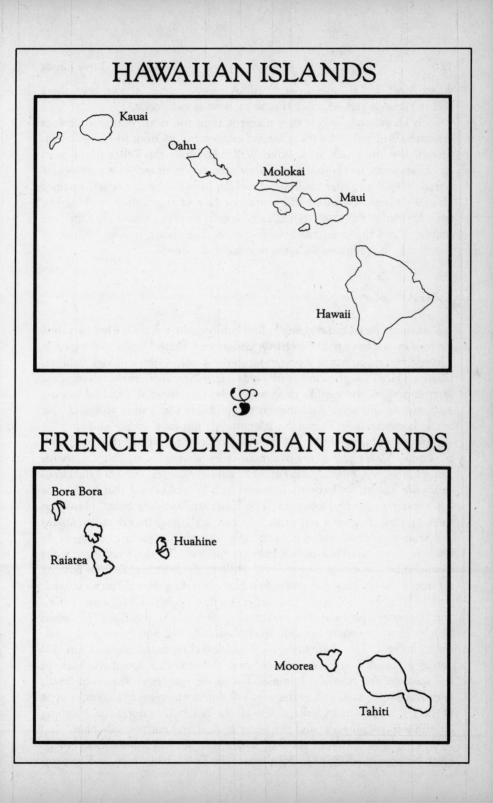

HAWAIIAN ISLANDS

Kauai

Oahu

Molokai

Maui

Hawaii

FRENCH POLYNESIAN ISLANDS

Bora Bora

Huahine

Raiatea

Moorea

Tahiti

floats alone, 2,400 miles from North America, people who've been there find the sounds and sights of Hawaii as close as next door.

Each Hawaiian island is very different from the next, posing a pleasant dilemma. Will you go for the color and excitement of Oahu, where surfboards literally line the beach at Waikiki? Will it be Maui, the Valley Isle, known for its smooth, shore-lining resorts? Maybe you're drawn to Kauai, where waterfalls spill into silent valleys, or the Big Island—the one actually named Hawaii—where volcanoes still shape the face of the landscape. Molokai, once known as the Forgotten Isle, now calls to couples searching for pure simplicity and that one true luxury—peace. The choice is yours. Whatever you decide, be prepared for some wonderful discoveries.

Oahu

Remember Jack Lord dodging bullets behind palm trees? Or Elvis swiveling his hips on a slab of gold beach? Or Gidget and Moon Doggie making up at a luau? Even if you're too young to recall the kitsch, Oahu will look familiar. Diamond Head's stern profile, surfboards skimming into shore, hotels standing at attention on the world's most famous beach—these Waikiki images are instantly recognizable. And though you probably won't want to spend your whole honeymoon in Honolulu, it's certainly fun for a couple of days.

Arriving in Honolulu has all the subtlety of being hit over the head with a coconut. Your plane is met by dozens of lei-bearing locals, your cab speeds past a harbor of Chinese junks, an old whaling ship, and enough catamarans to invade Tahiti, and you're deposited in a Waikiki hotel that very likely has a waterfall in the lobby and "The Hawaiian Wedding Song" playing in the elevators. You walk out onto your balcony (here, they're called *lanais*) and feast your eyes: stacks of surfboards lean against palms, outriggers fly towards shore, bikinied bodies bake in the sun. To the southeast, rocky Diamond Head juts out over the sea, while to the west, smoke from burning sugarcane rises beyond the downtown Honolulu skyscrapers. You've arrived.

Waikiki's beach—a string of beaches, really—is Oahu's biggest attraction, and it changes personality from strand to strand. At the Royal Hawaiian Beach (closest to most hotels), you'll find sailboats, aquabikes, and windsurfers to rent, plus surfing instructors, snorkeling outfitters, and muscled outrigger guides who'll steer you out over the surf, then speed you back on the wave-crested ride of a lifetime. Things are quieter at Kapiolani Beach Park and Sans Souci, and to the west you'll find a man-made lagoon in front of the Hilton Hawaiian Village. On all the beaches, tanning and splashing are the primary pursuits, and the water is clear and outrageously blue.

When you've had your share of sun, a pair of attractions within beach-range beckon: the campy hip-wigglings of the Kodak Hula show, in Kapiolani

Park (weekdays, 10 A.M.), and the hiking trail at Diamond Head, leading up the crater's inside slope to a panoramic view well worth every puff. You'll work up an appetite, so head to the Colony Surf Hotel, where Tom Selleck has his morning omelette.

Mixed in with the glass towers and acres of parking lots of downtown Honolulu, you'll find museums, galleries, and gardens with distinctly Hawaiian appeal. The most intriguing: Iolani Palace, a Renaissance-style reminder of the last days of Hawaiian royalty; and the Bishop Museum's specifically Pacific displays—feather capes, carved war gods, and a 55-foot-long sperm whale. From the museum, a double-decker bus can shuttle you to the four-masted square-rigger Falls of Clyde, a gorgeous example of nineteenth-century ship building. And Honolulu boasts two organized tours worth taking: a walking tour of Chinatown (departing Tuesdays at 9:30 A.M. from the Chinese Chamber of Commerce), into open-air markets, past pool halls, sex parlors, and noodle joints filled with earnest slurpers; and the National Park Service's tour of Pearl Harbor, where the USS *Arizona* lies silent beneath the waters.

Intense and lively as Honolulu is, there's a whole other Oahu that demands to be explored. Heading east past Diamond Head, you'll pass wealthy suburbs, lush rain forests, and cliffside homes of the rich and famous. Beyond lies a simple, very peaceful landscape of small churches, family homes, and surfy beaches. Novice surfers make their way to the strand at Waimanalo; Kaupo Beach is long, lapped by very gentle waves; Makapuu's big crests are ideal for body surfers; and Hanauma Bay Beach boasts excellent snorkeling and tall palms for resting in the shade. A must-make stop: the Nuuanu Pali Lookout, where ancient Hawaiian warriors leapt to their deaths (King Kamehameha was heading their way), with glorious views of the Koolau Mountains and the dramatic Windward coast.

Continuing along the eastern tip of the island, deep green cliffs sliced with waterfalls give way to clear seas and coral reefs. Stop to snorkel at Kaneohe Bay, or continue north to the Polynesian Cultural Center, where seven Pacific cultures have been transplanted to a compound owned and operated by Brigham Young University. There, Tongans work with *tapa* cloth, Tahitians weave grass skirts, and young Maori men toss *tititorea* sticks. Further along the north shore, you'll come to Sunset Beach, where waves of astounding size draw champion surfers, followed by Waimea Falls Park, a tranquil enclave of rust-red waterfalls, lush nature trails, and rare Hawaiian flora. Last stop before taking the center road back to Honolulu: the town of Haleiwa, once a simple seaside hamlet, and now, despite an influx of back-to-basics '60s types, a place that really does seem forgotten by time.

Happily exhausted, a bit red on the shoulders and freckled about the face, Oahu honeymooners view nights as a chance to sit back, admire each other, and let the entertainment come to them. Catamarans set sail on cocktail cruises, laden with drinks and *pupus*, skimming the copper ocean with Honolulu's skyline blazing in the light. Hotel restaurants offer elegant splurges, and downtown Honolulu eateries, from noodle houses to nouvelle Hawaiian spots, provide local flavors. The big Polynesian shows at the major hotels can be fun, but if you're turned off by gimmicks, best leave them to the septuagenarian set. Ditto with most Oahu luaus—the *imu* oven and basic food is authentic enough, but commercialization has taken out much of the heart. Instead, you might join young rockers at Wave Waikiki, or the jazz lovers at Trapper's in the Hyatt Regency.

FACTS TO GO ON 🗲

☐ Getting there: Among the airlines that make frequent mainland-Oahu runs are United, American, Western, Continental, TWA, Northwest Orient, Pan Am, and Delta.

☐ *Bride's* Best Beds

● *Halekulani:* One of Waikiki's finest, a place of seamless, creamy comforts (Prince Charles has stayed here), where even the bathtubs come with an ocean view. Expensive.

● *Hyatt Regency:* Twin towers of sophisticated looks, superb shopping, not to mention Regency Club floors that pamper you with concierge service, complimentary cocktails, and spectacular suites. Expensive.

● *Royal Hawaiian:* Wedged like a pink petit four among Waikiki's highrises, the charm of this mature hotel (pink inside and out) lures lovers back year after year. Expensive.

☐ For more information, write: Hawaii Visitors Bureau, 2270 Kalakaua Avenue, Room 801, Honolulu, HI 96815. Or call (808) 923-1811. (There are also offices in Los Angeles, San Francisco, Chicago, and New York.)

Maui 🌺

As far as honeymooners are concerned, Maui is mecca, the island woven into thousands of newlywed dreams. What put it there? First, although several of its beaches are backed by huge resort hotels, much of the island's hilly contour remains as nature intended it, untouched by man. Second, it not only boasts one of the happiest port towns in the Pacific—the old whaling town of Lahaina—but a variety of eye-popping excursions fit for Harrison Ford. And finally, Maui is so twentieth-century efficient—with direct flights from the mainland, a network of highway-smooth roads, plus restaurants whose wine lists are heavy enough to flatten a coconut—that all the uncertainty and stress of faraway travel melts away like shaved ice in the noonday sun.

Honeymooners tend to settle in at one of Maui's three vacation areas. Largest is Kaanapali, a "master-planned" resort. Meaning that instead of a confused jumble of condominiums, fish houses, and motels, you'll find an organized tropical fantasy: several handsome high-rise hotels, a tasteful shopping center, seafood restaurants where torches flame at night and reservations are *de rigueur*, all backed by a batch of palm-fringed beaches. Smaller and somewhat more upscale in tone is Kapalua. Though it has only one real hotel to its name (a veritable stunner), its neighboring resort community called Napili offers a choice of "barefoot" staying options—hotels and condominiums alike—which go easier on your budget. Third is Wailea, basking on some of the island's sunniest (and driest) shores. There, in addition to first-class hotels, tennis-lovers discover what must be the only grass courts in the Pacific, while golfers can tee off on courses traversed by ancient lava walls. There's a fourth—albeit very isolated—place to base yourselves (*retreat to* is really more like it). Hana, at the end of one of the world's more venturesome roads, is true backwater Hawaii, a heavenly combination of lush ranchland, rust-red cinder cones, and silent beaches to which some of Hollywood's more notable artists escape.

Next to the traditional beach sports—swimming, outrigger-riding, surfing, *et al*—renting a car and touring is Maui's biggest honeymoon pleasure. The roads are generally excellent, the scenery is often spectacular, and it's a great way to take a break from the fierce Hawaiian sun.

A trio of real musts: first, Haleakala Crater (21 miles in circumference, it's the largest dormant volcano on the planet). To be there at sunrise, steel yourselves for a 4 A.M. wake-up call. Hotel vans motor off in the predawn dark, pumping passengers with coffee and breakfast rolls. Huddled at the summit, you wait for the show to begin. Mark Twain called it "the sublimest spectacle" he ever saw—something like the aurora borealis skimming across the moon. If there's one sunrise to wake for in your life, this is probably it. Sleep-ins can drive up later for pony rides into the crater or, perhaps most appealing of all, exhilarating bike rides down the mountain, past protea fields and up-country pastures.

A second touring route takes you past Kaanapali and Kapalua to the far northern tip of the island. Scenes along the way: endless pineapple fields, velvety valleys, swarms of surfers riding impossibly big waves. Ask your hotel to pack a picnic and pause at D. T. Fleming Beach Park (do not, however, be tempted to swim—the water is much too rough). Then head to Honolua Bay, to see some of Maui's best surfers ride the waves (there's no sign, but if you spot several cars pulling off into the pineapple fields, just follow). On the way home, treat yourselves to drinks at the Kapalua Bay Hotel's posh

Bay Club; set on a lava peninsula slapped by aquamarine water, people call it one of the island's best.

Your third option takes steady nerves, a reliable rental car, and should ideally be spaced out over a couple of days. It's the aforementioned road to Hana, 52 miles long, with 617 curves—most of them hairpin—and 56 one-lane bridges. Nerve-wracking it may be, but it's also one of the most beautiful drives in the world. Banyan and leki leki trees form an olive canopy and waterfalls splash down moss-softened rock, while sunbathed beaches tease you from the shore below. In Hana itself, splash around the Seven Pools, buy postcards at the Hasegawa General Store, and pay your respects at the almost-hidden church behind which Charles Lindbergh is buried. If you can, plan to overnight at the Hotel Hana Maui (make sure you reserve well in advance), a tranquil temple of true Hawaiian hospitality.

The first part of a Maui night never really varies: a Pacific sunset, maybe a torch-lighting ceremony, a drink with pineapple wedges perched on top. After that, almost anything can happen. Polynesian luaus, grill-your-own steak dinners, candlelit four-course meals, room service on your terrace; during a weeklong honeymoon, chances are you'll sample some of each. Finally, a walk on the beach, a nightcap, and sweet dreaming to the rhythm of the Maui surf.

FACTS TO GO ON ♋

☐ Getting there: United Airlines has daily nonstop service to Maui from Los Angeles, San Francisco, Chicago, and Seattle (winter only). American has direct flights from Dallas/Fort Worth, Los Angeles, and Chicago. These plus Continental, Northwest, and Pan Am all schedule nonstop or direct Honolulu flights from dozens of U.S. cities. From there, inter-island carriers make the quick hop to Maui.

☐ *Bride's Best Beds*

● *Kapalua Bay Hotel:* In Kapalua, this elegant beauty lures with deep-dish comforts, graceful plantation looks, and outstanding service. The villas are expansive and expensive (they're designed for families, not honeymooners), but if you've got the cash, they're heaven on earth. Expensive.

● *Hyatt Regency:* In Kaanapali, this fantasy of fish ponds, waterfalls, and orchid gardens is a tourist destination in itself. Along with the comfortable rooms in three separate towers and complete sports facilities, there's the Hyatt trademark—a huge, free-form pool with a slide, grottoes, and cascades. Expensive.

● *Stouffer's Wailea Beach:* In Wailea, with glorious gardens, a dreamy beach, and comforting rooms in an ocean-view tower or beachfront wing. Expensive.

- *Maui Inter-Continental Wailea:* A huge, posh resort complex, with rooms in a low tower and in smaller buildings scattered through a lush, landscaped maze. Expensive.
- *Hana Maui:* In Hana, this exclusive, newly renovated hotel is one of the gems of the Pacific, with real Hawaiian quilts on the beds, truly gourmet dining, and a personable, pleasurable round of activities, from breakfast trail rides to backpacked picnics. If you possibly can, take a few wedding-gift checks and splurge on a stay here. Very expensive.
- *Westin Maui:* Millions of dollars have transformed the old Maui Surf Hotel into a dazzling new resort, with a tremendous pool, loads of artwork, and full watersports program. Expensive.

☐ For more information, write: Maui Visitors Bureau, P.O. Box 1738, Kahului, Maui, HI 96732. Or call: (808) 871-8691. (You could also contact the Hawaii Visitors Bureau—see page 122).

Hawaii

Raw, fearsome scenery and a number of cushy resorts give the Big Island (a.k.a. Hawaii) a Jekyll-and-Hyde personality. As soon as you leave the airport, your car radio fuzzes out and you're surrounded with brittle black lava for as far as the eye can see. It's an immediate clue that the Big Island isn't your typical Pacific garden spot. But before you know it, you'll spot splendid oases of palms and fish ponds beside the distant water's edge. And once you check into your chosen resort, you'll realize that all that black lava not only serves as a dramatic contrast to your hotel's luxury comforts, but that it also gives the Big Island a beauty all its own.

Most visitors coming to the Big Island for romance stay on what's known as the Kona—or farther north, the Kohala—Coast; the names are almost interchangeable. There is one town in the area, Kailua, of limited interest unless your tastes run to shopping malls. Otherwise, on this western end of things, resort life is about the only life around.

So who's complaining? You can start your day with breakfast on the lanai, forking up sweet pineapple and savoring Kona coffee—it's grown right here on the Big Island. Then you'll probably be drawn to the water, where hefty Hawaiian he-men are waiting to show you the ropes on mini-outriggers, windsurfers, and catamarans. They'll also set you up with snorkel equipment so you can come face-to-face with exotic fish you thought only swam in aquariums.

There's plenty in the way of simple relaxing, too; Hawaiian resorts typically come strung with hammocks, edged with chaise lounges, and stocked with enough beach towels, inflatable rafts, and sand mats to cushion all of Southern

California. Which doesn't mean, however, that there isn't room to stretch
out alone. (Why do you think they call it the Big Island?)

What else will you find in Kona/Kohala? For starters, most of those emerald
green patches belong to golf courses. Dramatically difficult holes have been
carved out of lava fields and perched above churning surf to create some of
the world's most beautiful courses. There's also a good deal of tennis, and
resorts here have even managed to make Laykold pretty, by planting bushes
of lemon bougainvillaea and by shading the "gardens" with striped canvas
awnings.

But no matter how gorgeous your resort, before long, you're going to feel
itchy. You'll have heard stories—of how the first Polynesians arrived here
in their double-hulled canoes, of Pele (the volcano goddess) and her nasty
temper, of hidden valleys that look like Eden before the fall. Impelled by a
mix of legends and landscapes, you'll want to rent a car and see some of
these wonders yourselves. The Big Island is not only the most easily explored
member of the Hawaiian chain (lots of room to roam and excellent roads),
it has some pretty amazing sites to see.

First, you'll want to get the volcanoes out of your system. In Volcanoes
National Park (a full day's excursion from the main resort area), two of the
world's most active volcanoes are presently taking what, in geological terms,
amounts to a catnap. Major eruptions in the last three years have literally
changed the shape of the Big Island, adding acres of new waterfront real
estate. Things have been pretty calm of late, but walking or driving through
the park can still be a dramatic interlude, especially when you start spotting
signs warning about steam vents and cracks in the road. A visitors center
gives you a good grasp of the explosive phenomenon, but to really appreciate
the power of a volcano, you'll have to get out there and look at the real
thing—a landscape as desolate as a playground at midnight.

If you're feeling a bit unsettled, spend a while in Waimea, where the picket
fences and grazing cattle plant you firmly back on earth. This northerly part
of the island may look more like Nebraska than Bali Hai, but the cowboys
(here, they're called *paniolos*) are pure Hawaiian. You can snoop around the
vast Parker Ranch's visitors center, even see a summertime rodeo. If you've
rented a four-wheel-drive car, you may be able to make it up the Saddle
Road to Mauna Kea, where, believe it or not, there's snow-skiing between
December and May.

Finally, for a look at the lush, luscious valleys and secret waterfalls that
you may have thought Hawaii was all about, drive further east to the Hamakua
Coast. Route 19 traces the island's northeast edge and gives you neck-wrench-
ing views of jade valleys and lacy waterfalls. There are a couple of stops you
might want to make: Akaka Falls, to the east, steeped in Hawaiian legend,
and the Waipio Valley, to the west, whose neat taro fields, black sand beach,
and a pair of silvery waterfields are quintessential Hawaii. You can eyeball

the valley from a small lookout, waving off the butterflies; get a closer look on the world's scariest jeep ride; or even stay the night at the Waipio Motel— three rooms and one communal shower.

Assuming your headquarters are more deluxe, you'll probably want to spend several Big Island evenings right in your hotel, since resorts are fairly well spread apart, which makes lounge hopping a nuisance. When you do want to make the effort, be sure to call ahead for reservations. If you want to dress down and go native, tuck into the multiethnic platters at the Ocean View Inn; it's in the heart of Kailua, and the crowd is as mixed as the menu. In general, Big Island restaurants and bars close early; you could cap the night by sneaking into the pool for a swim, sharing a drink on your lanai, or just using your imagination.

FACTS TO GO ON 𝕲

☐ Getting there: United offers direct service to the Big Island of Hawaii. On most other airlines—Pan American, American, Delta, and Continental—you'll deplane in Oahu and catch another flight to the Big Island.

☐ *Bride's* Best Beds

● *Mauna Lani Bay:* This glossy hotel is Hawaii's nod to modern design, and a gorgeous one; you'll find his-and-hers bath areas in the cool pastel rooms, and a walking trail that skirts royal fish ponds and lava tubes. Expensive.

● *Westin Mauna Kea Beach:* Gracing the island's most beautiful beach, this elegant-looking resort offers a 1,000-piece art collection, fishing from a 58-foot catamaran, and shuttle service to Parker Ranch for horseback riding. Expensive.

● *Kona Village Resort:* This could be a Polynesian summer camp for rich adults. You stay in a private *hale* on the beach, complete with thatched roof, graphics by island artist Peggy Hopper, and coconut Do-Not-Disturb signs. They also offer enticing wedding/honeymoon packages. Expensive.

● *Kona Surf:* A less expensive staying option, with all sorts of nice touches— landscaped rock pools, queen-sized beds, and Hawaiian art. Moderate.

☐ For more information, write: Hawaii Visitors Bureau, 180 Kinoole Street, Suite 104, Hilo, HI 96720. Or call: (808) 965-5797.

Kauai 🌺

Memories of Kauai are washed with an emerald glaze. Ginger flowers perfume the valleys, lush and lovely as a Rousseau painting. Rivers run slowly, bordered with giant ferns and orchids. Resorts seem so thoroughly tropical, they'd revert to jungle if gardeners weren't so quick with the pruning shears. It feels like a place that just woke up and is still blinking away the sleep. Naturally gorgeous and development-wary, Kauai may be the fantasy island of this fantastical chain.

Poipu, Wailua, and Hanalei are Kauai's chief resort areas. Up in the north, Hanalei's scenery defies most cameras—colossal cliffs topped with rainbows, silent valleys planted with taro fields, a string of beaches melting into a broad blue bay. Its newest place to stay is the Princeville resort complex, complete with luxury condominiums, tennis courts, and a plush hotel.

Wailua, midway down the east coast, is the island's most popular destination. With a superb beach, groves of coconut palms, and a crop of staying places fit for almost any newlywed budget, Wailua could be tomorrow's Waikiki. But chances are it won't—resorts tend to be modest in scale, and happy to stay that way. The Fern Grotto, Wailua's big tourist attraction, can be crowded and commercial beyond belief; a more pleasant excursion might be a hike around Wailua State Park, taking a dip in the swimming hole.

Poipu, on the dry southern shore, boasts nonstop sunshine and a wealth of wide beaches. Rustling fields of sugar cane are punctuated with comfort-minded resorts, but most of the south coast is still rooted in agriculture. A walk around towns like Koloa or Kekaha—especially when the crawling cane trucks drive through—will show you a Hawaii that, despite tourism, really hasn't changed much.

Whichever area you choose to base yourselves in, the must-take trip is to the Na Pali coast, a 14-mile stretch of dense, tropical valleys, immense green cliffs, and small beaches virtually guaranteed to be yours alone. No roads lead to Na Pali; your only recourse is a helicopter tour (very expensive, but the exhilaration, the rush of adrenaline, and the pure wonder of the ride are unquestionably worth it) or one of Captain Zodiak's sturdy rubber raft cruises (May through September).

You'll probably want to spend some time poking around Hanalei town, with its Mission House Museum and complex of Hawaiian crafts shops. You might discover a waterfall or two—Opaekaa Falls, near Wailua, is very accessible. Perhaps you'd like to whale-watch from a stripe-sailed catamaran. Or go horseback riding into the mountains and along the north coast. Many resorts offer the full spectrum of water sports—snorkeling, surfing, and sailing—and you'll find five fine golf courses as well as tennis courts at hotels and condominiums alike. But most of the time you'll find yourselves content to spread a couple of towels on the beach, pull out a good book, and work on those Pacific tans.

Sunset brings on standard Hawaiian entertainment—luaus, Polynesian dancing, island music—but with a distinctive, homey flavor. Don't miss the traditional torch-lighting ceremony at Coco Palms resort, or the impromptu

Hawaiian parties at Tahiti Nui, in Hanalei. The island's most elegant dining possibilities include the Coconut Palace, at Coco Palms; Plantation Gardens at Kiahuna Plantation, on Poipu Beach; and the nearby Tamarind.

FACTS TO GO ON

☐ Getting there: Most honeymooners land first in Honolulu (*see* Facts to Go On—Oahu) and then take smaller commuter flights to Kauai.

☐ *Bride's* Best Beds

● *The Waiohai:* In Poipu, this modern resort on a beautiful beach tempts with exotic amenities and a luxuriously eclectic decor. Expensive.

● *Sheraton Princeville:* In Hanalei, its allure combines American-style comforts with spectacular views from the rooms. Expensive.

● *The Cliffs:* A condominium complex in Hanalei, these breezy apartments perch atop cliffs overlooking the Pacific. Moderate.

● *Coco Palms:* In Wailua, this is the landmark place to stay—part pampering resort and part Disneyesque Polynesian fantasy. Expensive.

● *Westin Kauai:* A colossal new resort whose reflecting pool is home to a team of white marble horses. Expensive.

☐ For more information, write Hawaii Visitors Bureau, 3016 Umi Street, Room 207, Lihue, HI 96766. Or call: (808) 245-3971.

Molokai

Population: 6,576. Traffic lights: none. Staying places: half a dozen. If you're looking for real seclusion, the kind of peace and quiet you didn't think you could reach by plane, then Molokai could be for you.

From the air, the highest sea cliffs in the world seem cushioned with miles of moss. Black and gold beaches are splashed by white foam. Four waterfalls shimmer like silver ribbons in the deep green interior. And acres of rippling cane fields dominate the western plains.

Given Molokai's classic good looks, you might wonder why so few tourists set foot here. The first people to settle Hawaii avoided Molokai's eastern cliffs and western dryness; the *kahunas* (magic men) who finally populated the place kept superstitious Hawaiians at bay; and then, a leper colony was set up at Kalaupapa, which slammed the door as far as "normal" island development goes.

Obviously, things have changed. In the 1970s, a good portion of western farmland was sold for resort development, and travelers today will find a lovely golf course, riding stables, a scattering of tennis courts, and beaches for whiling away an afternoon. To the east, you'll find snorkeling, scuba diving, and safe swimming in coves and lagoons. Fishing and hunting are major activities, and the hiking is marvelous. But basically, Molokai is a place for honeymooners with a taste for simplicity and Old Hawaii.

Touring is a three-part series. You'll want to inspect the town of Kaunakakai, where the one main street is lined with wooden homes and a row of photogenic clapboard churches. You'll certainly want to explore the lonely east end, where royal fish ponds, ancient shrines, and the silent Halawa Valley create a sense of mystery and power. And by all means take the mule train down to Kalaupapa, the leper colony where Father Damien lived and died. While it's a hair-raising descent—and certainly not your standard honeymoon delight—we've yet to meet anyone who came away unmoved by its sheer spirituality.

FACTS TO GO ON

☐ Getting there: Most honeymooners fly first to Honolulu (page 122), then take an interisland flight to Molokai.

☐ Bride's Best Beds

● The Kaluakoi (formerly the Sheraton-Molokai): The biggest, most modern resort on the island. Its rooms boast American comforts and South Seas styling, all overlooking a stunner of a beach. Expensive.

● Ke Nani Kai: A condominium resort near the Kaluakoi, which offers large one- and two-bedroom units with complete kitchen facilities. Tennis courts, a huge pool, and a Jacuzzi are also on-site; you use the same beach as the Kaluakoi. Expensive.

☐ For more information, write: Hawaii Visitors Bureau, 2270 Kalakaua Avenue, Honolulu, HI 96815. Or call: (808) 923-1811.

French Polynesia (Tahiti)

Islanders who live on Bora Bora's Matira Beach can't help laughing: each day they witness a handful of determined travelers—people who've come thousands of miles from Tokyo, Vienna, or New York—make their way up the beach, plop down in the soft sand, and then launch into a ballad of oohs and aahs.

Undeniably, the scene is spectacular: the brazen aqua of a shimmering lagoon, the looming, green profile of Mt. Otemanu, the offbeat slant of bright-colored houses tucked into a verdant explosion of frangipani, mango trees, and palms. Matira Beach is one of many places in French Polynesia that conforms to our mind's image of Tahiti, an image sketched by postcards of emerald islands and flower-wreathed maidens, then filled in by Gauguin, Melville, and Maugham.

French Polynesia is aware of its unique place in the minds of foreigners. Today's Tahitians might zip about on shiny Hondas and Vespas, but they're completely prepared to give you the tropical paradise you've imagined. You'll stay in a thatched-roof *fare*, paddle around in outrigger canoes, learn to love *poisson cru* (raw fish marinated in coconut milk), served in shiny coconut shells. You"ll tie a bright, cotton *pareo* around your middle and put flowers in your hair. You can even arrange to be dropped off on a deserted *motu* (tiny offshore island) to play castaway for a day.

Those who say "an island is an island is an island—why go halfway around the globe when the Caribbean is right next door?" will learn that these islands are different. The surreal outline of their peaks, the gentle clarity of their pools, the beauty of their people set them apart. Budding from blue sea in rippling color, their jade towers wear cloudy haloes and successive necklaces of gold (the rim of beach), aquamarines (the calm lagoons), and diamonds (the offshore reefs, smacked by sparkling breakers). In French Polynesia, the word *lush* takes on new meaning. All cares dissolve with the power of the sun. And the endless Pacific all around lets you know that you're far, far away from any care or woe. For island lovers, there's no better place to be.

FACTS TO GO ON FOR FRENCH POLYNESIA

- [ ] Entry requirements: You must have a valid passport and an outgoing ticket to enter French Polynesia. You will also need a visa, given to you on arrival.

- [ ] Currency: You'll be paying with French Pacific Francs. Bring plenty of money; French Polynesia is quite expensive. Lunch for two costs $25–$30; dinner ranges from $50–$100 for two. Drinks are cheaper. There is no tipping.

- [ ] Language: French is the official language, but even high school French will get you where you want to go. Islanders speak Polynesian among themselves, and you'll be warmly received if you learn a few of their words. English is spoken at all of the larger hotels.

- [ ] For more information, write: Tahiti Promotion Board, 12233 West Olympic Boulevard, Suite 110, Los Angeles, CA 90064; or call: (213) 207-1919.

Tahiti

Tahiti is the biggest and busiest of French Polynesia's Society Islands, but beyond the bustle of capital city Papeete (Pa-pee-ay-tay), there's a good bit of unspoiled Polynesian scenery, too. Tahiti is where Paul Gauguin came to break from rigid European conventions, where Rupert Brooke wrote "Tiare Tahiti," and where Fletcher Christian and his *Bounty* band mutinied against Captain Bligh—all of which has endowed this island with a distinct notoriety. When people talk of running away from it all, they usually talk of running to Tahiti, even if they imagine an atoll more like the small, outer islands.

Most planes from California arrive in the wee hours of the morning. By the time you collect your baggage and go through customs, you'll have seen a hip-wiggling Tahitian welcome, watched the sky go from dark to glowing orange to soft morning blue, and you'll be draped with sticky-sweet leis. The perfume in the air makes it clear: you've landed in an exotic land.

Tahiti's modernization provides sharp contrast to the island's legendary landscape of jagged green peaks and palm-lined shores. The four-lane roads, buzzing traffic, and apartment complexes can sometimes intrude on the paradisiacal feeling, so travelers who've come to escape civilization *altogether* should use Tahiti simply as a jump-off point to the smaller, calmer islands of Moorea, Huahine, Raiatea, and Bora Bora. For those who enjoy the excitement of an active capital port, who are interested in the "real life" of paradise, who want wide territory to explore and numerous sights to see, Tahiti deserves more time.

Papeete buzzes, honks, and whistles through the early morning hours. Cruise ships and fishing boats tie up at the waterfront quay, nightclub owners sweep away the trails of last night's revelers, and Tahitian women with great baskets of blooms make leis in the shade. At the Marché Papeete, the main market (most active on Sunday mornings), butchers cleave cutlets on chopping slabs sliced from palm trees, and shiny fruits are laid out like still lives on wide tables. Scout out a *Herald Tribune* (it's your last chance for comics and sports scores if you're heading to the outer islands), have coffee or a beer in a Boulevard Pomare café, and dash off some bare-breasted postcards to the pals back home.

Tahiti's excellent transportation system makes the rest of the island very accessible for those who don't want to splurge on a rental car. Long blue open-air trucks make regular stops all around the island, taking you almost anywhere for little more than a dollar. Simply wave one down, and you're on your way to the outer reaches of the island.

One day, head out along Tahiti's south coast, stopping at the Musée de Tahiti et des Iles, with exhibits on the culture, flora, fauna, and history of these islands; at Paea for surfy beaches and shopping for handmade carvings and weaving at the Irihono Craft Centre; and further out, at the Gauguin

Museum and Botanical Gardens. Another day, do the north coast, weaving
up Tahara'a Hill, down past the lighthouse at Point Venus, stopping for a
splash in the Farrumai Waterfalls, then moving along to the peninsula, where
you can hike to Vista Point for one of the most spectacular views of Tahiti.
On the way back, stop off again at Point Venus and Matavai Bay; this historic
crescent, where Wallis landed in 1767, is a lovely spot to watch the setting
sun. Tahitian teens sing around guitars, French children cover their bodies
with silky black sand, and topless moms are never far behind, tossing the
children into the tranquil lagoon for a wash. The sun sets behind cloud-
crowned Moorea, its heavenly rays of gold, rose, and crimson gilding the
crests of the lagoon's ripples.

Nights on Papeete, as on all of these islands, can seem even more lovely
than days. The evening air is satin on tanned skin, and you'll sit back over
a leisurely meal (mahi-mahi prepared a dozen ways, fresh tuna, lobster,
escargots, and traditional French favorites), watching the moon spread a fan
of silver over the sea.

Papeete's after-dinner hours are filled with drum-pounding floor shows and
visits to discos that happily mix Tahitians, French sailors, and American
tourists on the dance floor. But if you've got discos at home, you might prefer
sitting outside, gazing up at the stars, and bathing in the chirpings, croakings,
and cawings of a South Pacific night.

FACTS TO GO ON

☐ Getting there: UTA French Airlines flies regularly from San Francisco
and Los Angeles, as does Continental. Air France also flies from Los
Angeles. Many planes bound for Australia or New Zealand (Qantas, Air
New Zealand) also fly into Papeete.

☐ *Bride's Best Beds*
● *Hotel Tahara'a:* A coral colored, terraced hotel, built into the Tahara'a
hillside, offering spacious, American-style rooms, flower-bordered patios,
and spectacular views of Moorea and the Matavai Bay. An elevator ride,
then a steep, winding staircase take you down to a beautiful black sand
beach. Expensive.
● *Hotel Sofitel Maeva Beach:* A French-accented hotel on a white, man-made
beach a few miles from Papeete. Expensive.
● *Tahiti Beachcomber:* Along with tennis, golf, and swimming pool, this
well-located hotel just outside of Papeete offers overwater bungalows.
Expensive.
● *Royal Tahitian:* On a lovely crescent of black-sand beach, you can choose
between motel-type units and beach bungalows.

Moorea

Though it's just a seven-minute plane ride or a 45-minute boat ride away, Moorea (Mo-ray-a) seems miles and years apart from the bustle of Papeete. In Papeete, the tall ship *Sea Cloud*, docked at the waterfront, is an odd-looking anomaly: a century-old square-rigger amid the buzzing of a twentieth-century port. But the same ship anchored in Moorea's Cook Bay seems perfectly placed against the backdrop of palms and peaks. Straight from *Typee* or *Mutiny on the Bounty*, it carries you back to the days of pure, balmy, South Pacific beauty.

The twin bays called Cook and Opunohu define Moorea's north coast, where most hotels and restaurants are located. On all sides of these long, sheltered harbors, steep hills covered with jungle rise to craggy ridges and volcanic towers. To get a feel for the splendid geography of Moorea, scooter up to the Belvedere lookout, where both bays and the surrounding hillsides are laid out before you in a blazing spread of blue and green. On the way down, you can stop to investigate a group of *marae* (ancient, sacred sites constructed from black volcanic stone), then whiz down the lush valley where cows happily graze through the pastoral scene.

Due to its proximity to Tahiti, Moorea gets a healthy tourist flow. Which means that you'll find a selection of hotels, as well as a wide choice of excursions (glass-bottom boat tours, sunset cruises, snorkel and scuba trips). Moorea's hotels boast a lion's share of Polynesia's overwater bungalows, which are well worth the added investment. Perched on stilts at reef's edge, they provide excellent dive-off points for snorkeling and splashing in the lagoon. Some even boast plexiglass floor panels, which you can open up to feed the phosphorescent fish that swim beneath.

Sightseeing doesn't take long. There's no main town; instead, stores and restaurants are spread all along the bumpy shoreline road. Aside from heading up to the Belvedere, stopping in at the Fruit Juice Factory and Distillery (even a rainy day seems brighter after tasting their potent pineapple liqueur), and browsing through hand-dyed *pareos* at roadside stands, beach-shopping is the main order of the day. And the choice is wide; all three prongs of Moorea's north side are frosted with intimate strands. A lunch stop at Les Tipanier's beach restaurant is highly recommended; with one of their fresh salads, a cool Hinano beer, and the eclectic company of barefoot-chic Europeans, you look out over the glowing lagoon, unable to wish for anything more.

As evening draws near, there's a good chance you'll see the square-rigged *Sea Cloud* or four-masted *Wind Song* approach. Sails puffed full, lovingly lit in afternoon's glow, these vessels can't fail to impress. Later, it's well worth venturing off hotel grounds to sample Moorea's best restaurants: sophisticated, open-air Oasis, where lagoon oysters, giant prawns, and smoked swordfish and blinis are served; Les Tipaniers, serving Italian fare with nouvelle variations; and Chez Michel and Jackie, just down from the Bali Hai, where delicious French specialties are delivered with notable speed. The nightly dance shows at some hotels can seem silly if you're squeezed into a crowd of flashing cameras, but from a starlit veranda of an overwater bungalow, the sound of drums and whoops and cries across the lagoon can sound very exotic indeed.

FACTS TO GO ON

☐ Getting there: From Papeete, Air Moorea flies to Moorea at frequent, if somewhat irregular, intervals. You can also take a boat from Papeete's waterfront.

☐ *Bride's* Best Beds

● *Sofitel Kia Ora Moorea:* Thatched bungalows dotted along a long white-sand beach house some of the most spacious, comfortable rooms on Moorea. Expensive.

● *Les Tipaniers:* Though it's not Moorea's fanciest hotel, it stands out for the quality of its food, its fun crowd, and laid-back charm. With a lovely white-sand beach. Moderate.

● *Bali Hai:* The pioneer Moorea hotel, with very nice overwater bungalows, attentive service, and a mature American clientele. Expensive.

● *Moorea Lagoon:* Redecorated, thatched-roofed bungalows along a lovely stretch of beach. Moderate.

● *Club Méditerranée:* Its full range of sports and activities, its all-inclusive pricing, and its fun-loving crowd makes it just right for newlyweds with partying and waterskiing on their minds.

Bora Bora

Surprise! Planes to Bora Bora don't land on Bora Bora, but on an offshore *motu,* from which you'll be ferried to this island of legendary beauty. As you wait at the airport's dock for the Louis Vuitton suitcases and overflowing crates of vegetables to be loaded on the boat, you gaze over a crystal-clear lagoon to a square-topped hunk of mountain covered soft and green. Mt. O'Temanu, Bora Bora's towering peak, follows you all over Bora Bora; it looms up behind beaches, it rises from veils of palm when you bike around the bays, and as the airport boat putts to the Viatape dock (where hotel buses collect you), it rotates, as if on a carousel, showing off its sweeping contours. Your fellow passengers sprawl out of the boat and perform incredible acrobatics to capture it on film. By the time you dock, everyone's tongue hangs out in anticipation.

After the boat ride, the bus to the hotel, and check-in, you're so ready to devour Bora Bora's beauty that you can only run to the beach. Wade into the glassy lagoon and dozens of fish, sun flashing on their brightly made-up sides, are happy to let you join them; they flirt and flicker all around. Float on your back: the horizon is clear, dazzlingly blue, with palm-fringed *motus*, a sparkling line of waves on the reef, and puffy white clouds strategically placed. The mountain behind you wears a skirt of lush-patterned jungle, fringed with leaning palms over the water. Birds gracefully swirl and caw. The sun tans you to the bone. *This* is what you came for.

Visitors do their best to experience Bora Bora from every conceivable angle. You can tour the island-rimming road—an afternoon of scouting quiet beaches (Matira Beach is the loveliest), snapping rolls of film, and poking through Viatape Village when everyone comes to buy warm *baguettes*. You can sail out into the lagoon; most hotels have outrigger canoes to paddle, others have windsurfers, and some have elegant outrigger sailboats with tanned skippers who'll take you anywhere. Motorboats shuttle you to Bora Bora's numerous *motus* for snorkeling, sunning, and barbeque lunches. And everywhere, the lagoons, the arc of the bays, and the mountain profile firmly anchor you in the South Pacific.

Bora Bora's extreme beauty makes it popular for its small size. Much of the shoreline road has a well-groomed look and a fair share of thatched bungalow hotels. Several restaurants provide pick-up service (a hysterical affair, with flower-crowned divers swerving to avoid crunching crabs), which helps since taxis are expensive. And dinner is always an event: a foot-stomping island band plays at Chez Christian; Hotel Bora Bora stages all-out barbeques; Club Med produces lively buffets with flowing wine; and at Bloody Mary's (where Angie Dickinson and Juliet Prowse have dined), the host introduces you to the mahi-mahi, unicorn fish, and parrotfish you'll eat, stroking their slippery sides and describing their flavors as they stare from a bed of ice.

Later, you could go dancing at Le Refice, Oa Oa, or Club Med (they'll let in nonguests who buy drink beads at the door), or watch any of the hotel-sponsored dance shows. But early mornings are gorgeous on Bora Bora, and an evening lying on the beach, staring up at the South Pacific sky, and heading early to your bungalow bed, gives you the chance to see the splendor of dawn.

FACTS TO GO ON 🦢

☐ Getting there: Air Tahiti schedules regular flights to Bora Bora from Tahiti and the other Society Islands. There are also boats that sail to Bora Bora from neighboring islands, but the schedules vary, so inquire at your hotel.

☐ *Bride's* Best Beds

● *Hotel Sofitel Marara Bora-Bora:* A lovely hotel with garden, beach, and overwater bungalows in the nicest part of Bora Bora, near Matira Beach, with complete watersports facilities and excursions (snorkeling, sunset cruises, shark-feeding). Expensive.

● *Hotel Bora Bora:* Without doubt, the most elegant hotel on the island. Beautifully landscaped grounds, immaculate, well-appointed garden, beach, and overwater bungalows, and a gorgeous beach with the nicest beach restaurant on the island. Expensive.

● *Hotel Matira:* Bungalows on Bora Bora's best beach, kitchen facilities, a charming waterside Chinese restaurant, and reasonable prices make it a favorite. Moderate.

● *Club Mediterranée:* With room for just 80 guests, it's one of Club Med's smallest properties, and their regular boat service to beautiful Motu Tapu draws raves from the people who stay there. All-inclusive pricing makes this a good Bora Bora buy. Moderate.

Raiatea 🦎

Tahiti, Moorea, and Bora Bora are regular stops on the French Polynesian tourist track, but Raiatea (Rye-a-tay-a) receives fewer visitors. Consequently, this dramatically peaked island retains a laid-back, genuinely friendly attitude. That, plus its spectacular mountains, its charming town of Uturoa and sister island, Tahaa, make Raiatea a very inviting stopover.

Uturoa, the capital port, is arguably the nicest town in these islands. You'll want to spend some time wandering through its old-fashioned, open-air market, surrounded by a moat of watermelons, which bustles most on Wednesday, Friday, and Sunday mornings. In stores, the razor-neat rows of cans, the shelves of farming tools, the spools of rope and wire, all imply a great productivity on this, the second-largest of the Society Islands. When the *Wind Song* docks in town, you'll find a beautiful crafts market set up right by their gangplank, with rows of bright-dyed *pareos* and beautiful coral jewelry. In the streets further back from the waterfront, no-frills restaurants and billiard halls provide glimpses of an island life essentially unaffected by tourism.

You won't find an abundance of beaches, so take to the water for a snorkeling trip, scuba excursion, or an afternoon adventure on one of the offshore *motus*—an experience you'll remember always. The Bali Hai, the only resort-style hotel on the island, sets up a number of other interesting excursions: visits to Raiatea's *marae*, outrigger journeys up the Faaroa River, and guided treks up Mt. Temehani, the island's highest point. At this mountain's peak, you'll be treated to a spectacular view of Raiatea, Tahaa, and further on the horizon, Bora Bora. It's also the only place to find the *tiare apetahi*, a white flower whose five petals symbolize the hand of a Tahitian maiden who was never allowed to marry her true love, an island prince.

At night, venture into town (it's only a short walk from the Bali Hai) for dinner at Hotel Motu's harbor-view restaurant. If the *Wind Song* is in port, this restaurant's arched windows provide a view of palms, white-lit rigging, and a wide Pacific moon that's impossibly romantic. You'll pass through Hotel Motu's card room on the way out; the tables of sunburnt poker and bridge players will have you giggling all the way home. But don't laugh too loud, because you might want to join them tomorrow night. It may be the most nighttime action in town.

FACTS TO GO ON

☐ Getting there: Air Tahiti provides regular service to Raiatea from Tahiti and the other Society Islands. There is also frequent boat service to and from other islands.

☐ *Bride's* Best Beds

● *Bali Hai:* The biggest hotel on Raiatea, and the only one that comes close to being a resort. Garden and overwater bungalows have nice views, though they could use some loving attention. Expensive.

● *Hotel Motu:* Right in the center of Uturoa, this white cement hotel is neat, clean, and extremely welcoming—with a surprisingly good restaurant. Moderate.

Huahine

All of the Society Islands boast beautiful scenery, but the landscape of Huahine (Hoo-a-hee-nay) is particularly wonderful. Actually two islands (Huahine Nui and Huahine Iti) connected by a small bridge, Huahine's towering peaks, knuckly ridges, and deep green valleys make keeping your eyes on the road while touring a spectacular challenge. It boasts French Polynesia's most impressive collection of archeological sites, and its low-key atmosphere—similar to that of Raiatea—makes Huahine's welcome especially warm.

At the northwest side of Huahine Nui (Big Huahine), you'll find Maeva, where the island's best *marae* are located. You'll approach along Maeva Lake, a wide inland lagoon ringed with palms. Some *marae* occupy a tranquil, mystical site at the edge of the lake; others are scattered up a hill.

Heading south, you can stop in Fare, Huahine's principal town, which is a blink-you-miss-it sort of place. Wander through, but don't dawdle; the really good stuff is further along.

As you scooter along the island's west coast, you'll rise up into hills, passing walls of toothy, green peaks, and spreading valleys with palm-lined bays. The beauty culminates where the two islands meet to create one of the most incredible vistas in French Polynesia. Steep, jungle-covered slopes sweep up from all sides of twin bays, and lines of palms and drooping vines trace the flow of water and land.

After crossing the bridge, your goal on Huahine Iti (Little Huahine) is Avea Bay, at the southwest tip of the island. Its beach is splendid—a huge crescent of silky white sand, with only a small hotel and a few houses tucked into the shoreline palms. Along with Bora Bora's Matira Beach, it ranks as one of the nicest strands on these islands. You're infused with a sense of great peace just basking on this tranquil bay. A beautiful child comes up to chat, not the least bit fazed if you can't comprehend her French and Polynesian burblings. When you walk along the water's edge, you meet only a fisherman sorting his nets and a woman who jumps up from her pot to smile and wave. Your footprints make a solitary trail on the smooth curve of sand.

FACTS TO GO ON

☐ Getting there: Air Tahiti schedules regular flights to Huahine from Tahiti and other Society Islands. You can also take a boat from the other islands.

☐ *Bride's* Best Beds

● *Relais Mahana:* Its superb location on Avea Bay, Huahine's most beautiful beach, makes it a favorite, but it's not fancy. Twelve bungalows along the beach, with a selection of watersports, and a French menu. Very isolated. Moderate.

● *Bali Hai:* Huahine's most polished hotel, with its own *marae* on the premises, well-tended beach bungalows, a beautiful pool, winding streams, and lush landscaping. A very nice place. Expensive.

● *Hotel Bellevue:* A no-frills hotel up in the hills with a glorious view of Maroe Bay. Ask for a poolside bungalow rather than a room in the main hotel. Inexpensive.

11
THE CONTINENTAL U.S.A.

From the shore of the Pilgrims' landing to the regal Pacific Coast, from New England's mossy mountains to crusty Southwestern canyons, America's glory blazes like no other land's. Just think of the silvery mountain sheen of an Ansel Adams photograph or the desert pastels of a Georgia O'Keeffe canvas. Or the type of quintessential country town that Norman Rockwell loved to paint. It's the America of poets and painters, of history books and Hollywood westerns. The America Kate Smith must have pictured when she sang "God Bless America."

Regional romance is the big U.S.A. story. As we rediscover the homegrown tastes of America—the Creole cooking of New Orleans, the blue corn tortillas of Santa Fe, Maine's just-caught lobster—we're also taking a fresh look at America's premier honeymoon destinations. Consider the sunstruck southeastern states. You could spend a week or more lazing away on palm-shaded beaches, playing golf or tennis from dawn till dusk, and sipping piña coladas under a silver moon. In the Northeast, you might splurge on a stay in the country's largest city, bike through New England landscapes, or investigate Colonial towns that haven't changed much in 200 years. The Rocky Mountain states invite you to join rodeos, hot-air balloon rides, horseback treks through valleys of wild flowers. Or you might explore the wooded hills, glimmering lakes, and treasured resorts of our clear-eyed midwestern states. In America's Southwest, you'll find country-and-western bars, slow-talking cowboys, and the dramatic mesas, cloud-piled skies, and giant cacti of picture books. Way out west, you can sample the star treatment in a Pacific hideaway, coast along breathtaking Big Sur, or sample the wines of Napa and Sonoma. And that's just to start. America's wedding-trip possibilities are practically endless. One is bound to match your dream.

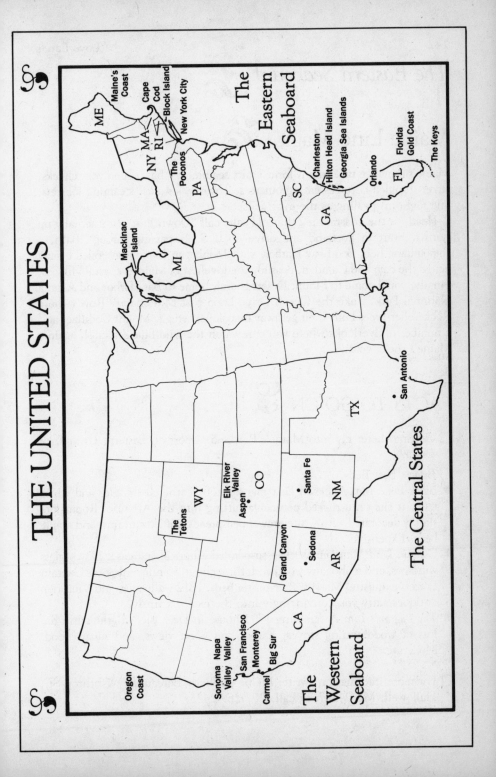

THE UNITED STATES

The Eastern Seaboard

Maine's Coast
Cape Cod
Block Island
New York City

ME
NY MA
RI

The Poconos
PA

Charleston
Hilton Head Island
Georgia Sea Islands

SC
GA

Florida Gold Coast
The Keys
Orlando
FL

Mackinac Island
MI

San Antonio
TX

The Central States

Elk River Valley
CO
Aspen

WY

Santa Fe
NM

The Tetons

Grand Canyon
Sedona
AR

Oregon Coast

Sonoma Valley
Napa Valley
San Francisco
Monterey
Carmel
Big Sur

CA

The Western Seaboard

The Eastern Seaboard

Maine-Line Magic

Maine's romance takes many forms: salty sea breezes that redden your cheeks, silver-shingled cottages gazing out to sea, widow's walks, steaming lobsters, and foghorns pealing as the mist whispers in.

Head for the coastal area that old salts call "Down East" (it's actually up north). Start in Portland and drive up U.S. 1, passing through Bath, a shipbuilding hub; Boothbay Harbor, with Monhegan Island's unspoiled beauty across the bay; and Camden, possibly the loveliest of Maine's coastal villages. Finally, you'll come to Mount Desert Island, home to Bar Harbor and Acadia National Park. Take the Ocean Drive Loop past Millionaire's Row (where Rockefeller-types built their getaway mansions), craggy Mount Cadillac, and a number of overlooks where you can watch the wild blue sea crash against Maine's rocky coast.

FACTS TO GO ON

☐ Getting there: Fly into Maine's Portland airport on Eastern, United, or Delta.

☐ *Bride's Best Beds*
● *Black Point Inn:* A Down East mansion of weathered shingles and white trim, it sits on a rugged peninsula jutting into the Atlantic. Rooms are simply decorated with white crewel bedspreads, ruffled curtains, and maple beds. Expensive.
● *Captain Lord Mansion:* With a suspended elliptical staircase, blown-glass windows, and mahogany woodwork throughout, Kennebunkport's Captain Lord is exquisite. Massive four-poster beds, 1812 wallpaper, and Victorian antiques carry you convincingly into the past. Expensive.
● *The Pilgrim's Inn:* A rambling 1793 house in Deer Isle, Pilgrim's Inn has lots of woodburning stoves, harbor and pond views, and superb food. Moderate.

☐ For more information, write: Maine Publicity Bureau, 97 Winthrop St.; Hallowell, ME 04347; or call (207)289-2423.

Candid Cape Cod

That little spit of land poking out from Massachusetts is New England's sandbox, where Bostonians play all summer long. Settle someplace that overlooks the glassy bay or the Atlantic, and devote at least a few days to exploring. Start in the south and proceed east to Hyannis (lots of shops, galleries, cafés, plus a dose of Kennedy-compound mystique) and Chatham, a quintessential Cape town with its lighthouse, handsome yachts, and sailboats. Or discover the Cape's north side, with Sandwich (famous for glass), Barnstable (dunes, beaches, a pretty harbor), elm-shaded Yarmouth, and Dennis, where the summer playhouse is worth an evening.

From Orleans at the Cape's elbow, carry on through Eastham, where you can stop to find out more about the National Seashore and its lunar-looking dunes. Continue up the Cape, stopping in Wellfleet (good seafood restaurants), then up to Provincetown, an eclectic hamlet of funky shops and partying people. And try to visit one of Cape Cod's offshore islands; Nantucket and Martha's Vineyard are restful havens with the Cape's natural beauty and none of its tourist-strip hubbub. With cobbled streets, sea captains' mansions, tranquil harbors, and spreading beaches, they may be the most romantic of all.

FACTS TO GO ON

☐ Getting there: Fly into Boston and pick up a rental car for the one-hour drive to the Cape Cod Canal—the entrance to the Cape. Or arrange to connect with one of PBA's (a division of Continental) flights to Hyannis, Provincetown, Nantucket, or Martha's Vineyard. You can take a ferry from Woods Hole or Hyannis to either offshore island.

☐ *Bride's Best Beds*

● *Queen Anne Inn:* In Chatham, a grey-shingled inn with lovely rooms looking over Oyster Pond Bay. The inn's private boats can take you to Monomoy Island, a nature preserve. Expensive/Moderate.

- *Charlotte Inn:* On Martha's Vineyard, it's a charming white clapboard sea captain's home in the village of Edgartown. Choose from antique-furnished rooms in the main house, the Carriage House, or the Summer House. Expensive/Moderate.
- *Jared Coffin House:* On Nantucket, this Greek Revival house is one of the town's centerpieces. Expensive/Moderate.

☐ For more information, write Cape Cod Chamber of Commerce, Junction of Route 6 and 132, Hyannis, MA 02601; or call: (617) 362-3225.

Beckoning Block Island 🦋

On Block Island, quiet pleasures are king. In grassy moors, birdwatchers scan the sky; on Mohegan Bluffs, a painter brushes his canvas with a wash of Atlantic blue; at Crescent Beach, peace-seekers soak up the salty tranquility. An hour-and-15-minute ferry ride from Rhode Island's southern tip, Block Island offers windswept relief from trend-following eastern cities. One trend, though, snuck across the Sound: renovation. The grand hotels in New Shoreham, the island's tiny village, have been snapped up—and spruced up—with remarkably romantic results.

Most days you'll devote to all-out relaxing, stretched on a sun-blessed curve of beach. When you feel the urge to explore, use bicycles to get around. Visit Settler's Rock, where the first visitors arrived in 1661, the North Light at Sandy Point, and the Palatine Graves, where ships sank like coins tossed into a fountain. Then wander around the Maze's gentle footpaths and the dramatic Mohegan Bluffs—cliffs that rise 200 feet from the sea. They're crowned with a brick castle lighthouse that flashes green into the night.

FACTS TO GO ON 𝒮

☐ Getting there: Fly into Green Airport in Providence, Rhode Island. From there, drive south to Point Judith and catch the Block Island Ferry. Or book charter seats on New England Airlines to fly directly from Green Airport to Block Island.

☐ *Bride's* Best Beds
- *Hotel Manisses and 1661 Inn:* Two charming inns, run by the same family. Hotel Manisses is a Victorian showplace in town, with stained glass, flowered wallpaper, and a Jacuzzi-ed bridal suite. If ocean views are your primary goal, choose the 1661 Inn, the Manisses' simpler sister hotel, right up the hill. Moderate.

☐ For more information, write: Block Island Chamber of Commerce, Drawer D, Block Island, RI 02807; or call: (401) 466-2982.

Nonstop New York 🌀

Its skyline is breathtaking. Its bustling streets are heaven for window-shoppers, art-lovers, and people-watchers alike. So a New York honeymoon is bound to be dazzling.

Start your city-seeing with a shopping stroll down Fifth Avenue (from 59th to 34th Streets). Then amble through Greenwich Village, where historic townhouses, theaters, and cafés line the streets. Explore SoHo's renovated warehouses, now home to art and fashion's cutting edge. Pick a Broadway show and dine later, maybe in Chinatown, Little Italy, or in a once-in-a-honeymoon, four-star French spot like Lutèce or Le Cirque. Another day, art-out on Museum Mile (the stretch of Fifth Avenue from 79th to 104th streets), cross Central Park with its whirling roller skaters, kite-flyers, and sun-soakers, then munch your way down the West Side on trendy Columbus Avenue.

Of course you'll want to visit the standard tourist sites—Rockefeller Center (its Rainbow Room has reopened to great fanfare), the Empire State Building, and Lady Liberty. But look beyond these postcard images and you'll see the many different faces of the metropolis. Consider the East Village, where artists, punks, students, street people, and limousine-hoppers all mix in a clattery swirl; or the Sheep Meadow, in Central Park, where you're sure to meet someone, whether it be your best friend from third grade, or Larry Locksmith, who'll deliver a lengthy monologue about why you need window bars; or any of the hundreds of fashionable restaurants, where your waiter at lunch might be the leading man in the Off-Broadway play you saw last night. Whether you're hoping for the sweet-hued New York of carriage rides and champagne toasts, or the real-life New York of lines and crowds and lights and noise, you won't be disappointed.

FACTS TO GO ON 🌀

☐ Getting there: Most airlines fly in and out of New York's Kennedy and La Guardia airports, as well as Newark's airport, just across the Hudson.

☐ *Bride's Best Beds*

● *The Stanhope:* Newly renovated, with sumptuous suites overlooking the Metropolitan Museum of Art. Expensive.

● *The Pierre:* Sitting at the lower corner of Central Park on Fifth Avenue, it's one of the most exclusive hostelries in the city. Park-view rooms are the nicest and priciest. Expensive.

- *The Ritz-Carlton:* A small hotel on Central Park South that offers an older, clubby atmosphere. Request a park-view room. Expensive.
- *The Carlyle:* Just a block away from the Whitney Museum, this Upper East Side hotel is where the elite meet for tea and to listen to Bobby Short play in the Café Carlyle. Expensive.
- *Morgans:* The small, elegant, modern rooms are usually filled with entertainment people (its penthouse is Cher's second home). Expensive.

☐ For more information, write: New York Convention and Visitors Bureau, Two Columbus Circle, New York, NY 10019. Or call: (212) 397-8222.

The Poconos

Once upon a time, these rural Pennsylvania hills were no different from many others. Farmland rolled on for miles, dotted only by the occasional town, house, or forest-fringed lake. Then the wedding-trip industry hit, and the Poconos became the honeymoon capital of the world.

Splendid countryside accounts for part of the appeal, but what makes the Poconos unique is a collection of couples-only retreats that are the antithesis of 80s minimalism. In shag-covered playpens with mirrors and velvet drapery, just-married couples soak in heart-shaped tubs and sip bubbly on huge, red beds.

While the whole concept of honeymooners-only resorts may sound odd, it makes practical sense. The man behind the idea—a Pennsylvania farmer named Von Hoevenberg—felt that newlyweds would feel most comfortable surrounded by other newlyweds. In the 1940s, when his Farm on the Hill opened, he was probably right. And even today, while honeymooners feel more at ease, the "we're all in this together" camaraderie can be equally important. More than any other group of resorts, the hotels in the Poconos have made an art of putting newlyweds on pedestals.

Take, for example, the kind of rooms they've devised. They're not meant for family reunions. Champagne-glass-shaped whirlpool baths and round beds are ensconced in rooms that sometimes come without a single window (but *with* the freedom to pretend it's nighttime any time of the day). If a cabin in the woods is more your style, you'll find them sporting four-poster beds and working fireplaces. And if you've ever wanted to tan yourselves all over, there are suites with private terraces designed just for that.

All Pocono honeymoon resorts schedule group activities throughout the day. There's always some kind of sporting event—a volleyball game or an archery tournament—that you can join, watch, or ignore. There are pools for swimming and lakes for waterskiing and rows of lounge chairs on which to stretch out with a magazine. If you're honeymooning in winter, ski slopes, frozen lakes, and white forests beckon you into the cold. And any time of year, indoor sports centers—with gym equipment, swimming pools, skating rinks, and even miniature golf courses—mean that a rainy day needn't dampen your spirits.

The people who built the Poconos realized that nights are as important as days, and their resorts boast on-site clubs and discos that rival those of some entire towns. A magician will perform one night, a belly dancer the next, and show bands (they sing, tell jokes, even organize contests) round out the week. Some of the larger resorts import "name" talent from New York, and all have after-hours discos for couples who aren't quite ready to call it a night. Then again, Pocono evenings are also times for being alone together, on moonlight strolls through garden paths and on balconies just an arm's length from the stars.

One of the nicest aspects of a Poconos honeymoon (and one of the reasons you'll feel so free to do anything that you like) is that one price pays for just about everything. The cost of your stay will not only include your room, but most of your meals, your sporting equipment, plus parties and hayrides, nightclub admission, even taxes and tips. The only things you'll pay extra for are drinks, souvenirs, and phone calls. You can take out a canoe, soothe yourselves in a sauna, and sit down to dinner without reaching into your wallets even once.

FACTS TO GO ON

☐ Getting there: The Poconos are just a two-hour drive from New York or Philadelphia. You can also fly into Allentown/Bethlehem or Wilkes Barre/Scranton airports; connections usually go through Atlanta and Pittsburgh. (Eastern and USAir fly in from most parts of the U.S. and Canada.)

☐ *Bride's* Best Beds

● The best Pocono room is the one that has the features (heart-shaped or champagne-glass tub? Private indoor pool or steamroom?) that you want. For information on Pocono resorts, drop a postcard to the Pocono Mountains Vacation Bureau, 1004 Main Street, Stroudsburg, PA 18360. Or call: (800) POCONOS.

Classic Charleston

Antebellum homes, winding cobblestoned streets, and magnificent flowering gardens are a few of this South Carolina town's many charms. The honeymoon appeal is exploring a city that tends to its twentieth-century business amid storybook southern settings. In Charleston, history and romance go hand in hand.

Start your sightseeing with a clip-clopping carriage ride past gracious mansions, antique churches, and oak-studded parks. Historic homes open for touring include the Nathanial Russell House with its incredible spiral staircase; the Edmonston-Alston House, overlooking the harbor, and the Calhoun Mansion, which boasts 35 fireplaces—visit at least one. Afterwards, stroll along the brightly painted houses on Rainbow Row (inspiration for *Porgy and Bess*), and visit Fort Sumter, where the first shots of the Civil War were fired. At Magnolia Plantation and Gardens, you can bike, boat, or hike through acres of blooms. And Boone Hall, a few miles from town, is where *Gone with the Wind* was filmed; its mansion and grounds offer well-preserved glimpses of a silver-screen South.

FACTS TO GO ON

☐ Getting there: American, Delta, Eastern, Piedmont, and United fly into Charleston.
☐ *Bride's* Best Beds
● *The Battery Carriage House:* The small guest rooms in this carriage house of a Charleston mansion have become romantic favorites. Oriental rugs cover polished floors, canopied beds invite midday napping, and breakfast is served in the gardens on silver trays. Expensive.
● *Two Meeting Street:* A very pleasing mansion filled with antiques, Oriental rugs, and four-poster beds. Moderate.
● *The Lodge Alley Inn:* This old warehouse has been transformed into a lovely inn with fireplaces, exposed brick walls, and windows that frame Charleston's best historic vistas. Moderate.

☐ For more information, write: Charleston Trident Convention and Visitors Bureau, P.O. Box 975, Charleston, SC 29402; or call: (803) 577-2510.

Hilton Head Island

This South Carolina island beckons newlyweds with an astonishing sports scene, miles of uncrowded beaches, and balmy temperatures year-round. You can take your pick of four sport-happy "plantations"—Palmetto Dunes, Sea Pines Plantation, Shipyard, and Port Royal—which are actually resort communities shared by hotel guests and private home owners.

Spend days serving tennis balls on hard or clay courts (even grass in some places), teeing off on any of a dozen golf courses, sailing the bluer-than-blue waters, or lounging on a white-sand beach. When you feel like taking a break, head into Savannah for a day of sightseeing, or drive up to Harbour Town for souvenir shopping. Along the way, you'll pass scenes right off the pages of *National Geographic*: long-legged cranes perfectly reflected in glassy water, marshlands and dunes stretching off in every direction, and sunsets that turn everything cotton-candy pink. To really get away from it all, ferry over to pristine Daufuskie Island—there's not a neon light, asphalt road, or private car in sight. Back on Hilton Head Island, nights start off with seafood feasts, move on to dancing, and end with strolls on the beach. At high tide, you can practically see the water dripping off the rising moon.

FACTS TO GO ON

- ☐ Getting there: Fly into Savannah and drive 45 minutes north to Hilton Head Island.
- ☐ *Bride's* Best Beds
- ● *Sea Pines Plantation:* The first resort on Hilton Head island, Sea Pines offers a wide room variety: the older Hilton Head Inn, plus villas, town-houses, or cottages elsewhere on the plantation. Some think that the Treehouses are the most romantic of all. Expensive.
- ● *Hotel Inter-Continental Hilton Head:* One of the newer Hilton Head hotels, it offers the chain's worldy refinement in a resort setting. Expensive.

- ☐ For more information, write: Hilton Head Chamber of Commerce, P.O. Box 5647, Hilton Head, SC 29938; or call: (803) 785-3673.

Georgia's Islands

On Georgia's southern coast, four Golden Islands lure newlyweds with sun, sand, and sea. Each offers its own romantic flourishes.

Jekyll Island tempts with the tradition of tycoons. Fifty years ago, Rockefellers, Vanderbilts, and Morgans used Jekyll as their exclusive winter retreat; today, the mansions they built are open for tours. St. Simons invites you to sample southern history, from the ruins of Fort Frederica and the Lighthouse Museum to Epworth-by-the-Sea. Sea Island delivers luxe resort living, southern style; its Cloister Hotel has coddled so many newlyweds that it's become a tradition. Back-to-nature couples head for Little St. Simons; only 24 guests can visit the island at any one time, lured by the salt marshes, palmetto thickets, and untouched shores, home to alligators and 200 species of birds.

FACTS TO GO ON ᘓ

☐ Getting there: Fly in to Jacksonville or Savannah, and drive one and a half hours to the Golden Islands. You can fly to Brunswick from Atlanta on Atlantic Southeast Airlines.

☐ *Bride's* Best Beds

● *The Cloister:* This comforting world of manicured lawns, white arches, bubbling fountains, and Spanish moss has been coddling honeymooners for generations. Along with the beautiful beach and a fine sporting spread, you'll find elegant dining, horse-drawn carriages, afternoon teas, and cheek-to-cheek dancing. Expensive.

● *Little St. Simons Island:* The hotel with the same name is the only place to stay on this nature-loving island. With rooms scattered through the main lodge and three outbuildings, it's happily secluded. And staff naturalists will show you around the island, pointing out armadillos, deer, and hundreds of birds. You can also ride horseback, swim at the beach, hike, and windsurf. Expensive.

☐ For more information, write: Brunswick's Golden Isles Tourist and Convention Bureau, 4 Glynn Avenue, Brunswick, GA 31520; or call: (912) 265-0620.

Outlandish Orlando ᘓ

If you think Orlando is just for children, you're in for a surprise; it's one of the most popular honeymoon destinations in the state. Why do so many newlyweds flock to this patch of fantasy in central Florida? Walt Disney World's Magic Kingdom and EPCOT Center, for starters. Sheer terror provides the excuse to clutch each other in Space Mountain or the Haunted Mansion, and the only person—yes, there is a person under those ears—who could possibly come between you is Mickey Mouse, posing for a snapshot. In EPCOT's Future World, America's wealthiest industries put together jaw-dropping technological displays, and World Showcase's fun- and food-filled global village takes you round the world in 80 minutes instead of 80 days.

But Disney's isn't the only world in Orlando's universe. Sea World and Boardwalk and Baseball both orbit nearby, and Wet 'n Wild's water slides are among the fastest and splashiest anywhere. For a break from all the man-made hoopla, head to Alexander Springs for tubing and canoeing. Or there's the Ocala National Forest, surrounded by sprawling horse ranches. And if you're still looking for a way to keep that piece of wedding cake fresh for your anniversary, consider a side trip to the Tupperware Museum.

FACTS TO GO ON ♋

☐ Getting there: American, Continental, Delta, Eastern, Northwest Orient, Pan Am, Piedmont, TWA, United, and USAir all fly to Orlando, along with a flock of smaller airlines.

☐ *Bride's* Best Beds

● *Hyatt Regency Grand Cypress:* An atrium where streams bubble, music fills the air, and glass elevators whir up and down, plus the hotel's showpiece pool—a sprawling oasis with waterfalls, suspension bridges, Jacuzzis, water slides, and a grotto bar—make it a glitzy Orlando favorite. Expensive.

● *Disney's Polynesian Village Resort:* With a pair of pools, the Seven Seas Lagoon, and palm trees everywhere, this Disney resort gets top honeymoon billing. Also important: its proximity to the Magic Kingdom on the monorail line. Expensive. Also check out *Disney's Grand Floridian Beach Resort*, opening in summer 1988.

● *Chalet Suzanne:* This family-run inn in nearby Lake Wales offers a tranquil honeymoon base. Nestled into palms and rosewood by a private lake, each of the Chalet's rooms has been decorated with treasures from all over the world. And there's a very appealing honeymoon package. Moderate.

☐ For more information, write: Orlando Convention and Visitors Bureau, 7680 Republic Drive, Suite 200, Orlando, FL 32819; or call: (305) 345-8882.

The Sun-Gilded Gold Coast 🦚

People who've never been to Florida think the whole state looks like the Gold Coast. It's a mix of high-rise hotels, mile-long beaches, and palm-lined avenues, populated by lotioned suntanners by day and pastel-dressed vacationers by night. While Fort Lauderdale's beach bunnies couldn't be more different from Palm Beach's society set, people on the Gold Coast are unified in their quest for a sunny, social escape from the rest of the world.

Miami reigns as the queen of the coast. Like Rio de Janeiro and Waikiki, this tropical metropolis combines seaside pleasures with big-city thrills. And thanks to replenished beaches, a hit TV show, and some new hotels that specialize in cosmopolitan style, Miami is back in the honeymoon spotlight.

Miami's unique blend of people—Cuban cigarmakers in Little Havana, Perrier-sippers in Coconut Grove, retirees in white Lincolns everywhere—gives it the pulse of diversity. While sunning and splashing on the world-famous beach might be your primary diversions, you'll find a number of enticingly shady retreats: Villa Vizcaya, a Renaissance-style mansion with gardens to wander in; the Metro-Dade Cultural Center, a museum complex designed by Philip (no relation to Don) Johnson; and shopping meccas like Mayfair-in-the-Grove, with the designer boutiques of Paris and Beverly Hills. Just across the MacArthur Causeway is the heart of Miami Beach's Art Deco district, where streamlined facades are colored like cotton candy and poked through with glass blocks and porthole windows.

On the Fort Lauderdale strip, sun-baked teenagers herd into bars, wave from Camaros, and rub oiled shoulders. Festivity, you'll find, runs deep through the veins of this sea-loving city, just north of Miami. Pastels are applied to a canvas of condos, while canals weave under bridges, through marinas, and past million-dollar homes. With enough yachts to stretch for miles, enough theme parks to play in till you drop, and enough restaurants to feed a small country, Fort Lauderdale cruises on a happy, high-voltage plateau. A peace-loving hotel is a honeymoon necessity, and water-view restaurants offer plenty of romance: a table by the Intracoastal Waterway, chilled champagne, and a parade of slowly gliding boats against the sunset's tableau.

Pirates saw the rocky inlet of Boca Raton (it means "mouth of the rat") as the ideal place to hide and lay low with their booty. The architect Addison Mizner saw Boca Raton, north of Fort Lauderdale, as the perfect site for a society retreat by the sea. The Depression stopped most of his dreams before they started. But his Cloister Inn made it just under the wire, opening to one of the greatest society bashes ever. Just months later, Mizner went broke, yet the town has gone on to become one of the nation's wealthiest communities. Its waters are filled with well-polished yachts; its Royal Palm Polo Club fields a championship team; and the Cloister Inn lives on at the end of palm-lined Camino Real.

The Palm Beach question: how could there possibly be so many Rolls-Royces, million-dollar mansions, and acorn-sized diamonds in a single place? Money—and lots of it—answers this and all questions about Palm Beach. It's one of the few bastions of old wealth left in the country, and residents keep the jeweled aura pristine with laws that prohibit such vulgarities as jogging without a shirt, hanging clothes on a line, and placing "sale" signs in shop windows.

Palm Beach pastimes include afternoons at the polo fields, lunches at Petite Marmite, and browses through stores on if-you-have-to-ask-you-can't-afford-it Worth Avenue. And a drive down South Ocean Boulevard shows you just how much money can buy; sprawling mansions look to sea, the most notable being Mar-a-Lago, the home of late raisin-bran heiress Marjorie Merriweather Post. So polish up your credit cards, borrow Uncle Fred's Mercedes, and prepare yourselves for the horsey set.

FACTS TO GO ON ∾

☐ Getting there: A wide selection of airlines fly into Miami, Fort Lauderdale, and West Palm Beach from most U.S. cities.

☐ *Bride's* Best Beds

● *Grand Bay Hotel:* A sleek new pyramid-shaped hotel in Miami's Coconut Grove, with a lobby full of polished antiques, leather chairs, and brass-framed mirrors. The Grand Bay boasts bay views from balconied rooms, pool, health club with sauna and Jacuzzis, two superb restaurants, and a branch of Regine's nightclub on the top floor. Expensive.

● *Fontainebleau Hilton:* Since its creation, this mega-hotel has been the centerpiece of Miami Beach. And a multi-million-dollar facelift gives it fresh honeymoon appeal. Expensive.

● *Marriott's Harbor Beach Resort:* Tops in Fort Lauderdale because of its modern appeal, beach (silky sands right outside the door, with no busy road to cross), comfortable ocean-view rooms, and attractive honeymoon packages. Expensive.

● *Boca Raton Hotel and Club:* Mizner's Spanish-style palace is the hotel's centerpiece, and recent renovations have restored its former glory: the lobby's Gothic arches, the purple stained glass, and the Spanish antiques all look as elegant as they did on opening night. Choose from rooms in the landmark Cloister, the high-rise tower, or the newer Beach Club. Expensive.

● *The Breakers:* Designed by the architect of New York's Waldorf-Astoria, this oceanfront palace is the reigning monarch of Palm Beach resorts. The belvedere towers were patterned after Rome's Villa Medici, the fountain after one in Florence's Boboli Gardens, and everywhere you look, Renaissance features take cues from Italy's grand *palazzi.* Expensive.

☐ For more information, write: Greater Miami and the Beaches, 555 17th Street, Miami Beach, FL 33139; or call: (800) 641-1111.

The Keys

The overseas highway is a white ribbon stretching miles over aqua sea; driving it south to Key West feels like a journey to the world's edge. Curious scenes breeze by: a bridge stretching over seven ocean miles without a scrap of land beneath, pelicans perching on guardrails, fishermen casting lines from old railroad beds. On the way down, stop in Key Largo (stormy scenes with Bogart and Bacall made it famous) to dive at the John Pennekamp Coral Reef State Park; at Islamorada for superb sport fishing; at Bahia Honda's recreation center for beachside tent sites so beautiful that even city slickers are tempted to set up camp. Finally, you'll come to Key West, the gleaming pendant on this island chain.

Here at the southern end of things, creaky wooden houses are made of parts you've seen elsewhere—New England's widows' walks, the Caribbean's gingerbread, New Orleans's balustrades. Familiar signs—a grocery store, a laundromat—ground you in reality, but jumbled together with upscale stores, clanky bars, and tangly vines, it's more like an illogical daydream. Key West may seem slightly run down at first. But before long, you'll love its weathered look like a favorite pair of faded jeans. The island has been around; its history reads like a tall tale, with hurricanes, treasure seekers, writers, and notorious parties. And everyone's in the mood to chat about it.

By all means, check out established sights (Hemingway's house, Audubon House, Mel Fisher's Treasure Museum, with the awesome riches of just one wreck) on the Conch Train tour. But Key West demands participation, and you'll want to be more than voyeurs. So the best idea might be to ditch the tour and have a drink. In a town made up of die-hard hippies, native-born conchs (pronounced "conks"), smooth-talking Bahamians, gays from all over, and northerners fleeing the snow, a clink of glasses and down-the-hatch seems to be the uniform salute to any event.

As sunset draws near, head to Mallory Square, where the crowd is gathering. As the sun turns the sky to fire and beer cans pop, a chorus of clicking cameras ushers in another Key West night.

FACTS TO GO ON ℒ

☐ Getting there: Eastern and Piedmont fly into Key West, with connections in Miami. You can also drive three hours down the Overseas Highway from Miami.

☐ *Bride's* Best Beds

● *Casa Marina:* Built by Henry Flagler as the glamorous finale to his overseas railroad, with renovations by Marriott designed to recall the glory of the era. Expensive.

● *Pier House:* An atmosphere of sophistication, a topless beach, and some of the happiest restaurants and bars in town make Pier House a favorite of both visitors and locals alike. Right in the center of Key West's action, the hotel's contemporary lines hug some of the island's best (albeit snuggest) sands. Expensive.

☐ For more information, write: Florida Keys and Key West Visitors Bureau, P.O. Box 1147, Key West, FL 33041; or call: (800) FLA-KEYS.

Central States: The Midwest, the Rockies, and the Southwest

The Towering Tetons

Grand Teton mornings seem nearly prehistoric. Eerie and theatrical, mist rises from a purple lake and pines trace a flowing line. The background for the scene: the looming Teton mountains themselves, their sharp peaks and snow-filled crags glowing pink in the light of dawn. If you weren't in love already, the sight could send you flying straight into each other's arms.

Grand Teton National Park, in Wyoming's northwest quadrant, is a summer magnet for peak-seekers and cross-country caravans. At first, you'll just want to daydream on the Tetons' regal rise from the valley's floor. But the sight will soon nudge you into action, so look into raft trips on the Snake River, sailboat rentals on the lake, and the 200 miles of hiking trails. Horseback riding can be set up too—trots to lakeside groves, gallops through flowery meadows, even morning trail rides that end up with a cowboy-style breakfast of steaming coffee, ham 'n eggs, and fluffy flapjacks. The only experience that can match it is a moonlight stroll, the Tetons shimmering into the blue of the night.

FACTS TO GO ON

☐ Getting there: Fly Delta or American into Jackson Hole, Wyoming, and rent a car for the drive to the Park.

☐ *Bride's* Best Beds

● *Jenny Lake Lodge:* The most exclusive of park accommodations, where guests check into comfortable log cabins to feel reassured by the handmade quilts and the braided rugs and to sit in silence on Teton-view terraces. Expensive.

● *Spring Creek Ranch:* A luxurious resort set atop a Teton-viewing butte in Jackson Hole. Expensive/moderate.

☐ For more information, write: Superintendent, Grand Teton National Park, P.O. Drawer 170, Moose, WY 83012; or call: (307) 733-2880.

Colorado Cabins

Surrounded by mountains in the Elk River Valley, the Home Ranch offers total seclusion and rugged Rocky Mountain splendor. No telephone, no TV sets—just 600 acres of whispering aspens, regal peaks, and bright blue sky.

At the Home Ranch's center, a big log cabin is the place to take meals (hearty fare like roast chicken, prime ribs, home-baked bread) and meet your fellow guests. Nestled into the nearby woods, your private cabin comes with a woodburning stove, Navajo rugs, and a hot tub on the deck for bubbling under a star-spangled Colorado sky.

Daytime diversions: horseback riding, cross-country skiing, sleigh-riding, hiking, and fishing—all depending on the season. For nightlife, there's little beyond the aforementioned dinners and hot tubs. But with a crackling fire and two snifters of brandy, you've got a recipe for home-cooked after-dark doings that would make any disco seem dull.

☐ Getting there: Fly into Steamboat Springs on Continental Express, connecting from Denver, and a Home Ranch staff member will pick you up.

☐ *Bride's* Best Beds: Home Ranch. See above. Expensive.

☐ For more information, write: Home Ranch, Box 822-K, Clark, CO 80428; or call: (303) 879-1780.

All-Season Aspen

The little mining town of Aspen is booming again. Victorian miners' homes have been painted in every color of the rainbow, grand landmarks like the Wheeler Opera House and the Hotel Jerome have been renovated to their former glory, and enough fancy boutiques have sprouted up to keep you shopping through every off-slope moment. The quartet of ski areas—expert

Aspen Mountain, beginner's Buttermilk, eclectic Aspen Highlands, and sprawling Snowmass—offer a ski run for every ability and taste. To say nothing of cross-country skiing, dog-sledding, snowmobiling, and soaking away in hot tubs and heated pools.

While everyone knows the skiing is great, summer is Aspen's unsung hero. When the snowy blankets melt, sparkling streams begin to flow, the mountains grow warm and green, and wildflowers carpet the meadows. Hike a peak and be awed by the rugged Rockies' panorama, raft down roaring rivers, get your fill of tennis, golf, and horseback riding. Summer also turns Aspen into a cultural hub: Along with ballet and theater, the prized jewel is the Aspen Music Festival, featuring nine weeks of classical music, opera, and contemporary works by internationally renowned musicians.

FACTS TO GO ON

☐ Getting there: Fly into Denver and connect with a Continental Express or United Express plane to Aspen. The beautiful mountain-viewing drive from Denver to Aspen takes 4½ hours.

☐ *Bride's* Best Beds

● *The Snowmass Club:* Set in the mountain-skirted resort village of Snowmass (about half an hour from town), the Snowmass Club offers all the luxuries and sports options of a major resort with easy access to Aspen's in-town action. Expensive.

● *Hotel Jerome:* Even if you don't stay here, you must stop in for an after-dinner drink one night. Recently renovated, this landmark Victorian shines brighter than ever. Moderate.

☐ For more information, write: Aspen Resort Association, Visitor Information, 303 East Main Street, Aspen, CO 81611; or call: (303) 925-1940.

Serene Sedona

The approach to Sedona is so magnificently scenic, you may want to pull over on the road to take pictures. Mesas tower tall, and sandstone buttes are punched up from the horizon like modern sculpture. But hold back, because you'll find that the closer you get, the more spectacular this Arizona wonderland really is. Everywhere you turn, terra-cotta rocks and cliffs tower above junipers, cypress, and piñon pines. To really appreciate it all, sign on one of Pink Jeep Tours' thrilling two-hour excursions that take you up, down, and all over the region's red rocks (hold on tight—they're not kidding when they talk about a 45-degree grade). Just north of town, you can hike around Oak Creek Canyon, take a ride down Slide Rock (a natural water chute in the middle of the canyon), or just snap photographs of the inspiring scenes. In the actual town of Sedona, the replicated Mexican village called Tlaquepaque offers a bonanza of silver shops, glass artisans, boutiques, and restaurants.

FACTS TO GO ON ℘

☐ Getting there: Fly into Phoenix (most major airlines fly there) and drive about 2½ hours north.

☐ *Bride's Best Beds*

● *Auberge de Sedona:* A classy covey of log cabins with Provençal accents, canopied brass beds, stone fireplaces, and private porches. Fine dining in the creekside restaurant is included in the room rate. The "hillivator" climbs up to the Orchards Inn, a sister resort with two pools and a Jacuzzi. Expensive.

☐ For more information, write: Sedona Information, P.O. Box 3768, West Sedona, AZ 56340; or call: (602) 282-1117.

The Gigantic Grand Canyon ℘

Majestic and moving it may be, but romantic? Quite. Especially if you consider our favorite Grand Canyon honeymoon, combining the peace of a canyon-view room with the excitement of rafting the raging river that sculpted this natural spectacle. Settle in on the canyon's South Rim, open all year; you can cruise the Village Loop, hike the Bright Angel Trail, take a mule ride down into the canyon, or, for the very best canyon views, take a sightseeing flight in a helicopter or small plane.

After a few days of admiring this all, you'll be ready to take the plunge. Down, down, down you go, past stripes of sand and limestone, where passing years are marked by sedimentary layers filled with fossilized ferns and lizard footprints. At the canyon's bottom, the mighty Colorado, which looked like a pretty ribbon from up above, displays its canyon-carving force. Sign up with Grand Canyon Dories, Arizona River Adventures, or OARS Inc. for a river journey that you'll never forget.

FACTS TO GO ON 🐚

☐ Getting there: Fly into Phoenix (most major airlines fly there) and drive 4 hours to the canyon.

☐ *Bride's* Best Beds

● *El Tovar:* The canyon's oldest, most comfortable hostelry, perched on the South Rim. You'll be well situated for sightseeing, as well as simple gazing at the wonder outside your bedroom window. Expensive.

☐ For more information, write: Arizona Office of Tourism, 1480 Bethany Home Road, Phoenix, AZ 85104; or call: (602) 255-3618.

Spellbinding Santa Fe 🐚

Surrounded by a landscape of terra-cotta mountains and cattle-dotted grasslands, this chic New Mexican town is a bonanza of shops, earthy art galleries, and cafés. Start exploring its warren of narrow streets and low adobe buildings, stopping at the Palace of the Governors (the oldest public building in the U.S.), the Museum of Fine Arts, and the San Miguel Mission, which dates back to the year 1610. In between, shop for Indian pottery, jewelry, and basketry in dozens of small shops; Canyon Road, the soul of Santa Fe (a.k.a. the Arts and Crafts Road), is where you'll find the biggest concentration of galleries.

Take some time from shopping and sightseeing to explore the country outside of Santa Fe. The incredible spaciousness of earth and sky is home to several ghost towns, Indian cliff dwellings, ruins, and over half a dozen pueblos. Summertime honeymooners can take in the Santa Fe Opera (call way ahead for tickets) or drive up to Ten Thousand Waves, a Japanese bathhouse in the foothills, for a soak in a private hot tub. For a great Mexican meal, cruise up to Rancho de Chimayo; the trip—especially at sunset—is something you'll remember always.

☐ Getting there: Fly into Albuquerque (many major airlines fly there) and drive one hour north to Santa Fe.

☐ *Bride's* Best Beds

● *Rancho Encantado:* Just eight miles out of town, this resort has a wonderful away-from-it-all feeling. In the adobe buildings, you'll find fireplaces, hand-woven rugs, and painted tiles. Tennis, swimming, and horseback riding complete the picture. Expensive.

● *La Posada:* Centered around a Victorian house with a restaurant and bar, La Posada's landscaped grounds are dotted with private *casitas* and Santa Fe–style rooms. Moderate.

☐ For more information, write Santa Fe Visitors Bureau, P.O. Box 909, Santa Fe, NM 87504; or call: (800) 528-5369.

Spanish-Style San Antonio 🐉

If Dallas is Texas's most famous city and Houston its biggest, San Antonio takes the prize for Texas-style romance.

Start off where Crockett, Bowie, and Travers ended—at the Alamo, as moving a sight as ever. The Paseo del Rio, San Antonio's peaceful pedestrian thoroughfare, is nearby; walk down the stone steps to a riverside promenade where sunbeams filter through pecan and cypress trees to dapple café umbrellas. After browsing the boutiques and galleries, take a riverboat cruise and then cross over to El Mercado, a Mexican-style market where you can buy piñatas and terra-cotta figurines.

Mexican food lovers may have more than shopping on their minds. Whether you're into basics like nachos and tacos, or if you'd like to try nouvelle variations with spicy accents, or even if all you care about are salt-rimmed margaritas round the clock, you'll find a huge number of eateries that meet any taste or budget.

☐ Getting there: Many major airlines fly into San Antonio.

☐ *Bride's* Best Beds

● *La Mansión del Río:* With its Spanish styling, riverside location, swimming pool, restaurants, and classic wedding-trip comforts, La Mansion del Rio attracts more than its share of honeymooners. Expensive.

● *Menger Hotel:* Open since 1859, its antiques, next-door-to-the-Alamo location, and New Orleans–inspired facade make it one of the city's most handsomely historic hotels. Teddy Roosevelt frequented the bar. Moderate.

☐ For more information, write San Antonio Convention and Visitors Bureau, P.O. Box 2277, San Antonio, TX 78298; or call: (800) 531-5700.

The Western Seaboard

Big Sur Briefing

Big Sur defies photographers. Because no matter how wide the lens, how precipitous the angle, there's no capturing this California shore's heart-catching drama. For 90 miles, Highway One twists and plunges past parched canyons, sweeping meadows, and steep cliffs that fall sharply into the foam. The whole drive takes four hours or so, with a few stops along the way; try the Big Sur Inn for lunch with a 60s flavor—waitresses wear dashikis and the Beatles play on. Then press towards Kirk Creek with its bluff-top picnic sites, the sequoia redwoods at Salmon Creek, and San Simeon, where Hearst Castle invites you to see what unabashed excess is all about.

FACTS TO GO ON

☐ Getting there: Fly into San Francisco, and drive south on scenic Highway One or on speedier Route 101. Or you can fly into Monterey from San Francisco or Los Angeles (United makes the run), and drive from there. Big Sur is a 300-mile drive from Los Angeles.

☐ *Bride's* Best Beds
● *Ventana Inn:* Just south of Big Sur State Park, Ventana's stylish cedar ocean-view buildings make wonderful honeymoon bases. And they're made even better by Japanese hot tubs and an elegant, natural decor. The restaurant serves noteworthy fish and fowl. Expensive.
● *Deetjen's Big Sur Inn:* Some call it rustic, some call it funky; this woody, rambling inn is definitely unique. Moderate.

☐ For more information, write: California Tourist Information, P.O. Box 9278, Van Nuys, CA 91409; or call: (800) TO-CALIF.

Carmel and Monterey 🦎

This pair of artful coast-hugging hamlets have been favorite retreats for generations of Californian honeymooners. Their natural beauties are immense—towering granite cliffs, cypress-forested headlands, and the great navy Pacific.

Start your touring with a look around Monterey. Fisherman's Wharf and Cannery Row of Steinbeck fame have been scrubbed and prettified, and now they house craft shops, seafood cafés, and paneled pubs. The Monterey Bay Aquarium will give you a diver's-eye view of the marine life below, and there are historical sights to see, including a thoroughly creepy jail.

Carmel's charming eccentricities—a ban on neon, house numbers, and traffic lights—have kept the town perfect as its postcards. It's a felony to cut down a tree here, so Ocean Avenue resembles not so much a street as a park, lined with cypress, pines, and flower beds. Inns and restaurants are tucked away in Hansel-and-Gretel cottages and red-tiled adobes, and an astounding number of bakeries, antique shops, and maritime galleries hide in the brick-lined alleys just off the main drag. There's a perfect little beach at the foot of the avenue, and the surrounding scenics are splendid, especially at wildly beautiful Point Lobos State Reserve (bring binoculars to spy on the sea lions and otters). The biggest nightspot around is Mayor Clint Eastwood's own Hog's Breath Inn, where outdoor fireplaces and heaters warm the flagstone patio on even the coolest nights.

FACTS TO GO ON 🎷

☐ Getting there: Fly into San Francisco and drive south for about two hours (depending on the traffic) along scenic Route One or speedier 101. PSA and United fly from San Francisco and Los Angeles into Monterey.

☐ *Bride's* Best Beds

● *Highlands Inn:* Perched on the cliffs four miles from town, sophisticated touches include stone fireplaces, bleached oak floors, and a contemporary decor in sea-inspired colors—mauve, heather, Pacific blue. Choose a spa suite (Madonna and Sean Penn honeymooned in one) and you have your own whirlpool with an ocean view. Expensive.

● *La Playa Hotel:* Just a few blocks away from the beach in Carmel, La Playa offers ocean- and-garden-view rooms with Mediterranean styling. Expensive.

● *Old Monterey Inn:* With its half-timbered walls, blazing hearths, and nook-and-cranny charm, it's a Monterey favorite. Moderate.

☐ For more information, write: Carmel Business Association, Box 4444, Carmel, CA 93921; or call: (408) 624-2522. Or write: Monterey Peninsula Chamber of Commerce, Box 1770, Monterey, CA 93942; 649-1770.

San Francisco Flirtations

No matter when you go to San Francisco, you'll be greeted by a city that coddles lovers in scenic complexities: steep hills and flat bays, rolling fog and gleaming sunshine, Victorian gingerbreads and tall glassy towers. Down each narrow street, over the crest of every hill, lies a different neighborhood waiting to seduce you with charm and vitality: Nob Hill, where railroad barons built their roosts; Union Square, with smart hotels and fashionable stores; Haight-Ashbury, made famous by Janis Joplin and the Grateful Dead twenty summers ago.

You might begin your city seeing at Union Square, the very fashionable heart of town. Lined with handsome palms, it is surrounded by flower stalls, deluxe hotels, and posh storefronts. Street performers juggle and play flutes on the sidewalks. Just minutes away, lacquered boxes and silky butterfly kites enliven the storefronts of Chinatown, as frenetically colorful a neighborhood as you'll find anywhere.

Chinatown leads to North Beach, an Italian neighborhood beloved for its traditional restaurants, bohemian coffee houses (Caffé Trieste still draws an arty set), and tiny boutiques. Next stop: Telegraph Hill and postcard views of the Golden Gate Bridge, Alcatraz, and the sailboats of Sausalito across the bay.

Tomorrow, climb on a cable car and hold on for dear life as it clangs down to Fisherman's Wharf, a jumble of tourists, crabcakes, and seagulls. You'll want to take the standard photographs, then wander over to the Cannery, a mecca for junk-food addicts, and Ghirardelli Square, a chocolate factory-turned-shopping complex that inspired a whole generation of urban mall-makers.

Another day, you might want to visit the city's Palace of Fine Arts, a terra-cotta–pillared complex that simulates the glory of ancient Greece, California-style. Its Exploratorium has been called the most fascinating science museum in the world. Or perhaps you'd prefer to head off to Golden Gate Park, with its green meadows, eucalyptus forests, buffalo herds, and spectacular ocean views.

FACTS TO GO ON ℭ

☐ Getting there: Most major airlines fly into San Francisco.

☐ *Bride's* Best Beds

● *The Inn at Union Square:* A small, personable, elegant place. Rooms are done in antiques, brass trimmings, and warm colors. There's a small lobby on each floor for afternoon tea and evening cocktails, and the penthouse suite has its own whirlpool bath and fireplace. Expensive.

● *Stanford Court:* A supremely comforting hotel on Nob Hill, where your every need is anticipated well in advance, and then met with style. Expensive.

● *Sherman House:* Highlighted by fine antiques, marble fireplaces, and a superb French restaurant, this beautiful white mansion looks over Pacific Heights to San Francisco Bay. Expensive.

☐ For more information, write: San Francisco Convention and Visitors Bureau, P.O. Box 6977, San Francisco, CA 94101; or call: (415) 974-6900.

Spirited Napa and Sonoma ℨ

Napa and Sonoma are California's most famous wine-growing valleys, and they make fantastic touring country. Though neither leads a very hectic life, Napa's long valley seems the busier of the two, while the vast territory of Sonoma County—stretching from forest to sea—encourages you to slow down and savor. Start your exploring with a guide from the local chamber of commerce leading to vineyards great and small: the sparkling cellars at Korbel (fun, informative tours, a highly romantic garden, champagne tastings, too); Cuvaison, with its lovely picnic area and excellent chardonnays; and Jordan, looking more like a French château than a West Coast winery (call ahead for an appointment). For the best picnic provisions, follow Sonoma County's *Farm Trails* guide (it's free at your hotel) to mushroom purveyors, U-pick strawberry fields, and game bird farms selling dressed partridge and quail eggs.

There's history to see at Sonoma's plaza, where the Bear Flag Republic was proclaimed in 1846; you'll find the state's northernmost mission and some elegant shopping. Visit General Mariano Vallejo's home, where Sonoma roses climb the gates. And pay your respects at Jack London's Home and Museum, which shelters a few of the writer's 600 rejection letters, and a handmade wake-up clock on his bedroom door. For some early excitement, take a balloon ride in the morning mist with champagne to follow. Balloon Aviation of Napa Valley and Air Flambuouant offer one-hour flights.

FACTS TO GO ON ♋

☐ Getting there: From San Francisco, it takes about two hours to drive to the Napa and Sonoma Valleys.

☐ *Bride's* Best Beds

● *Auberge du Soleil:* With elegant rooms scattered through nine Mediterranean-style villas, sophisticated decor, a restaurant serving some of the finest California cuisine around, and a hillside perch looking through olive groves down Napa Valley, it's wine country's honeymoon favorite. A swimming pool, Jacuzzi, tennis courts, and bike riding compliment the area's wine-tasting possibilities. Expensive.

● *Sonoma Mission Inn and Spa:* Boasting nearly 100 rooms of contemporary, natural-hued luxury and a spa that celebrities flock to, it's become one of the most sought-after vacation addresses in Sonoma County. Expensive.

● *Madrona Manor:* A dramatically styled Victorian inn, Madrona is loaded with antiques, and offers a very fine restaurant and wine cellar. Expensive/moderate.

☐ For more information, write: Napa Chamber of Commerce, P.O. Box 636, Napa, CA 94559; or call: (707) 226-7455. Or write: Sonoma County Convention and Visitors Bureau, 10 Fourth Street, Suite 100, Santa Rosa, CA 95401; or call: (707) 575-1191.

Coastal Oregon 🐚

Lush forest and verdant meadows sweep down the slopes, ending with a plunge into the Pacific. Blasting waves and wind have carved the shore's jagged edges and stark stone towers, and seals and whales find the chilly swells just right. Usually, the sun shines down through the Pacific spray. But sometimes, Oregon's refreshing mists turn into thrilling rainstorms, which some people consider to be more fun than the sun.

You might begin an exploration of Oregon's coast at Gleneden Beach, home of the Salishan Lodge, one of the most honeymoon-worthy hotels on this or any shore. From there, head south to: Depoe Bay, which lays claim to the world's smallest harbor; Cape Foulweather, with a splendid coastal view; and Devil's Punchbowl, where waves slurp and slap through a circle of rock. Between Newport and Florence, you'll pass the Heceta Light, a tall white lighthouse capping an impressive peninsula. Just south, you'll find the Sea Lion Caves, where you can elevator down a murky den loaded with the playful, barking beasts. At the Oregon Dunes National Recreation Area, you can hike or dune-buggy around the massive sand formations, right by Honeymoon State Park. You could end up at Gold Beach, with some of the state's most dramatic, rugged shoreline; its Cape Sebastion juts 700 feet out into the swirling sea.

FACTS TO GO ON 🐈

☐ Getting there: Fly into Portland (many major airlines will take you there) and drive 90 miles southwest.

☐ *Bride's* Best Beds

● *Salishan Lodge:* Set on a slope looking down to Siletz Bay, Salishan coddles guests in earthy elegance. You'll have your own fireplace, dreamy down pillows, and a balcony that looks down to the sea or through the trees. Expensive.

● *Tu Tu Tun Lodge:* An intimate, luxurious retreat set on the banks of the Rogue River. Expensive.

☐ For more information, write: Oregon Tourism Division, 595 Cottage Street N.E., Salem, OR 97310; or call: (800) 547-7842.

America's Grand Hotels

They are places that over the years have attracted enough lovers to fill stadiums. The tenet of their era: Bigger must be better. Hundreds can waltz in their ballrooms with room to spare. Corridors stretch the length of football fields. They boast towers and turrets, verandas and cupolas. Crystal glitters, polished floors gleam, and huge, arched windows frame perfect views: a wave-smacked beach, a tranquil lake, or a set of towering mountains.

Even though America's grand hotels play host to America's grand conventions (lots of company name tags, talk about widgets in the elevators), the dignity of these *grandes dames* remains intact. We never had royalty in America, but we *do* have palaces. Palaces designed with pleasure in mind. At all these hotels, you'll find golf courses, pools, tennis courts, and a wide variety of other sporty options.

Here are a few of the best:

Boca Raton Hotel and Club, Boca Raton, Florida: On Florida's fabled

Gold Coast, Boca's newer Beach Club and Tower compliment the original Cloister—an opulent, pink, Spanish-style castle.

The Broadmoor, Colorado Springs, Colorado: A sprawling resort complex overlooking a mountain-backed lake, with a pink, Mediterranean-style palace as its centerpiece.

The Cloister, Sea Island, Georgia: On a beautiful, beach-lined island, this white stucco, red-roofed mansion has become a honeymoon tradition.

The Grand Hotel, Mackinac Island, Michigan: Geraniums, flapping flags, and white wicker chairs line the long, colonnaded porch of this huge white hotel on the Straits of Mackinac.

The Greenbrier, White Sulphur Springs, West Virginia: A white Georgian hotel, which predates the Civil War, carefully set into rolling green hills.

The Homestead, Hot Springs, Virginia: A brick, southern-style hotel with huge white columns, set over warm mineral springs in the Virginia hills.

Hotel del Coronado, San Diego, California: The first hotel in the world to have electric lights, the Coronado's beachside turrets and terraces have become a San Diego landmark.

The Sagamore, Lake George, New York: A sprawling white clapboard hotel, overlooking the cool, clear Adirondack waters of Lake George.

12
MEXICO

Why is it that smiles seem to come easier down here? That laughs seem to ring louder, that passions seem to run deeper, and that life itself seems to be lived on a whole other plane? Colors seem brighter in Mexico; the brilliant sun-yellow of hibiscus, the rich primrose of an adobe wall, the startling blue of a Caribbean wave. Music soars as you've never heard it before: caressing notes from a solo guitar, a troubadour's aching ballad, the high-pitched blast of a mariachi's trumpet. Even flavors seem more vivid: salty-sweet margaritas, fiery chilis, tangy *mole* sauces. It's no wonder the romance of Mexico has called to couples from Mr. and Mrs. John F. Kennedy, who honeymooned here in 1953, to Rolling Stone Keith Richard and Patti Hansen, who were married in Baja 30 years later.

But back to the first question: Why? It's a combination of things—a blend of Latin machismo, Indian grace, and canny entrepreneurship which transforms your standard vacation into a fiesta. Where you'd normally find a box-shaped hotel room, Mexico gives you a fantasy of tiled walls, sunken tubs, and terraces reaching for the sea. Instead of dull Sunday buffets, mariachis herald you onto sun-splattered patios nearly awash in tequila. And on even the most remote and peaceable beach, someone is bound to come up and offer you a beer.

Mexico boasts a range of honeymoon possibilities that may be the widest—and wildest—in the world. You could spend a week basking on a snow-white Caribbean beach or on one of the Pacific's more exotic coves. You could investigate the mysteries of Mayan ruins or tour the Spanish colonial hill-country. You could watch for whales from Baja's boulder-strewn beaches or sample the cafés of dynamic Mexico City. No matter what kind of couple you are, Mexico has a place that's just right.

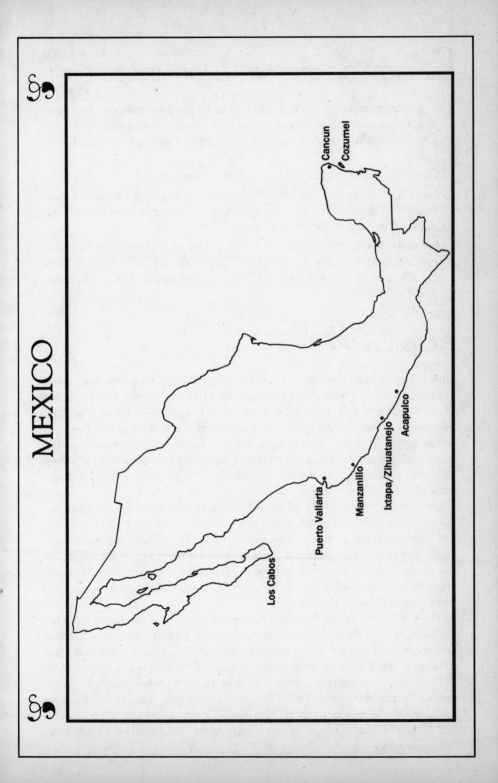

MEXICO

Cancun
Cozumel

Acapulco
Ixtapa/Zihuatanejo
Manzanillo
Puerto Vallarta

Los Cabos

FACTS TO GO ON FOR ALL OF MEXICO ℘

☐ Entry Requirements: You'll need proof of citizenship (passport, birth certificate, or voter's registration). You'll be issued a tourist card when you check in at the ticket counter. Hold it tight—you'll need the card to go home.

☐ Currency: The Mexican peso, which is in constant flux.

☐ Language: Spanish is the official language, though you can get by with English in most resort areas. Nonetheless, everyone will appreciate your efforts if you learn the Spanish basics.

☐ For more information, write: Mexico Ministry of Tourism, 405 Park Avenue, Suite 1002, New York, NY 10022; or call: (212) 755-7261. (There are also offices in Los Angeles, Chicago, Washington, D.C., Montreal, and Toronto.)

Acapulco 🐚

Unless you've been sleeping for the last 20 years, you've got at least a few impressions of Acapulco, that eternally swinging city of the Pacific. Some of them are probably even true: It is often beautiful—a broad blue bay, hillsides of pulsing lights, cruise ships at rest in the harbor. It can be glamorous, especially if you're ensconced in a *casita* at Las Brisas, still one of the world's most romantic hotels. And if your honeymoon dreams involve a deep Mexican tan and a heavy dose of nightlife, you probably won't be disappointed.

On Condesa Beach—*the* place for admiring and showing off taut, tan skin—barefoot girls approach with ceramic birds, parachutes waft overhead, and margaritas slip past your lips with a tang. You adjust your sunglasses, angle your towel, and wonder if there's time for a siesta before showering for the evening ahead. Maybe you'd prefer basking at poolside; recently, hotel pools have been gaining popularity over Acapulco beaches, where the souvenir vendors can be persistent.

The real beauty of an Acapulco honeymoon is that if you never stir from poolside, if your shopping is confined to hotel lobbies, even if you never venture beyond the tacos and tamales, you can still have a great time. But should you want a bit more, this city of one million people has plenty up its sleeve. Some couples rent a jeep and drive to the beaches which flank the town—Puerto Marques and Revolcadero to the south, and Pie de la Cuesta to the north. While not exactly Robinson Crusoe discoveries, the sense of real Mexico comes through in the fishing boats, the thatched food stands, and the families who come to spend the day. Caleta Beach, Acapulco's original resort area, is now a somewhat sleepy enclave that some consider more pleasant than the main tourist strip; boats leave from Caleta for Roqueta island, where the donkeys are rumored to drink beer.

If you don't mind a bit of noise, wander through the city's main market for a look at the brilliant chaos—tubs of flowers, stacks of rubber sandals, stalls piled high with sticky candy, silver jewelry, and Superman pinatas. And pass an hour or so in the town's main *zócalo* (square)—it's an easy introduction to a vital part of Mexican life.

Acapulco evenings can be very quiet affairs—cocktails on your balcony, a ride in a horse-drawn *calandria* decked with balloons. But one of the things that so many people come here for is the sheer wildness of the nights. They can begin with sunset by the beach at Pie de la Cuesta, the perfect spot to begin an evening. You can swing in a hammock, pop open a couple of beers, and witness one of nature's more flamboyant displays. Then ease into the city scene with a toast to the moon from a hotel bar. Restaurants start filling up around 9 P.M., and don't even think about heading out to dance before 11. Most discos don't open till then, and none are crowded before midnight. One favorite is Fantasy, near Las Brisas in the hills; other long-running reliables are BabyO, UBQ, Boccaccio's and Jackie-O. If you'd rather sit back and be entertained, the Gallery hosts a sweet-natured parade of female impersonators.

FACTS TO GO ON 🤟

☐ Getting there: Aeromexico, Mexicana, and American Airlines schedule frequent nonstop service to Acapulco from several U.S. cities, but if you're coming from the eastern U.S., you'll probably need to change planes— usually in Mexico City.

☐ *Bride's* Best Beds

● *Las Brisas:* Carved into the side of a hill, it's the eternal honeymoon favorite, a peaceful compound of pink-and-white *casitas*, private and semiprivate pools, and jaw-dropping views of the Pacific. Very expensive.

● *Acapulco Princess:* Sharing facilities with the Hotel Pierre Marques, and quite a ways from town, the Princess is a huge, pyramid-shaped luxury hotel with an open-air lobby, natural-looking pool, extensive sports facilities, and a gorgeous chunk of beach. Expensive.

● *Villa Vera Hotel and Racquet Club:* This in-town hotel sits on a hill above the hubbub and offers handsome whitewashed villas at relatively attractive prices. Expensive/Moderate.

Ixtapa/Zihuatanejo

Ixtapa is the resort, Zihuatanejo is the town. Together, they form one of the world's unique vacationlands.

Over 100 years ago, the Pacific fishing village of Zihuatanejo rivaled Acapulco for trade with the Orient. Gradually, it relaxed into its still-somnambulent state as a small, tropical port town, where a few cruise ships came calling and a couple of small hotels served the spotty tourist trade. Then came Ixtapa, an almost instant creation of the Mexican government. Conceptualized only 15 years ago, the resort now boasts over a dozen major beachfront hotels, a Robert Trent Jones golf course, a full-fledged tennis complex, shopping mall, and more swim-up bars than you can shake a maraca at.

Most couples mix the best of both worlds, taking in the snazzy show-off along with the quieter cousin. By bus or taxi, it's only 15 minutes from a smooth Ixtapa hotel to Zihuatanejo's long, main pier, where you can hire a fishing boat to take you on a hair-tangling ride over turquoise waters. And after noting that the townspeople really do take their own chairs to the movies, you can head back to your Ixtapa hotel for an air-conditioned evening of steak and vintage wines.

In Zihuatanejo, don't miss lunch on the beach or at the tempting little Villa del Sol hotel. Hire a boat to take you to the beach called Las Gatas, where you'll find a scuba instructor, a restaurant, and a regal past—a Mexican king brought his daughter here on holiday 600 years ago. Come back to wander the back streets, watch a girls' basketball game, and shop for silver and serapes.

In Ixtapa, days are classically resorty. You can golf a round, play tennis in the morning or twilight coolness, and maybe test your courage on a rope-tethered parachute pulled high above the waves by a trusty speedboat. La Puerta's shopping center overflows with ceramic Christmas ornaments, straw hats, onyx chess sets, and Mexican folk art. Later, find a patio with a view, watch the sky change from blue to golden, then plan on dinner in a swank hotel dining room or something more casual in Zihuatanejo.

FACTS TO GO ON

☐ Getting there: Aeromexico and Mexicana fly into Zihuatanejo, usually stopping in Mexico City or Guadalajara.

☐ *Bride's* Best Beds

● *Camino Real:* Boasting splendid modern architecture and a spectacular hillside site, this is Ixtapa's most dramatic hotel. All rooms boast seaview terraces (some with hammocks), grounds are lushly landscaped, and a private elevator takes you down to the beach. Expensive.

- *Villa del Sol:* This Zihuatanejo hotel is a relaxing favorite—bilevel villa suites, baths with Mexican tiles, terraces, and delicious meals. It's right on the La Ropa beach. Expensive.

Puerto Vallarta

For years, Puerto Vallarta was just another small fishing village; it didn't even have a name until 1818. Later, Richard Burton and Elizabeth Taylor came here during the filming of *Night of the Iguana,* and talk of their romance made headlines around the world. Today, some call Puerto Vallarta a little Acapulco. More and more luxury resorts are being built, designer shops have sprouted everywhere, and you can sample food from around the world.

Set about midway down the country's Pacific coast, Puerto Vallarta lies on 25 miles of glorious white sand beaches. Some are social strands like Playa del Sol, a carnival of musical combos, cocktail bars, and young Mexicans selling broiled fish on sticks. You'll find all manner of water sports including sailing, surfing, water-skiing, and parasailing. Other beaches offer total seclusion; try Chino Beach, Las Ampas, or Playa las Estacas for a very private picnic. You can go underwater at Los Arcos and overwater by boat. The *Serape* sails 2½ hours to Yelapa, an isolated beach town without a single road or car. For a look at the dramatic countryside all around—jungly mountains, sparkling waterfalls, and deep, green valleys—rent a jeep and head for Chico's Paradise up in the hills, where you can cool off in the gin-clear pools, talk to the parrot, and sample Mexican fare.

Since most hotels have sprouted to the north and south of town, the village itself remains essentially Mexican. A morning's walking tour will lead you past the busy town square, the crown-topped church, and dozens of attractive shops specializing in bright-colored sportswear and traditional crafts—rainbow-striped serapes, big baskets, and lots of pottery.

Nights usually start out with a pair of sundowners at one of the hotel bars. Or you might opt for a sunset cruise to Mismaloya. Once the sun has made its fabulous descent, move on to a fabulous dinner—an open-air seafood place set on a cliff or elegant Mexican food served in a mansion. Your hotel's nightclub is likely to make a nice nightcap, but at least once, sample the town's neon-zapped discos—Capriccio, DaVinci, or the City Dump.

FACTS TO GO ON 🎵

☐ Getting there: Aeromexico, Mexicana, American, and Frontier all fly to Puerto Vallarta, either directly or with a change in Mexico City or Guadalajara.

☐ *Bride's* Best Beds

● *Camino Real:* Combining the luxury of a total resort with a nice sense of privacy, it's a Puerto Vallarta favorite. Surrounded by gardens, a high-rise contains large, well-appointed rooms looking to sea. Expensive.

● *Hotel Garza Blanca:* With large suites and villas, either on the beach or a shuttle ride away, Garza Blanca tempts with luxury and privacy. Expensive.

Manzanillo 🎵

Not quite halfway between Puerto Vallarta and Acapulco, this dusty little fishing town doesn't quite look like a honeymoon dream. Its narrow streets are crammed with donkey carts, rickety pickup trucks, and sack-toting locals. But outside the busy port, you'll find spectacular scenery—deep green hillsides tumbling down to azure sea—graced with some of the most romantic resorts in all of Mexico.

Most well known of the group is the Mediterranean-styled Las Hadas, where parts of the movie *10* were filmed. Your room is likely to be a split level with a sun-washed terrace and a sweeping view of the bay or a jasmine-scented garden. If you're golfers, its ocean-hugging course may be a touchstone the rest of your lives. There's tennis, too, and a gigantic pool surrounded by chaise longues and umbrellas. Add fresh seafood and magnificent Mexican cuisine to the picture, and you can't lose. Nearby, you can stay in one of Club Maeva's one-bedroom villas and find absolutely everything you need—from a supermarket to a cinema—on the grounds. Another honeymoon favorite is El Pueblito, an intimate time-share resort furnished with ceramics, woven rugs, and Mexican touches.

Though you'll probably be happiest soaking up the rays and paddling around the sudsy Pacific, do build in a little time to explore town. Its stores spill over with Mexican handicrafts like embroidered dresses, straw baskets, and ceramic pots. Stroll around the back streets for the best photo opportunities. And plan to dine out at Manzanillo restaurants like Le Recif (French food, gorgeous ocean views), Osteria Bugatti (Italian and seafood dishes), and El Mariscal, an on-the-beach Mexican spot.

FACTS TO GO ON ✍

☐ Getting there: Aeromexico and Mexicana fly into Manzanillo with connections in Mexico City or Guadalajara.

☐ *Bride's Best Beds*

● *Las Hadas:* See text. Expensive.

● *Club Maeva:* See text. Moderate.

Los Cabos 🐚

At the very tip of Baja California (the long leg of Mexico that's an extension of California, U.S.A.), the familiar world comes to a halt. Barely an inch of rain falls each year. Great whales and marlin swim in the Pacific, while the sea of Cortez shimmers like a vast, blue pond. Cacti bristle on scrubby hills, and colossal rocks cast shadows on curved beaches. If you headed due south, the next piece of land you'd reach would be Antarctica.

While sports fishermen have known about it for years, it's only recently that Los Cabos—the peninsula's southernmost area, encompassing the towns of San José del Cabo and Cabo San Lucas—has taken its place in the Mexican resort scene. Today, couples come for more than a wrestle with a dorado. A collection of luxury resorts lure with swimming pools, beaches, tennis courts, breeze-fanned bars, and suites that open onto endless sea.

There are lovely beaches to discover—the series of tiny crescents at the Hotel Palmilla, the perfect half-circle of sand called the Playa Santa Maria (it's next door to the Hotel Twin Dolphin), and Playa de Amor, a secluded stretch reached only by boat, where the sea of Cortez meets the Pacific. Despite generally heavy surf, there are protected patches for snorkeling, and if you chance to look up rather than down, you'll find the sky hold its own diversions—rare land and sea birds riding the warm currents. Take an hour to walk around San José del Cabo, one of Mexico's prettiest, tidiest towns, where you'll find a block of shops, a shady *zócalo*, and a few antique municipal buildings. In Cabo San Lucas, the harbor and dockside *mercado* are the only real attractions, but if you're looking for silver earrings, Mexican cowboy hats, or wood carvings, it's worth a look.

At sunset, taxi into San Lucas to take in the fiery display from the Hotel Finisterra's Whale Watch Bar. While you'll probably eat at your hotel most nights, you'll find a number of enticing restaurants in both Cabo San Lucas and San José del Cabo.

FACTS TO GO ON

☐ Getting there: Aeromexico, Mexicana, and PSA fly into Los Cabos from Los Angeles.

☐ *Bride's Best Beds*

● *Hotel Palmilla:* It makes beautiful honeymoon sense. A tropically landscaped enclave of airy, Mexican-accented rooms, breeze-cooled bar, and enough sporting possibilities—pool, tennis, croquet, and a whole string of beaches—to keep you happy for days. No phones in rooms, so your wake-up "call" is breakfast delivered to your door. Expensive.

● *Hotel Twin Dolphin:* Dramatically handsome, with suntanned bodies draped around a pool surrounded by desert flora. Looking over the beach, the primary accents are stone, with painted replicas of primitive cave paintings. Expensive.

Cancún

If you close your eyes and try to picture *the* perfect beach, you'll see Cancún. About 15 years ago, the Mexican government selected this once-sleepy fishing village as the site of a master-planned resort. Their reasons: Floating off the Yucatán peninsula in the Caribbean sea, Cancún boasts an enviable expanse of beach, with fine white sand and the bluest, brightest water imaginable. By placing beach hotels on a barrier island, the resort area could be removed from urban hustle. And since Cancún was a blank slate, developers had free reign to design fantasy complexes for luxury-seeking tourists. Today, the results tower all around. Monumental hotels cater to all sorts of whimsies— Mayan pyramids, mirrored monoliths, Disneyesque versions of Mexican villages. With superb beaches, rustling palms, and air-conditioned everything, Cancún has become a Caribbean boom town.

You can practically live on the wide, white beach. Waitresses saunter up, rolling their Rs to make the offer of a margarita sound nearly poetic. Deep-tanned musclemen approach, asking if you'd like to ride a bright parasail across the sky. Others invite you to take a scuba diving lesson or to join a volleyball game. And as a background to it all, piña coladas crunch around in beach-bar blenders, mariachi melodies ride the breeze, and the waves roll in with soothing rumbles.

When you want to dry out a bit, you can putt around the golf course or play a set of tennis. If you're dedicated shoppers, plan to scout Cancún's numerous shopping centers, as well as the open-air stalls behind the convention center, where you can find specialties like *guayabera* shirts for men, *huipil* dresses, Panama hats, and handicrafts from all over Mexico.

You don't have to be history buffs to appreciate the area's bounty of ruins.

Ask your hotel about bus tours to Chichén Itzá, Tulum, and Coba, where you can scramble about the remains of ancient Mayan centers.

Chichén Itzá is the celebrity city; its El Castillo pyramid dominates the scene. Ninety-one steps lead up the terraced sides, and your guide will spout complex formulas, multiplying and adding to get significant sums like 52 and 365, which demonstrate the precision of the Mayan calendar. The Mayans gathered their knowledge of the seasons from careful stargazing, and their domed observatory, El Caracol, remains one of the ruin's most impressive structures. A bit closer to Cancún, Tulum is one of the prettiest Mayan sites—a time-softened fortress towering above Caribbean waves and a beach. Coba rises from tropical jungle to look more like something from Guatemala than a traditional Mexican site.

Back in Cancún, restaurants occupy two different camps. There are the hotel-zone restaurants (hotel-associated, elegant, requiring reservations) and the in-town restaurants (casual, less expensive), an inexpensive cab ride from your hotel. Later, head to a hotel nightclub, or stroll along the beach lit by a wide Mexican moon.

FACTS TO GO ON 🎧

☐ Getting there: Aeromexico, Mexicana, United, Continental, and American offer nonstop or direct service to Cancún from several U.S. cities.

☐ *Bride's* Best Beds

● *Hotel Camino Real:* For sleek, simple, sophisticated design, Camino Real is Cancún's most impressive hotel. Shaped like a low pyramid, one side faces the ocean, the other a tropical lagoon. Add tennis, pool, busy bars and restaurant, and you'll start to see what this first-class place is all about. Expensive.

● *Villas Plaza:* A cluster of pink-and-white villas with landscaped walkways, Villas Plaza looks like a gentrified Mexican village. Rooms are large, and look over Cancún's nicest stretch of beach—between Punta Cancún and Punta Nizac. Expensive.

● *Cancún Sheraton Resort:* A fabulous sporting complex, boasting suites that come with Jacuzzis and its own little Mayan ruin. Expensive.

● *Hyatt Exelaris Regency Cancún:* Known for its towering atrium and split-level pool, this round high-rise is a prime Cancún choice. Expensive.

Cozumel 🐚

In Mayan lore, this island off the coast of Mexico near Cancún, is where life began. In scuba parlance, it's one of the world's best dive sites. And in romantic terms, it's a pure delight, a blend of comfortable resort pleasures and unspoiled charm lapped by translucent Caribbean waters. Because Cozumel was developed as a haven for scuba divers, its atmosphere is essentially casual, with cut-offs and T-shirts outnumbering resort ensembles five-to-one. And a low-key, friendly feeling prevails. In barefoot beach bars, groups chat from table to table. Taxi drivers and bartenders strike up conversations; their smiles cancel out any language barrier. After just a few days here, you'll have made new friends.

Most hotels are on the western beaches, where you'll spend most of your time pursuing a Mexican tan. Scooters are available for touring, but be warned: The average scooter gas tank contains just enough gas to make it *almost* all the way around the island, so you might want to opt for a rental car or taxi-tour instead.

Start in San Miguel, Cozumel's central town. Restaurants and souvenir stores settle around the wide, sun-bleached square, and waterfront cafés make ideal spots to sip cold beers and watch the boats come and go. Then head down to Chankanab Lagoon, where lush botanical gardens provide jungle-shaded paths for quiet strolls. There's excellent snorkeling right off the beach and a selection of shady beach bars. Further down, Playa San Francisco is the island's most popular beach, but it can become noisy. More tranquil shores lie on the east coast of the island. The undertow here can be dangerous, so it's best to pick a protected spot like Punta Morena, whose thatched-roof beach bar serves some of the freshest seafood on the island.

Dry land is just half of the Cozumel picture. Right off the southwest tip of the island, Palancar Reef stretches for six miles through the clear Caribbean. Even if the thought of diving gives you the willies, gather your nerves and give it a shot. The descent into the submarine dream world, with waving sea fans, mushroom-shaped coral, and exotic-colored fish swimming up to your mask, is a thrilling adventure.

Cozumel evenings are enchanting. Head into town, where hanging out and breathing-in the evening seems to be the main order of business. Tucked between restaurants and shops, you'll see Cozumel homes opened up to the street: An old man adjusts his living room sofa so he can watch the passers-by; a huge family plays cards around the kitchen table; a young mother feeds her quiet baby while a Spanish love song plays on the radio.

After dinner, take a stroll along the harborside promenade. Moonlight washes San Miguel's eclectic waterfront so it resembles a misty movie set. Couples sit on the sea wall, whispering and kissing, while boats bob and slurp on their moorings. Stake out your own waterside perch, or follow the sound of music that drifts from alleyways and rooftop discos. In nightclubs tucked between sleeping homes, Cozumel carouses till dawn seeps through the sky.

FACTS TO GO ON ℘

☐ Getting there: Aeromexico, Mexicana, Continental, United, and American fly to Cozumel directly, or to Cancún first, followed by a brief flight to Cozumel.

☐ *Bride's* Best Beds

● *Hotel Mayan Plaza:* A large, ten-floor hotel with lovely rooms overlooking a palm-backed beach. Expensive.

● *Hotel Cozumel Caribe:* Large hotel on the beach, with nicest rooms in the newer tower section. Ask about enticing, all-inclusive packages. Expensive.

● *Hotel El Presidente:* Cozumel's original luxury hotel, with large attractive rooms, a big beach, full sports facilities. Expensive/Moderate.

● *Hotel Barracuda:* Fairly spartan decor, but beachview rooms and very attractive prices. Moderate.

13
CANADA

Look north: sharing our longest border and comprising skyscratching mountains, cosmopolitan cities, and miles of unspoiled seashore, Canada's vast honeymoon territory is as wide and dramatic as you'll find. The thunder of Niagara Falls may have first called to Americans, but lately the allure has broadened. Cities like Montréal and Vancouver entice food-lovers and shopaholics with European flavors and low prices; Canada's Rocky Mountains invite die-hard Colorado skiers to schuss on new slopes; and events like the recent EXPO and winter Olympics keep reminding us that Canadians know how to throw a good party.

Canada's sensations tend to be both foreign and familiar. Like the United States, Canada has drawn its citizens from all over the world. The result: French cafés, Scottish bagpipe players, sprawling Chinatowns, and totem poles left by the Indians who called Canada home centuries before either the squabbling French or British arrived. You can stay in a hotel reminiscent of a French château, snap photos of a distinctly British-looking changing of the guard, even wander through a Caribbean-accented marketplace. At the same time, you'll find small towns that look like Main Street, U.S.A. (a burger is never hard to find), and American pop songs fill the airwaves. Walk into a bar and ask for a list of imported beers and the waiter starts off with, "Budweiser, Michelob, Coors. . . ."

Whether your idea of romance is a blazing ski-lodge hearth, a winding coastal road, or daylong shopping sprees followed by elegant, four-course meals, Canada fits the bill. From the eastern tip of Newfoundland to the western coast of British Columbia, it's loaded with honeymoon possibilities.

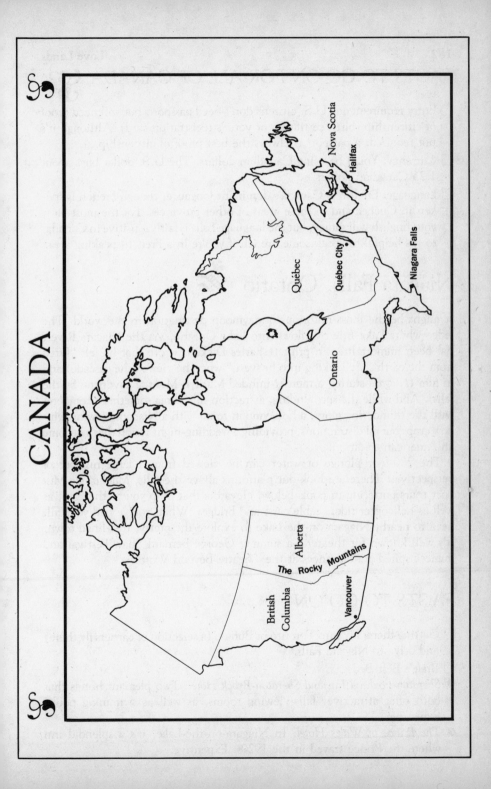

CANADA

Nova Scotia

Halifax

Niagara Falls

Québec City

Québec

Ontario

Alberta

The Rocky Mountains

British Columbia

Vancouver

FACTS TO GO ON FOR ALL OF CANADA ℘

☐ Entry requirements: U.S. citizens don't need passports but will need proof of citizenship (birth certificate or voter's registration card). Although it's not required, a passport is always the best proof of citizenship.

☐ Currency: You'll be using Canadian dollars. The U.S. dollar buys about 1.25 Canadian dollars.

☐ Language: English is Canada's dominant langauge, though French is spoken in Québec and in some areas of other provinces. For the most part, your English will suffice, but the language issue is fairly sensitive in Canada, so it's helpful to speak some French if you're in a French-speaking area.

Niagara Falls, Ontario

It might be the most notorious honeymoon destination in the world. The ledge where Lake Erie overflows into Lake Ontario, via the Niagara River, has been immortalized in print (Charles Dickens wrote that he felt "lifted from the earth . . . looking into heaven," when he viewed the cascade) and in film (*Niagara* starred a murder-minded Marilyn Monroe cavorting by the falls). And while the surrounding, attraction-filled area sometimes competes with the thundering glory, a honeymoon room with a Niagara-viewing window crops out all distractions, providing a wedding-night vision that's become an American tradition.

The 200-foot plunge of water can be viewed from a large number of perspectives: There are look-out platforms above the falls, *Maid of the Mist* boat tours puttering in pools below, elevators that drop you to the base, as well as helicopter rides, cable cars, and bridges. When you've had your fill, head to nearby Niagara-on-the-Lake to explore the pretty, tree-lined town. It's well known for theater—a summer George Bernard Shaw Festival and mime-inspired performances at the Theatre Beyond Words.

FACTS TO GO ON

☐ Getting there: Fly into Toronto or Buffalo (a selection of carriers fly there) and drive to Niagara Falls.

☐ *Bride's Best Beds*

● *Sheraton-Foxhead Inn and Sheraton-Brock Hotel:* Two pleasant hotels that both offer attractive, falls-viewing rooms, as well as swimming pools. Expensive.

● *The Prince of Wales Hotel:* In Niagara-on-the-Lake, it's a splendid inn where the Prince stayed in the 1920s. Expensive.

☐ For more information, write: Ontario Travel, Queen's Park, Ontario M7A 2R9; or call: (800) 268-3735.

Québec City, Québec

In Québec City, the province's capital, you'll want to spend your time within the walls of the tiny old quarter. Passing through its main gates is like entering an eighteenth-century dollhouse world, small and cozy, with old hotels and *pensions*, and streets full of restaurants and shops. It's lively, colorful, and very manageable.

Battles form a great part of Québec's history. For a cogent overview, there's a miniature reinactment at the Museé de Fort. But you don't have to know every date to enjoy a carriage ride on the Plains of Abraham. On the way, look for the "pigeon hotel," the city's imaginative solution for keeping its copper roofs clean.

Shopping is everywhere, especially concentrated in the lower part of town, reached by the steep steps of "Break-Neck" staircase, or the noisy funicular. Two parallel streets, Champlain, and Petit Champlain, and the even tinier *rues* in between, are full of one-of-a-kind shops. At Le Fil du Temps, you'll find elaborate dolls, handmade from their hair wigs to the hems of their handsewn silk petticoats. At Blanc d'Ivoire, on-site jewelers will work your design in silver with ivory or onyx in as little as a day. Sachem carries Québec art and handicrafts, and at the end of Petit Champlain, there's a hole-in-the-wall store that rents mopeds and one bicycle built for two.

Québec City comes alive at night. Music spills from sidewalk cafés as a young woman juggles with firesticks. On the Rue St-Anne, you can sit for a portrait in pastels, or pose for a lightning-fast caricature.

For other sights to see, you might think about reserving an afternoon for the farm country of Île d'Orléans (you'll need a car). Houses there have brightly colored roofs, used for easy ID in the days before postal-route numbers. Have lunch at La Goéliche, with its sunny, glassed-in terrace over the river. Or, depending on the season, fill up on strawberries, roasted corn, or apples at one of the roadside stands.

FACTS TO GO ON ℘

☐ Getting there: Air Canada offers the widest selection of flights to Québec City.

☐ *Bride's Best Beds*

● *Château Fronténac:* A grand, French Renaissance-style hotel, it's the traditional honeymoon choice in Québec City, looking over the St. Lawrence River (ask for a river-view room). Expensive.

● *Québec Hilton:* The gleaming tower of choice for high-rise hotel lovers. Expensive.

● *Manoire Ste-Geneviève:* An intimate, nine-room guesthouse with a very friendly owner, Mme. Corriveau. It's the nicest *pension* in town; if it's booked, you might want to try the St. Pierre, just down the street. Moderate.

☐ For more information, write: Québec Government House, 17 West 50th Street, New York, NY 10020; or call: (800) 443-7000.

Halifax, Nova Scotia 🐚

Ask anyone who's been there about Nova Scotia, and they'll talk about beauty. They'll describe miles of dramatic coastline dotted with salty fishing villages and centuries-old lighthouses. They'll rave about wooded headlands and green pastures that drop sharply into the sea. They'll paint pictures of apple orchards, glassy lakes, and beaches that turn pink at sunset.

Nova Scotia's capital, Halifax, crowds about a harbor at the base of a citadel-crowned hill. You'll need a couple of days to explore its tree-lined streets, waterfront downtown (shiny skyscrapers next to restored historic buildings), and handsome parks. You can take an orderly walking tour of Old Halifax (it starts at Privateer's Wharf) or wander happily on your own. It's an easy city to get to know and enjoy.

Stroll around the Historic Properties on the harbor's edge; it's full of galleries, crafts shops, pubs and restaurants. More shopping can be done at Scotia Square, the Maritime Mall, and Spring Garden Place. Visit Citadel Hill and its museums, and picnic in Point Pleasant Park, 186 wooded acres within walking distance of downtown. For a different perspective, sail aboard the *Bluenose II,* a replica of Canada's world-famous schooner; take a helicopter ride; or cruise the harbor with Halifax Water Tours. And when the sun goes down, pick up a copy of the current Metro Guide from your hotel or a tourist information booth for listings of nighttime happenings and the latest restaurants and hot spots in town.

After a few days in Halifax, you'll want to get out and explore the Nova

Scotian countryside. The Nova Scotia Travel Guide (free—it's published by Tourism Nova Scotia) maps out eight sightseeing trails through the province's seven vacation regions, including the Evangeline Trail, the Glooscap Trail, the Sunrise Trail, the Marine Drive, and a trio of routes on Cape Breton Island: the Cabot, Ceilidh, and Fleur-de-Lis Trails. The most popular driving route from Halifax is the Lighthouse Route, winding its way southwest along the sea, past rock-hewn fishing villages, breathtaking views, and seafood restaurants.

The first must-make stop on the Lighthouse Route is Nova Scotia's most photographed fishing village—Peggy's Cove. Here, everything conspires to please you: Sea gulls swoop down to the twinkling water, sea spray leaps from enormous boulders, and brightly painted wooden boats rock gently on washes of inky blue sea. From the boulder-bound lighthouse, you can mail postcards with the special lighthouse stamp. If hunger strikes, chow down on scallops, fresh haddock, or lobster at a cove-viewing restaurant.

Your next stop will be Chester, a small hamlet on the sea; houses are painted Wedgwood blue and green and the Yacht Club bathes in the summer sun. Further along the route, you can drive up to the Cape House Inn for lunch with a marvelous view of Mahone Bay, a multi-steepled town that's especially handsome in the honey-gold afternoon light. Down in town, you'll find lots of antique, gift, and craft shops. Still further along the trail, you'll come to the town of Lunenburg, looming high above a sparkling harbor. Then carry along the coast to Yarmouth, a bustling port and resort town with numerous places to stay, eat and play. From Yarmouth, the Evangeline Trail heads along the Bay of Fundy, through the fertile Annapolis Valley, and back down to Halifax.

FACTS TO GO ON ℰ

☐ Getting there: Air Canada flies in from New York to Halifax direct in summer months, through Montréal in other seasons, and from Boston to both Halifax and Yarmouth. From the rest of the U.S., Toronto and Montréal are connecting points. Or you can take a passenger ferry like the M/S *Scotia Prince* (newly enlarged with honeymoon suites) which makes the overnight run from Portland, Maine, to Yarmouth from May till October.

☐ *Bride's Best Beds*

● *Château Halifax:* Connected to Scotia Square's boutiques and restaurants, it's ideally located. There's a heated indoor/outdoor swimming pool, sauna, and rooms that look over the harbor and Citadel Hill. Expensive.

● *Sheraton Halifax:* Right in the heart of the historic district on the waterfront. Expensive.

- *The Tall Ships Inn:* A pretty Chester staying spot, just minutes from the water. On the Lighthouse Route. If it's booked, you might check the MacNeil Bed and Breakfast. Moderate.

☐ For more information, write: Tourism Nova Scotia, 129 Commercial Street, Portland, ME 04101; or call: (800) 341-6096 or (800) 492-0643 in Maine.

Canada's Rocky Mountains, Alberta

Snapping photos of the Canadian Rockies is like looking at your face in a doll's mirror; there's no way to get the complete image. Frame the picture one way, and you fit that fantastically craggy mountain into the shot, but you chop off the shimmering aqua lake. Frame it another way, and you get the lake plus a herd of grazing elk, but you miss the wall of snow-capped peaks. And the sky—it seems impossible to fit in enough of that brilliant, cloud-tumbled blue. The scene simply doesn't translate to a two-dimensional image; these mountains stretch to the stars and spread in all directions. They're a monumental sight.

The national parks called Banff and Jasper take you through the heart of the Rockies; a honeymoon in this part of Canada usually starts in Calgary, moves through Banff National Park, past Lake Louise and the Columbia Icefield Parkway, onto Jasper National Park. From there, you can either backtrack to Calgary, head over to Edmonton, or cross British Columbia to Vancouver.

Calgary is a cattletown turned oil city; as you approach it from the airport it resembles a miniature Dallas or Denver. It's pleasant but you'll want to move on to the mountains as soon as possible. A stroll through the Stephen Avenue Mall, a visit to the top of the 617-feet-high Calgary Tower, and drinks at the elegant Palliser Hotel are enough of Calgary for most honeymooners (unless you're visiting in early July, when the famed Calgary Stampede turns the city into a wall-to-wall rodeo).

Heading west to Banff, mountains rise from the flatlands—faces of sheer, grey stone with aprons of green pine. The town of Banff sits in a basin where the Spray and Bow River valleys meet. At the base of Tunnel Mountain, overlooking Bow Falls, the landmark Banff Springs Hotel bears the mark of an architect with visions of grandeur. A combination Scottish manse and French château, the huge, stone hotel is a maze of vaulted galleries, grand oil paintings, moose heads, leaded glass, and ocean-liner-sized dining rooms. Elk wander on the golf course, kilted men play bagpipes on the mountain-view terrace, and couples bubble away in the roof-top Jacuzzi.

In town, you'll find Banff Centre (where an arts festival runs in summer), a variety of restaurants, and gift stores with Indian trinkets, fur-lined moccasins, and jade jewelry. You can soak in the odorous waters at the Cave and Basin Centennial Centre or at the Sulphur Mountain Hot Springs, high on a hill. Take a gondola ride up Sulphur Mountain and you'll be treated to a spreading view of Banff, the Bow River, and Spray Valley—a luxurious sweep of pine stretching for miles. The mountains are the principal lures, and you can enjoy them while hiking, river-rafting, horseback riding, golfing, skiing, and biking.

Take the smaller road—1A—from Banff to Lake Louise. It's a quintessential car-commercial road, clinging to the mountainside with twists and hairpin turns. Midway, stop off at the Johnson Canyon Trail, where catwalks have been built into the side of a river-carved gorge, guiding you through deep chasms, over sparkling pools, and under misting waterfalls.

Lake Louise is glorious: a tranquil circle of bright, blue-green water backdropped by a V of pine mountains and a white wedge of glacial ice. Château Lake Louise, a massive hotel at the water's edge, feels a bit like Grand Central Station; *lots* of people tramp through to see the lake. Nonetheless, the wonder of having the lake outside your bedroom window makes it a honeymoon favorite. Louise is splendid to wake up to, her dark surface mirroring the white mountains and pink sky.

The drive from Lake Louise to Jasper is the most spectacular part of this journey. Along the Columbia Icefields Parkway, glacial tongues stretch down from the mountains to lick brazen aqua lakes. Elk and mountain goat graze at the highway's edge. And bold mountains pop up all around: perfect knife-carded wedges, castles with crags and turrets, proud points and razored flat-tops—all dressed in skirts of velvet pine. At the Icefield Information Center, you can pick up free information about hiking trails, scenic drives, and campsites (all of which are beautifully situated and well maintained).

Less tourist traffic makes it to Jasper than to Banff or Lake Louise, so a sense of complete calm prevails. Mountains stretch up on all sides, and the bubbling of the Athabasca River and honking of Canada geese are the only sounds you'll hear. You can take a gondola up Whistler Mountain, hike one of the hundreds of trails, or play 18 holes on an amazingly scenic golf course where each tee-off presents a majestic panorama of peaks and pines. Jasper Park Lodge is the most exclusive staying spot in these mountains. Its log cabins and contemporary suites dot the shores of Lac Beauvert ("beautiful green lake," a modest title, actually, for the heavenly setting). With this lodge as your comforting base, you can ski on nearby slopes, horseback ride through birch forests, paddle around the lake, or just sit in a bright-painted Adirondack chair at the water's edge and soak in the beauty of the place.

FACTS TO GO ON ✎

☐ Getting there: Air Canada schedules the most flights into Calgary; from there, rent a car for the drive into Banff and Jasper National Parks. Since there's just one main highway and a few smaller roads in the parks, it's virtually impossible to get lost once you're outside of Calgary.

☐ *Bride's* Best Beds

● *Palliser Hotel:* In the heart of Calgary, this grand railroad hotel is home to some plush, smartly decorated rooms. A fine city base. Expensive.

● *Banff Springs Hotel:* A veritable castle in Banff, with enough restaurants, dining rooms, shops, and sports facilities to fill a small town. The great stone hotel has a lot of character; most of the rooms are different, and many have been carved out with a great sense of humor. Expensive.

● *Château Lake Louise:* Its splendid location on the lake makes it a honeymoon favorite, and if the rooms are a bit tatty, the public areas are grand. Expensive.

● *The Post Hotel:* In Lake Louise Village, its rooms and dining room are far nicer than Château Lake Louise's, but it can't boast a lake view. Expensive.

● *Jasper Park Lodge:* An utterly peaceful retreat on the shore of Lac Beauvert. Gorgeous new suites and cozy cabins, a spectacular golf course, horseback riding, and tennis. A faithful clientele doesn't mind the very high prices. Expensive.

☐ For more information, write: Travel Alberta, Capitol Square, 10065 Jasper Avenue, Edmonton, Alberta T5J 2Z4; or call: (403) 427-4321 or (800) 661-8888.

Vancouver, British Columbia 🐚

In the same manner that New Yorkers alternately scorn and praise California, Eastern Canadians view Vancouver as their friendly, slightly flakey, but tremendously beautiful, West Coast counterpart. Backed by Grouse Mountain and tickled by the sea, Vancouver has earned a reputation as Canada's most attractive, and liveable, city. It resembles San Francisco more than Montréal or Toronto, and in much the same way that San Francisco acts as a magnet for American youth, Vancouver attracts students and young artists from all over Canada.

You might start with a visit to Gastown, the historic heart of the city. The seeds of Vancouver were planted here in 1866, when "Gassy" Jack Deighton built a barroom near a sawmill for the loggers. What was then a brawling boomtown has become a fashionable neighborhood of galleries, boutiques, and restaurants, where you can sip wine, eat homemade pasta, and shop, shop, shop.

Competing for attention, Chinatown draws you in to its *dim sum* restaurants and tiny, ginger-scented shops. Stanley Park, 1,000 acres of sea-bordered beauty, invites you to walk, bike, fly kites, or simply spread a picnic and lie in the sun. Robsonstrasse is an attractive shopping area to explore; settled by Europeans in the 1950s, it's the best place for *wurst*. If you're still hungry, head over to the Granville Island Market, where Vancouver's gourmets go in search of the pinkest salmon, the greenest lettuce, and the most aromatic cheese. And there's still the aquarium to visit, the Vancouver Art Gallery to explore, and the Grouse Mountain tram to ride for a stunning city view.

At night, you'll feast on seafood of all types—there's salmon galore in this part of Canada. Afterwards, Vancouver has a bit of nightlife for everyone: the symphony plays at the Orpheum, you'll find live bands at the Town Pump, and a mixed crowd mingles, drinks, and dances at Luv-a-Fair.

FACTS TO GO ON ℘

☐ Getting there: A host of major airlines fly into Vancouver. If you're coming from the East Coast, you'll probably connect through Chicago or Toronto.

☐ *Bride's* Best Beds

● *Four Seasons:* A Four Seasons' property, whose elegant rooms and suites boast magnificent views of both town and the surrounding mountains. Expensive.

● *Pan Pacific Vancouver:* Right on the waterfront, with a very impressive sports complex and lovely harbor views. Expensive.

● *Meridien:* Marble baths, glorious views, and pampering service make it an exceedingly comfortable Vancouver hotel. Expensive.

● *Hotel Vancouver:* Built in 1887, the Vancouver is the *grande dame* of town. Elegant and unique. Expensive.

☐ For more information, write: Tourism British Columbia, 1117 Wharf Street, Victoria, British Columbia V8W 2Z2; or call: (604) 387-6417.

14
EUROPE

The European dilemma: Where in this great weave of countries should you head? Rest assured that you really can't go wrong. Though twentieth-century Europeans can build modern eyesores as well as Americans can, virtually all of Europe is beautifully romantic. The main trick is not to spread yourselves too thin. Even if you've never been to Europe before, avoid the whirlwind five-countries-in-six-days tours. Concentrating on one area—maybe staying put all week, or combining a few days in a busy city with a stay in tranquil, quintessentially European countryside—works best for most honeymooners. You'll want the chance to go to a favorite restaurant a second time, or to linger till dusk at an unexpectedly romantic site.

Your European honeymoon can be put together in any number of ways. If time is short, compensate by going all-out in one place—staying at the Ritz in Paris, dining at three-star restaurants every night. If time's no problem but money is, head for traditional good-buy countries like Greece or Portugal, where even a plummeting dollar goes far. If you love the outdoors but don't want to spend your honeymoon in a tent, consider a bicycle tour, and stopping at cozy hotels each night.

Since we can't possibly describe all of Europe in one short chapter, we've opted to outline casually a group of honeymoon favorites—classic honeymoon cities and more peaceful country routes. All are places that would do any wedding trip proud. View them as little tastes—appetizers that leave you hungry for more.

EUROPE

Classic Honeymoon Cities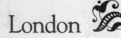

London

Eccentric and elegant, London lives up to many expectations. The taxis are so big you could set up house in the backseat. The Changing of the Guard is enough to make you vote for monarchy—almost. And gazing at the Houses of Parliament, you feel as though you're on the edge of history.

Consider a neighborhood-by-neighborhood approach. You'll probably want to start in Mayfair, where London's most expensive shops, hotels, and restaurants congregate. Regent, Oxford, and Bond streets are the area's most tempting avenues of acquisition; the biggest attractions are Fortnum & Mason for tea at the soda fountain and the silliness of being served by salesmen in morning coats; Liberty for print scarves, ties, picture frames, and anything else you can cover with flowery fabric; Asprey & Company, specializing in extravagant jewels (this is where the royal family gets theirs). Mayfair's mews and sidestreets are home to wine bars and pubs, and if you walk west, you'll come to Hyde Park; on fine days, it's London's favorite lunchtime rendezvous.

Another handsome shopping route takes you from Hyde Park Corner down Knightsbridge to Brompton Road, where Harrods holds forth. Follow Beauchamp Place to Sloane Street, habitat of the notorious Sloane Rangers with their Gucci loafers and pearls. If you want to lunch in their midst, try downstairs at the General Trading Co.; there's a nice outdoor patio for warm-weather dining. For couples who like their clothes and food a bit funkier, Kings Road is lined with dozens of boutiques and a few truly notable stores like Academy, which sells avant-garde British creations such as silk ties painted with tropical fish. Avoirdupois makes a dramatic lunch spot—warm salads, potatoes stuffed with caviar and cream, and champagne by the glass.

Eventually you'll feel compelled to see a museum or two. The eclectic Victoria and Albert's maze of galleries is highlighted by the Great Bed of

Ware, a roomful of Raphael cartoons, and the gory *St. George and the Dragon* altarpiece; trying to find your way out of the museum can be an adventure in itself. Don't miss the Elgin Marbles at the British Museum; Westminster Abbey's hundreds of tombs and memorials—a history lesson in stone; or the Tower of London, rife with tales of torture.

Make a point of sampling London's theater offerings. Pick up a copy of *Time Out*, and you'll know what's happening all over town. West End theaters put on shows most like Broadway's, and though the National Theatre and Barbican (home of the Royal Shakespeare Company) have lately been staging Broadway-type shows of their own, they're usually places to go for revered classics, daring new pieces, and dazzling productions of Shakespeare's best work. Backroom theaters all over town (often located above, in back of, or next door to pubs) stage both classics and innovative works by young playwrights; attending one of these plays will show you just how much young London loves theater, and tickets can often cost less than renting a videotape back home.

FACTS TO GO ON ℘

☐ Getting there: You'll find a wide choice of airlines (British Airways, TWA, Pan Am, American, Air India) flying to London's Heathrow Airport; British Caledonian, Delta, and Virgin Atlantic fly you to Gatwick.

☐ Entry requirements: You'll need valid passports, but visas are not required.

☐ Currency: You'll be paying with pounds sterling.

☐ Language: English.

☐ *Bride's* Best Beds

● *Ritz:* One of London's poshest hotels, boasting a fabulous location—down the block from Fortnum & Mason, a five-minute stroll from the shops of Regent Street, next door to Green Park (Buckingham Palace territory). Very expensive.

● *Savoy:* Comfortable, spacious rooms, a true sense of history, and attentive service make it a London favorite. Very expensive.

● *Blake's:* Victorian on the outside, trendy as can be on the inside, it's an intimate favorite among the young and the restless. Expensive.

● *Hazlitt's:* Three historic town houses joined to form a charming small hotel in the theater district. Moderate.

☐ For more information, write: British Tourist Authority, 40 West 57th Street, New York, NY 10019; or call: (212) 581-4700.

PARIS ♋

You could spend weeks in Paris and not see it all, so make some selections early on. The city's museums are among the world's best. Stop in at the Louvre to see the Mona Lisa and the Venus de Milo—just two of the museum's thousand-plus masterpieces. Venture into the Marais, one of the city's most beautiful neighborhoods, where you'll find the Picasso Museum, seventeenth-century mansions open to visitors, and a flock of youth-minded boutiques and restaurants. Head over to Le Centre Pompidou, loaded with contemporary canvases and video installations (Les Halles, a *Blade Runner*–like urban mall, is right around the corner). And don't forget churches (rose-lit Nôtre-Dame, wedding-cake Sacré-Coeur), shopping (elegant Rue du Faubourg-St.-Honoré, fabulous flea markets at Place d'Aligre and Montreuil), and French feasting (legendary Tour d'Argent, tony Taillevent, and hundreds of bistros all over town).

Explore, but don't hesitate to close the guidebook and savor daily Paris touches—the smell of warm bread wafting from *boulangeries*, lilting voices of schoolboys at play, and walks through twisting streets with cobbled alleys and courtyards. Let the clink of glasses from arch-covered cafés lead you on a tour around Place des Vosges. Focus on children launching sailboats in a Tuileries pond. Notice, on your way home after partying Saturday night, how every turn seems to reveal a couple kissing in the street. Paris turns everyday existence into sensory delight.

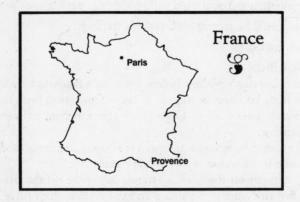

FACTS TO GO ON ℘

☐ Getting there: A host of major airlines, Air France, TWA, Pan Am among them, fly regularly from major U.S. hubs to Paris.

☐ Entry requirements: You'll need valid passports, as well as visas from the French consulate nearest you (Boston, Chicago, Detroit, Houston, Los Angeles, Miami, New Orleans, New York, San Francisco, and Washington, D.C.).

☐ Currency: You'll be paying with French francs.

☐ Language: French. To make snippy waiters a bit more personable, do your best to learn some.

☐ *Bride's* Best Beds

● *Crillon:* One of Paris' *crème de la crème* hotels. Rooms viewing Place de la Concorde are pieces of honeymoon heaven. Very expensive.

● *Ritz:* On oh-so-aristocratic Place Vendôme, the Ritz is—for many wealthy patrons—the *only* hotel in Paris. Half the fun of staying there is being able to say you're staying there. Very expensive.

● *Bretonnerie:* One of few hotels in the fun, fashionable Marais, it charms with beamed ceilings and cozy furnishings. Moderate.

☐ For more information, write: French Government Tourist Office, 610 Fifth Avenue, New York, NY 10020; or call: (212) 757-1125.

Rome 🐚

Act 1: Southern Trastevere, Rome's "village." You are wandering in the late-afternoon light, past an open-air mechanic's shop, past cheerful *trattorie,* past a one-room market displaying inflatable canoes, soccer balls, and giant boxes of Dash. At a second-story window, the local diva sings a few phrases from a familiar score. Mamas hush their quarreling children. You smell something wonderful—warm bread and rosemary. It could be the perfect setting for a spaghetti sauce commercial.

Act 2: Via Condotti, Rome's most fashionable street. Your shopping bags are heavy with Armani clothes and Pratesi linens. You sit at a café, call for a couple of lemon sodas, and watch the parade—wealthy matrons dripping gold chains, elegant businessmen sprinting across the street, gaggles of foreigners consulting maps. You're intent on finishing postcards, but a red handbag catches your eye and you're off, American Express card flashing in the sun.

There are lots of Romes. At first, you're overwhelmed with the top level—the slick, stylish glamour of modern Italy. But just beneath the surface gleam

remnants from a gloriously sensual Renaissance, and beneath that, the solemn beauty of Romanesque bell towers. Go deeper below the Middle Ages, and you'll find memories of early Christians. And deeper still, Rome's trademarks—ruined temples, arches, and baths—invite you to step back 1,500 years and more.

You'll want to do it all—skip down the Spanish Steps, wander through the Colosseum, gaze up, up, up at the dome of St. Peter's, toss coins and soak sore feet in the Trevi Fountain. But since the joys of Rome are often the joys of the table, you'll find some of your most memorable moments come over a bottle of Frascati wine and a tomato-and-mozzarella salad. A trio of musts: a chocolate *tartufo* at Tre Scalini, on the Piazza Navona, served with a view of terra-cotta buildings, wrought-iron balconies, Chinese-red geraniums, and Bernini's splendid fountain; a rooftop dinner at the Hassler or Eden hotel, from which you see the swallows swooping as domes and steeples fade to a skyline of shadows; late-night coffee at one of Doney's sidewalk tables on the Via Veneto, while all of Rome takes its evening stroll.

FACTS TO GO ON

- ☐ Getting there: Alitalia, Pan Am, and TWA all regularly fly from major U.S. cities to Rome's Leonardo da Vinci Airport.
- ☐ Entry requirements: You'll need valid passports, but no visas are required.
- ☐ Currency: You'll be paying with lire.
- ☐ Language: Italian. Try to learn some; Italians get a great kick out of hearing you speak their language, no matter how feeble your attempts.

☐ *Bride's* Best Beds

● *Hassler–Villa Medici:* Offering the best location in town (at the top of the Spanish Steps), a jet-set clientele, stupendous views from high-up rooms and the rooftop restaurant. Very expensive.

● *Eden:* Its extremely nice staff makes it a favorite luxury choice for staying, drinking (on a lovely rooftop patio), and dining. Two brothers own and manage the place, and they invite *Bride's* readers to stop by and see the hall porter with questions about Rome. Expensive.

● *Grand Hotel:* Part of the posh CIGA chain; visiting heads of state stay here. Expensive.

● *Parco dei Principi:* Modern in design, near the Via Veneto and Borghese Gardens; its quiet feel makes it a calm honeymoon choice. Moderate.

☐ For more information, write: Italian Government Travel Office, 630 Fifth Avenue, Suite 1565, New York, NY 10111; or call: (212) 245-4822.

Venice

If you've been to Venice with friends, you know its art, food, and charm. You may even have known romance. But it is only as a lover that you *really* know the city—a place to be savored and made yours.

Reconcile yourselves to getting lost and take off, crossing bridges, veering down alleys, letting yourselves stray over to a pretty group of café umbrellas or into the light coming from an open square. Venice's canals—the essence of romance—are a pathfinder's hell. Even Venetians get confounded.

It is always easy to find your way back to Piazza San Marco, where, every once in a while, the pigeons seem to fly in sync with the café orchestras. This may seem the time to sit down and order a Bellini (champagne and peaches), but first take a good look at the Basilica di San Marco, with its shimmering mosaics; one shows how relics of St. Mark were smuggled into Venice under a layer of pork. If you like art, or history, or both, take a tour of the Doges' Palace (doges were Venice's rulers), linked to the old prisons by the Bridge of Sighs.

It's a rare Venetian who's taken a gondola ride—considered much too expensive and touristy. But since you're on your honeymoon, you have every right to indulge in this pretty nonsense. Bring plenty of lire (it's roughly $50 an hour). Or go native and hop a *vaporetto* (a motorboat—the closest thing to a city bus) as it cruises along the Grand Canal or out to the islands.

You won't want to stop on the funeral island of San Michele, but it is strangely beautiful, with its black hearse gondolas and ladies carrying bouquets of flowers. Much more cheerful is Burano, the island known for its lacemakers. Its houses are a paintbox come to life—lavender, blue, mustard, olive, brick-red. Wander off the main canal, and you'll see sweet scenes of everyday life: pots of daisies on a white windowsill; a mother jiggling her baby's carriage; children in rubber boots looking for mussels. If you love fine linens, this is the place for lace bedspreads and embroidered napkins.

Torcello is a very different island, almost abandoned save for an extraordinary restaurant. Torcello's Byzantine cathedral shelters a tall, elegant mosaic Madonna. The church next door feels more intimate, and if you come on a Saturday, you may see a bride heading down the gravel path there on her father's arm. This could be the setting for a final Venetian splurge: lunch at Locanda Cipriani. First order drinks and take them into the garden. You can see how the zucchini and roses are doing, and then sit on a bench admiring the backdrop—the Byzantine roofs of the church and cathedral. If you choose your seats carefully, it will be quiet, except for the buzzing of bees and the faint clink of cutlery, and as the scent of herbs floats out of the kitchen, you'll know you've arrived.

FACTS TO GO ON 🜋

☐ Getting there: Fly Alitalia, Pan Am, or TWA into Milan, and board a train for Venice.

☐ Entry requirements, currency, language: See Rome.

☐ *Bride's* Best Beds

● *Cipriani:* The finest hotel in town is not *in* town; the Cipriani maintains its chic privacy on an island five minutes from Piazza San Marco. Pampering touches are everywhere: white peaches at breakfast in the summer, padded, fabric-covered walls in the bedrooms. New junior suites have big sundecks. Very expensive.

● *Gritti Palace:* With elegance aplenty, this Renaissance palace is famed for its canalside dining. Expensive.

● *Danieli:* It lures with a Gothic courtyard and a storied past—a fourteenth-century doge used to call it home. Expensive.

☐ For more information, write: Italian Government Travel Office, 630 Fifth Avenue, Suite 1565, New York, NY 10111; or call: (212) 245-4822.

Vienna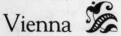

Three of man's most important pursuits—music, art, and food—are Vienna's lifeblood. Cab drivers, businessmen, and waitresses alike flock to the Philharmonic and the Symphony, to the Vienna Boys' Choir, to light operetta at the Volksoper, and to elaborate evenings at the Opera House.

Spend a day or two simply indulging. Cafés and pastry shops are a way of life in Vienna, so you should savor as much as possible. Café Landtmann is the oldest, most ornate coffee spot; painters hang out at the Café Museum; and a bohemian crowd frequents Café Hawelka. For pastry, Hotel Sacher's sinful Sachertorte has become a legend, Demel will send treats to your friends back home, and Kurcafé-Konditorei im Oberlaaer Stadthaus is acquiring a reputation as Vienna's best dessert den.

With a potent dose of chocolate in your blood, it's time to explore. The heart of Vienna rests inside the Ringstrasse, or Ring—wide boulevards that follow the lines the medieval city walls once traced. Visit the "dancing" white Lipizzaner horses at the Spanish Riding School; step inside the glittering Museum of Fine Arts (Kunsthistorisches Museum) with its rooms of Breughels and luminous Raphaels; climb the towers of St. Stephen's Cathedral for a Vienna vista. When you're ready to eat again, The Three Hussars (Zu den Drei Husaren) is Vienna's most elegant eatery, and sausage stands all over town purvey good, inexpensive eats.

FACTS TO GO ON 🎵

☐ Getting there: Royal Jordanian (ALIA) flies nonstop from New York to Vienna. Austrian Airlines, as well as other European airlines (Swissair, Lufthansa, KLM), fly from European hubs to Vienna.

☐ Entry requirements: You'll need valid passports, but no visas are necessary.

☐ Currency: You'll pay with Austrian schillings.

☐ Language: Austrians speak German, though many in tourist areas also speak English.

☐ *Bride's* Best Beds

● *Sacher:* The 100-year-old Sacher boasts rococo styling, personable service, and one of Vienna's best addresses. Though the rooms are not huge, the elegance of the building and its elite clientele make it a wonderful Vienna staying spot. Expensive.

● *Bristol:* Its large, luxurious rooms look over the Ringstrasse. A top-notch Vienna hotel. Expensive.

☐ For more information, write: Austrian National Tourist Office, 500 Fifth Avenue, New York, NY 10110; or call: (212) 944-6880.

Amsterdam 🦁

Amsterdam seems like a carnival ride. Hurrying taxis and hordes of cyclists in a city designed for slow-moving barges give it a wild, weaving pulse. While shopping on some streets you may find yourself crowded up against spike-haired punks and rosy-faced grandmothers. Beer-drinkers and sun-soakers fill the squares. And on narrow stone bridges, artists restore their creative juices with a toke and a gaze into the impressionistic ripples of the canals. With musicians on every street corner, stores loaded with blue and white delft, gabled canal houses poking every which way, and baked goods that'd do Alice B. Toklas proud, Amsterdam is one huge, happy party.

Some romantic respite from all the hubbub: Spread a picnic in Vondelpark, among the tulip blooms and shady groves. Or seek out a Sunday-morning coffee-concert for a gentle reintroduction to daylight after a wild Saturday night. Splendid museums (the Rijksmuseum, home of Rembrandt's *Night Watch;* the modern Van Gogh Museum, with an admirable collection of the master's work; the Stedelijk Museum, Amsterdam's contemporary art space)

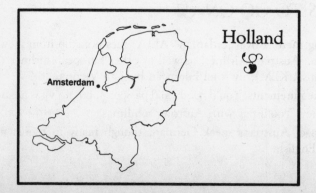

Holland

Amsterdam

offer moments of quiet enlightenment if you arrive early in the day. You'll spend many hours exploring the nooks and crannies of canal-rimming streets— pausing on bridges, snapping photos of strangely peaked roofs, peeking into residential barges (some brightly bohemian, others architect-designed). A visit to the Anne Frank House should not be missed; prepare to be deeply moved.

When it comes time to eat, Amsterdam sets a beautiful table. Not only can you gobble *rijsttafel* (an Indonesian rice dish, an Amsterdam specialty), but festive narrow streets serve up an international buffet. Head to Sama Sebo for *rijsttafel*, Dorrius for Dutch, the Oester Bar for seafood. You'll also want to sample Amsterdam's "brown cafés"—warm, informal spots for imbibing (Randeraat's is a romantic favorite). Nightlife centers around Leidseplein and Rembrandtsplein, where clubs, pubs, and smoky cafés offer a music and a crowd to please every (we mean *every*) sensibility. And hokey nighttime canal cruises, under sparkling bridges, past row after row of drowsy canal houses, earn Amsterdam a permanent place in the Honeymoon Hall of Fame.

FACTS TO GO ON ☙

☐ Getting there: KLM offers the widest variety of U.S.–Amsterdam flights.

☐ Entry requirements: You'll need valid passports, but visas are not required.

☐ Currency: You'll be paying with guilders (a.k.a. florins).

☐ Language: Dutch is the national language, but most people in Amsterdam also know English.

☐ *Bride's* Best Beds

● *Amstel:* One century old, overlooking the canals, it tops the list for old-fashioned grandeur. With a lovely restaurant, fine rooms, and friendly staff, romance is assured. Expensive.

● *Apollo:* Oriented toward the canals—the lobby opens onto one, the bar looks over five. Expensive.

● *Pulitzer:* A group of old canal houses were gutted, then woven together to make this twisty, quirky, hotel. Expensive.

☐ For more information, write: Netherlands National Tourist Office, 355 Lexington Avenue, New York, NY 10017; or call: (212) 370-7360.

Dublin

In theaters and pubs, and on sidewalks, you'll be seduced by a language that really does lilt. Dublin is as welcoming a city as you'll find anywhere, especially at sunset, when the Georgian squares and the buildings of Trinity College seem gilded, lit from within.

To begin, you'll want to wander freely and check out pubs like O'Donoghue's and the Bailey. But when you feel that some proper exploring is called for, pick up a copy of *Tourist Trail* and follow the signposted route to little Halfpenny Bridge (the nearby Bad Ass Café is a young lunch spot); Trinity College, whose library contains the luminous Book of Kells; Merrion Square, where both Oscar Wilde and William Butler Yeats once lived, bordered by Georgian buildings whose fanlight-crowed doors are a deep rainbow of reds, greens, and blues.

You might step inside the National Gallery, home to Hubert Pugh's earthy *Elegant Figures Drinking and Smoking in a Brothel.* Round the corner lies the National Museum, with its splendid collection of Celtic gold—necklets, torcs, and eight lustrous balls—conjuring up strange visions of ancient people shimmering against the rocks and the green.

Some Dublin moments you really shouldn't miss: an hour's stroll in St. Stephen's Green, where all the city seems to take lunch; an evening at the Abbey Theatre, where the Irish literary renaissance found its home; and a pint at Mulligan's (the country's best Guinness), Doheny & Nesbitt's, or Davy Byrne's, where Leopold Bloom had his Gorgonzola and burgundy. For major meals, Patrick Guilbaud's and Le Coq Hardi are among Dublin's most elegant eateries; the Celtic Mews is candelit, quiet, and somewhat less pricey. The Abbey, out of town in the seaside village of Howth, caters to locals and tourists alike in its warm pub, dim-lit restaurant, and spirited ballad room.

FACTS TO GO ON ஒ

☐ Getting there: Aer Lingus flies direct from New York to Dublin.

☐ Entry requirements: You'll need valid passports, but no visas are required.

☐ English is spoken everywhere, though Irish (Gaelic) is the official national language. Nowadays it's spoken mainly in the west.

☐ Currency: You'll be paying with Irish pounds (Punts).

☐ *Bride's* Best Beds

● *Shelbourne:* Dublin's finest address. The junior suites, with pretty antiques, elegant baths, and half-canopied beds, are very romantic. Expensive.

● *Berkeley Court:* Just out of town amid green gardens, this is Dublin's most luxurious staying spot. Expensive.

☐ For more information, write: Irish Tourist Board, 757 Third Avenue, New York, NY 10017; or call: (212) 418-0800.

Country Charmers

England's Cotswolds

Some of the most beautiful British honeymoons happen in the Cotswolds, west of London. Pick up a car from Heathrow and you can be in the midst of honey-gold towns and manicured fields in about an hour. While busloads of charm-chasing tourists descend on the shoppes of Broadway and Stratford-upon-Avon, you might prefer a four-street hamlet like Woodstock, where quail hang outside butcher shops and The Feathers invites you to bask in bedrooms that are a study of country chic. Then take days at your own pace—maybe see Blenheim Palace, where Churchill was born, a rambling estate surrounded by parkland that looks like an oil painting come to life. Head for the Slaughters—Upper and Lower—where you can spend an hour or two peeping in windows and drinking up their unstudied charm. Burford is full of expensive antique shops and ancient almshouses; Moreton-in-Marsh retains an honest, working atmosphere; Chipping Campden's restored streets show you the details of English life a century ago. But to really understand the gentleness of the country, abandon your car and walk a piece of the Cotswold Way, a series of footpaths that lead through pastures, walled-in fields, and Roman ruins, and lets you encounter the land as pilgrims did in Chaucer's day.

FACTS TO GO ON ℘

- ☐ Getting there: You'll enter the Cotswolds after a short drive from London's Heathrow Airport.
- ☐ Entry requirements, currency, language: *See* London.
- ☐ *Bride's* Best Beds
- ● *The Feathers:* Our favorite Cotswold hideaway, in Woodstock, with nooks and crannies to get lost in, blazing hearths, and a pair of companionable dogs. Expensive.
- ● *Cottage in the Wood:* A mansion in Malvern, the epitome of English country life. Expensive.

- ☐ For more information, write: British Tourist Authority, 40 West 57th Street, New York, NY 10019; or call: (212) 581-4700.

France's Provence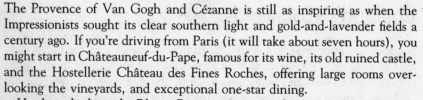

The Provence of Van Gogh and Cézanne is still as inspiring as when the Impressionists sought its clear southern light and gold-and-lavender fields a century ago. If you're driving from Paris (it will take about seven hours), you might start in Châteauneuf-du-Pape, famous for its wine, its old ruined castle, and the Hostellerie Château des Fines Roches, offering large rooms overlooking the vineyards, and exceptional one-star dining.

Head south along the Rhone River to Avignon, for a tour of the immense Palace of the Popes, some dawdling time in Place de L'Horloge cafés, and a browse among the antique shops. Next stops: the Pont du Gard, a remarkable Roman aqueduct between Nîmes and Arles (bring swimming things, the river is clear and cool); Nîmes, with its Roman amphitheater; and Tarascon, famed for its medieval château and a must for lovers of Souleiado's hand-blocked fabrics—the local workshop sells them at about one-third of prices at home. In Arles, take a turn through the Arletan Museum; slightly dusky and almost deserted, it will give you an in-depth view of the land.

Driving due east, you'll come to Les Baux, site of the most famous court of love of the fourteenth century; now in ruins, it is surrounded by lunar landscapes of unearthly beauty. Then, straight on to the city of Aix-en-Provence, where you'll applaud the street performers on the shady Cours Mirabeau; pay your respects at Cézanne's small atelier; and sup in a bistro serving fresh-from-the-garden Provençal fare.

FACTS TO GO ON ꧁

☐ Getting there: Fly into Paris and head south; or jet into Marseilles (Air France flies there), pick up a car, and drive north to Provence.

☐ Entry requirements, currency, language. *See* Paris.

☐ *Bride's* Best Beds

● *Hôtel d'Europe:* A sixteenth-century palace in Avignon, loaded with antiques and tapestries. Moderate.

● *Oustaù de Baumanière:* In Les Baux, this superb hotel's flowers, sports facilities, and excellent restaurant mean that it's often booked months in advance. An unforgettable place. Expensive.

● *Hôtel Jules César:* In Arles, once a convent, it's now a comforting hotel with a fine restaurant. Moderate.

☐ For more information, write: French Government Tourist Office, 610 Fifth Avenue, New York, NY 10020; or call: (212) 757-1125.

Spain's Andalusia 🌿

Southerly Andalusia is Spain at its most classically romantic. Whitewashed villages seem in danger of tumbling down mountainsides, orange blossoms explode over patio walls, pitchers of cool sangría wait to restore tired travelers.

Start in Seville, the ultimate Spanish town, where flowers bloom in mad profusion, young girls practice flamenco in white courtyards, and guitar notes spill out of smoky taverns. You can get a bird's-eye view of it all from atop the Giralda, an ancient Muslim minaret. A short walk will bring you to the fourteenth-century Alcázar (palace). Spend some meandering time in its acres

Spain

Andalusia

of artfully landscaped gardens with their wide terraces, graceful fountains, and arcades of lemon and orange trees. And there's still more to see: an old Jewish quarter, the Barrio de Santa Cruz, laced with antique alleys and ringing with wine-induced song; Parque María Luisa, a park on the banks of the Guadalquivir River, fine for a cool stroll in the late afternoon; and Calle de las Sierpes, a street reserved for pedestrians and lined with shops.

After a day or two, take off for Granada, with an overnight stop at the small mountain village called Ronda. Granada can be deceptive at first glance. Modern and businesslike, it will make you wonder why you bothered. One look at the Alhambra will tell you why. A palace of stunning beauty, it is the Moorish rulers' tenderest gift to Spain. Take a morning to wander about the complex of sun-splashed patios and gilded chambers, past reflecting pools that were once filled with quicksilver, and through royal bedrooms where sultans napped. The next day you might explore the Moorish neighborhood called the Albaicín (white houses, flowers, pocket-sized plazas) or drive up the road leading to Sacromonte, where Gypsies live in whitewashed caves.

Finally, Córdoba teases your senses to life. Its cobbled streets, wrought-iron grilles, and gold-stoned mansions could be the background for a love story. Start at the Mezquita, a grand mosque built by the Moors and later "improved" by the Christians, who plopped a Baroque cathedral into its center. Still, the original beauty is wondrously intact—a forest of pillars and red-and-cream arches, with a gilded prayer niche and streams of sunlight and shadow. Make your way to the Alcázar, where Ferdinand and Isabella received Columbus before his famous voyage. Its garden is a fantasy of cypress trees, goldfish ponds, and wide terraces. Follow the flowery streets of the Judería to the square called El Zoco; once a *souk*, it is now home to a handsome craft center and a modest café. After a bit of *tasca*-crawling in the student quarter and a dinner of lamb and honey, ride a carriage home under the Andalusian moon.

FACTS TO GO ON 𝕾

☐ Getting there: Fly Pan Am, TWA, or Iberia to Madrid, then board a connecting Iberia flight to Seville.

☐ Entry requirements: You'll need a valid U.S. passport, but no visas are required.

☐ Currency: Pesos.

☐ Language: Spanish.

☐ *Bride's* Best Beds

● *Alfonso XIII:* A grandly restored, palatial place in Seville, with fountains, hand-painted tiles, and beautiful service. Expensive.

- *Parador Nacional de San Francisco:* In Granada's Alhambra, the San Francisco Convent is a museum of a hotel that you'll love. Book *far* in advance. Moderate.
- *Parador Nacional de la Arruzafa:* A contemporary garden-set *parador* (government-owned inn) just outside of Córdoba. Moderate.

☐ For more information, write: National Tourist Office of Spain, 665 Fifth Avenue, New York, NY 10022; or call: (212) 759-8822.

Central Portugal

With towering castles, red-roofed towns, and acres of olive groves, Portugal offers a number of dramatically romantic—and surprisingly economical— touring routes. This, through the country's central hills, is our favorite.

Sintra, a short drive from Lisbon, welcomes you with a pair of pretty castles. From the center of town (twisting cobbled streets, exquisite tilework), you can hike up to the mountain perches. The first *castelo* is a Moorish mass dating back to the seventh century, proudly looking over the countryside; inside, thick stone walls lead up to a ceiling painted with magpies, commissioned by a king to laugh at ladies-in-waiting who gossiped below. Farther up the hill, the Palácio da Pena boasts yellow minarets and a fabulous view of Lisbon and the sea.

Heading out of Sintra, you'll drive through storybook countryside. Windmills spin, red-tiled roofs bake in the sun, and horse-drawn carts clop to market. Head for Óbidos, a polished-up medieval hamlet, walled on all sides, with streets so narrow that you can stretch to touch buildings on both sides. At one end of town, you'll find stairs that lead up to the top of the city ramparts, from which you'll look down on the ancient white and orange village.

Portugal

From Óbidos, head to Batalha, site of the Santa Maria de Vitora monastery. It's a grand place, all turrets and buttresses, oddly contrasting with the sounds of old pop songs floating in from the adjoining square. Then stop for a brief visit at the fishing village of Nazaré, where you'll be one of many camera-snappers. The broad slab of beach, boats painted in bands of green, yellow, and red, and the fishermen going about their daily net-repairing make it a lovely interlude.

From there, it's a hair-raising drive (it wouldn't be a honeymoon without one) to the Buçaco Forest, whose sky-reaching cedars tower into enchanted colonnades. The Hotel Palácio, in the middle of the forest, is one of the high points of this entire tour; the palace was once a hunting lodge, and now it's a dream of a hotel with crystal chandeliers, arches, tilework, and suites straight out of your honeymoon fantasies. Stay as long as you can.

From Buçaco, head into the mountains—tall, majestic, with great polished boulders, and purple and yellow wildflowers. Then, down to flat, dry terrain on roads lined with cork and olive trees. Steer toward Estremoz—all white-washed buildings whose doorways rise like stairs on steep, cobbled streets. An overnight at the Pousada da Rainha Santa Isabel will leave you feeling like royalty.

On your way back to Lisbon, you'll drive through flat country—all wheat and sheep, with cloud-ruffled skies and bells ringing in the wind. If you're not quite ready to reenter busy Lisbon, make one last stop in Évora—a sleepy town whose Pousada dos Lóios provides yet another fairy-tale night.

FACTS TO GO ON 🎀

☐ Getting there: TAP (Air Portugal) and TWA fly to Lisbon from New York. Pick up a car at the airport, and you're off.

☐ Entry requirements: You'll need valid passports, but visas are not required.

☐ Currency: You'll be paying with escudos.

☐ Language: Portuguese (good luck!), but with some hand-waving, diction-ary-flipping, and pointing, you can eventually get by with English. Learn whatever Portuguese you can.

☐ *Bride's* Best Beds

● *Hotel Palácio de Seteais:* In Sintra, it was once a king's summer home; now it's an exceedingly romantic inn. Moderate.

● *Pousada do Castelo:* In Óbidos, this inn has just six rooms, so reserve early. It's gorgeous. Moderate.

● *Hotel Palácio:* In the Buçaco Forest, its fantasy setting, princely rooms, and lavish meals make it out of this world. Moderate.

- *Pousada da Rainha Santa Isabel:* In Estremoz, with grand oil paintings, massive vaulted ceilings, and spectacular views of town. Moderate.
- *Pousada dos Lóios:* Once a convent, now yet another stunning, impossibly romantic inn, in Évora. Moderate.

☐ For more information, write: Portuguese National Tourist Office, 548 Fifth Avenue, New York, NY 10036; or call: (212) 354-4403.

The Italian Riviera

It may sound fearfully glamorous, but Italy's Riviera can be as unpretentious as a town you can't reach by car (no roads) or a walk to a lighthouse bordered by evergreens. Before Liguria (the region of the Italian Riviera) became chic, its seaside villages were nothing more than fishing towns—albeit very beautiful ones. It is this side of the Riviera that honeymooners love.

Having heard that, you'll probably want a hotel in a resort town: in Portofino, the real jewel hereabouts, or in Santa Margherita, an inexpensive bus ride away.

Arriving in Portofino by night is like walking into an Italian opera set. Frescoed houses hug the harbor—a semicircle of five- and six-story buildings painted rose, lemon, and cantaloupe. Sleek yachts tie up at the docks; you could jump from their decks into the boutiques. Tanned couples relax in harborside cafés, on low chairs originally designed for fishermen repairing their nets. A castle glows on a hill. It is all reflected in the water, doubling the magic.

Santa Margherita is a less exclusive resort, but still a stunner. Young Italians whiz by on motorbikes; older ones on bicycles. In the fish market, sardines, squid, and snails lie in great piles. Down on the public beach—a strip of gray pebbles—an elderly woman in a polka-dot dress sits on a fishing boat, while her grandson eats a sandwich, oblivious to the hundreds of sunbathers around them.

Honeymooning here is a matter of sampling the restaurants (order the *tagliatelle al sugo di pesce*—seafood pasta—at the Trattoria dei Pescatori; and try anything at Batti), doing the shops (Fendi, Mario Valentino), and getting tan. But one day, take the train to Riomaggiore for a walk back through the Cinqueterre (Five Lands). It's an all-day hike, showing you a side of Italy that's all but gone—five villages living on natural time, fishing, farming, and holding their ears as the trains whistle by.

Riomaggiore's "Street of Love" leads by the sea (sometimes so green it looks like food coloring) to Manarola, where you can make your first stop—perhaps for bread and wine. The main street is lined with fishing boats in crayon colors. Manarola to Corniglia is a tough, fragrant walk through a whole landscape of dusty pastels. You can stop for a swim just before entering Corniglia, which involves a walk up what seems like the longest staircase on earth. The reward: a café, a bottle of chilled wine, and a smiling waiter who could have been dressed by Missoni—proof that even in a town without cars, Italians know their style.

FACTS TO GO ON

☐ Getting there: Fly Alitalia, TWA, or Pan Am to Milan, then take a train to Santa Margherita Ligure–Portofino.

☐ Entry requirements, currency, language: *See* Rome.

☐ *Bride's* Best Beds

● *Splendido:* In Portofino, set on a hill overlooking the water. Terraces offer a view of olive trees and the aqua-blue port; the pool is big and cool; the food is some of the best in Italy. Very expensive.

● *Grand Hotel Miramare:* In Santa Margherita; honeymooners are welcomed with flowers and champagne. Expensive.

☐ For more information, write: Italian Government Travel Office, 630 Fifth Avenue, Suite 1565, New York, NY 10111; or call: (212) 245-4822.

Greece's Cyclades

Not a cloud in the world dares float across these skies all summer long. Each day is clear, bright, and blindingly blue. In the Cyclades, just one family of Greece's fabled isles, you can go to the beach every day—guaranteed. Beyond that, it's up to you. On the island of Mykonos, for example, a special list of

dos and don'ts applies: If you want to dance on tables, you do; if you want to try on a fabulous fur coat, even though it's 90 degrees, you do that, too. If you don't want to wear a bathing suit, you don't; if you don't want to get up until one in the afternoon, you don't do that either. (Since Mykonos nightlife is pretty wild, you'll be in good company). Mykonos loves to outdo itself—the beach named Paradise is done one better by another called Super Paradise.

Days on Mykonos are meant for leisure, pure and simple. What is there to do but roll out of bed, eat breakfast at an hour when you'd normally eat lunch, head to the beach as the sun mellows in the afternoon, watch sunsets with your drink of choice, dine in any of a score of open-air restaurants, then dance until dawn seeps through the sky? Nothing. A beautiful nothing that can be interrupted, if you like, by visiting any of the island's 300 churches or by poking through shops or by simply admiring the sheer beauty of Mykonos town—a jumble of whitewashed cubes, accented by bright blue railings and the even brighter blue of the sea.

To the people who stay all summer long, nothing can surpass Mykonos. But others find the unabashed strutting that some visitors indulge in, as well as the sheer abandon of the nighttime scene, a bit overwhelming. Not to worry, for there are plenty of islands to choose from. The temples and mosaics of Delos beckon to those with history on their minds. Santorini is another true beauty, with the cliff-perching town of Thira, wonderful beaches, and Akrotiri—a whole town that lay buried until recent excavations. And that still leaves partying Ios, peace-loving Amorgos, fertile Naxos, Andros, Tinos, and a host of others. If you've got islands on your mind, you've come to the right place.

FACTS TO GO ON ⚐

☐ Getting there: First, fly to Athens. Olympic Airways flies from Athens to Mykonos and Santorini. Boat service from Piraeus, the port of Athens, can bring you to almost any island you choose.

☐ Entry requirements: You'll need valid passports, but no visas are required.

☐ Currency: You'll be paying with drachmas.

☐ Language: Greek, but you'll find English is spoken where you need it.

☐ *Bride's* Best Beds

● *Caro Tagoo:* On Mykonos, near the harbor. Moderate.

● *Leto:* On Mykonos, in town. Moderate.

● *Atlantis Villas:* On Santorini. Expensive.

☐ More about beds: We've listed a few hotels on the islands, but the Cyclades are famous for their own beauty rather than that of their accommodations.

Hotels tend to be simpler, and less expensive, than in other resort areas. Some people prefer to (a) rent clean, cheap rooms from local families (they meet you at the boat or plane with offers), or (b) rent a villa (contact the Greek National Tourist Organization for details).

☐ For more information, write: Greek National Tourist Organization, Olympic Tower, 645 Fifth Avenue, 5th Floor, New York, NY 10022; or call: (212) 421-5777.

Ireland's Connemara and County Clare 🦡

Luckily for you, Shannon International Airport sits in the heart of western Ireland. Surrounded by mossy fields and the remnants of great castles, it's smack in the middle of grand touring country. Rent a car and head off (on the left-hand side, *please*) to what may be the world's greatest gift to jet-lagged romantics: Dromoland Castle, in Newmarket-on-Fergus, a handsome temple of hospitality. Spend a day strolling the velvet lawns, cantering over the hills, maybe taking in Bunratty Castle with its medieval chambers. While Bunratty's nightly banquets are a bit too orchestrated for some tastes (though we defy anyone not to be moved by the music—or the snuff), the laughs at Durty Nellie's are as genuine as the pub's intensely Irish clientele.

Heading north into County Clare, you encounter a land of stone-striped fields, silver bays, and meadows yellow with blossoming gorse. Route 18 leads north to Ennis; from there turn west, toward the seaside town of Liscannor, with its flagstone-fenced farms and narrow, boat-slapped harbor. A bit farther north lies a monument to Cornevilus O'Brien ("Horny Corny" according to the locals) and the Cliffs of Moher. Aquamarine water crashes against a wide ribbon of cliffs while seagulls drift across the striated face. On a clear day, you can see the Aran Islands; if not, console yourselves with apple tart and cream in the cottagelike tourist office.

Then wend your way to the Burren, where orchids and cranesbill bloom in a lunar landscape, and intrepid hikers sometimes come across the graves of early Christian hermits. Corkscrew Hill will lead you to Gregan's Castle hotel and on still to Ballyvaughan, where a covey of rentable cottages invites you to abandon your itinerary and get into country life—fishing, touring, and spending evenings at Moran's, in Kilcolgan, a waterside pub noted for its snugs (tiny rooms for private imbibing) and Galway oysters—sweet as the sea itself.

The city of Galway enchants with its musical pubs, back lanes, and approachable scale. Spend a few hours browsing through town; don't miss Kenny's for Irish books and Stephen Faller for Claddagh rings—two hands clasping a heart. Claddagh itself, across the river, is the oldest part of town. Other sights include the crumbling Spanish Arch; the Lynch Memorial Window, where a skull and crossbones marks the spot of a notorious hanging; and Lynch's Castle, a sixteenth-century townhouse.

You might pop into the pub called Seagan Ua Neachtain; its slightly seedy benches are often filled with actors from the Druid Theatre, intellectuals, and "those who fancy themselves such," as one bartender puts it. Other good imbibing spots: Cullens, featuring very traditional folk music; King's Head, lighter, with plenty of audience participation. For serious sustenance, the Malt House serves fish in a cozy setting and sends ladies home with a flower.

Leaving Galway on the western coast road, you drive through the resort town of Salthill ("Slots of Fun") to Connemara, a land of ancient ways and throat-catching beauty. Stone walls run helter-skelter down to the water, mountains and sea meet in the mist, and a pewter light washes everything— one-room cottages, limpid bays, hills purple with heather. Most Connemara folk still speak Gaelic and live exceedingly simple lives—fishing, raising bullocks and sheep, cutting peat from black fields. If you're tempted to stay awhile, estatelike hotels such as The Zetland and Cashel House make exquisite bases. Then you're free to really discover a pair of perfectly mated wild swans, frothing waterfalls, inky, cold streams, and valleys as green as Shangri-la. All in all, it's as pensive a landscape as the old fishermen who lean on their canes and stare out to sea.

FACTS TO GO ON 🔊

☐ Getting there: Fly Aer Lingus to Shannon International Airport, then pick up your car.

☐ Entry requirements, langauge, currency: *See* Dublin.

☐ *Bride's* Best Beds

● *Dromoland Castle:* In Newmarket-on-Fergus, it's a temple of hospitality whose rooms are open to paying guests. It features an 18-hole golf course, horseback riding, and beautiful gardens. Expensive.

● *Great Southern:* In Galway, a large, comforting Victorian hotel on Eyre Square. Expensive.

● *Cashel House:* In Cashel, this blue-trimmed beauty has its own tennis court and romantic, peaceful gardens. Expensive.

● *The Zetland:* In Cashel, overlooking a tidal lake, surrounded by thick woods. Expensive.

☐ For more information, write: Irish Tourist Board, 757 Third Avenue, New York, NY 10017; or call: (212) 418-0800.

15
CRUISING

Today's cruise ships are a privileged breed. Now that airplanes fly millions all over the globe, these luxury-loving vessels are free to pursue lives of pure pleasure. When it's freezing back home, they're prowling Caribbean ports in search of the perfect beach, the sweetest lobster, the tangiest rum punch. In summer months, they head to Alaska for cool mountain sojourns. Like socialites who spend winters in Palm Beach and summers in Newport, cruise ships ply the world's waters decked out in party finery, always ready for a ballroom whirl or black-tie party.

Cruising's life of leisure has prompted experimentation. Some lines have built bigger ships (or enlarged old ones) to make room for *more* on-deck pools, *more* discos, and *more* gourmet eateries. Other lines have added smaller ships to their collections—sleek craft that slip into secluded ports where the biggies can't go. Bolder itineraries mean that cruise ships dock all over the world: South America, Mexico, the South Pacific, Europe, Alaska, Africa, plus dozens of Caribbean combinations. So whether your heart's set on an Atlantic crossing, a cruise up the Nile, or a sampling of sunny, tropical ports, you'll find at least one ship—if not a small fleet—that's heading your way.

With hundreds of cruise ships and even more itineraries, a thorough cruise study could fill a whole book. So instead of drowning you in details, our look at sea life takes a two-pronged approach. First, we'll check out the shipboard scene, introducing you to the universal cruise experience. And then, we'll take a look at three different types of popular cruises—a transatlantic crossing, a Caribbean sailing, and an Alaskan adventure. Whatever ship you choose, you'll find that cruising's primary allure remains constant: the slow-going allure of approaching exotic lands from a most romantic viewpoint—the sea.

Love at Sea

Your first shipboard impressions will generally confirm the old clichés. Yes, that perky blonde in acrylic high heels is your social director. Yes, decks have exotic names like Acapulco, Riviera, and Monte Carlo. Yes, stars like Anna Maria Alberghetti will entertain you. Yes, you'll have a lifeboat drill, complete with ringing bells, floppy lifejackets, with some serious instruction plus a dose of black humor. And yes, the food is everything you've heard— delicious, abundant, and served up to eight times a day by an exceedingly gracious crew.

A steward will teach you the quickest path to your cabin through a maze of corridors. The cabin itself may look smaller than in brochures (cruise company photographers are adept with wide-angle lenses), but examining the unique touches of ship design (raised door jambs; tables edged to keep things from skidding off; Lilliputian sinks and showers) will provide lots of amusement.

Mornings usually start with a moment of disorientation upon awakening (an "if it's Tuesday this must be St. Thomas" kind of feeling). Look out the porthole, and you'll see either waves splashing by or a pretty harbor where you'll spend the day. While you were asleep, one of many shipboard elves will have slipped a newsletter under your door; it tells you about where you are, what activities are scheduled for the day, and whether dinner will be theme-oriented, black-tie, or casual. The first choice you'll face: whether to enjoy a full breakfast in the dining room, a buffet on deck, or room-service coffee and croissants in your cabin.

Your day's options spread like the sea itself. In port, there'll be a bonanza of excursion possibilities—bus tours, helicopter rides, horseback treks, snorkeling expeditions, river journeys, and in-town shopping sprees. Aboard, whether in port or at sea, there'll be a wide range of options. Depending on the size and character of your ship, you'll find exercise classes, slide shows, movies, lectures, bingo games, shuffleboard tournaments, cooking classes, and the like. You always have the option of simply pulling a deck chair into the sun and basking in your own good fortune.

Evenings usually begin with drinks in a sea-viewing lounge, where everyone compares the day's adventures. You'll move on to dinner in the dining room, where there's an early sitting and a late sitting (most honeymooners prefer the late one). Perhaps you'll have a table for two, but usually passengers are seated at group tables; by the time you debark, you'll have some new friends. (If you can't stand your tablemates, the maître d' can change the seating plans.)

After dinner, you'll have more choices to make. There's probably a crooning cabaret extravaganza in one nightclub, quiet piano music in another, and a spirited magic show in a third. Discos tend to get lively later at night. The casino always provides some fun; you can see how long you can make $20 last at the blackjack tables or watch the diehards fritter away big bucks. There'll be a midnight buffet, graced by a huge ice sculpture or a champagne waterfall, where you can fill up once again. On some nights there'll be special parties; you'll be amazed how even the most reserved passengers shed their inhibitions on masquerade nights (a shy secretary dons harem pants and does a belly dance; a retired couple dresses up as Sonny and Cher to sing "I Got You, Babe"; and a woman from Arkansas shakes pom-poms and belts out her college hog-call cheer, "Pig, pig, pig, sooooeeeeeuuuy!"). If you prefer peace and quiet, walk out on deck to watch as the ship slices through water. A wide moon and the shimmer of the sea itself make a powerfully romantic potion.

Three Sea Journeys

A Caribbean Cruise

The velvet-green islands and pure turquoise seas of the Caribbean call to more cruise passengers than almost any other place in the world. Because Caribbean cruises are so popular, newlyweds will be faced with a fantastic choice of ships and routes, ranging from Royal Caribbean's giant *Sovereign of the Seas,* which sails from Miami to popular ports like San Juan and St. Thomas, to Windstar Sail Cruises' intimate *Wind Star,* which sails from Fort-de-France, Martinique, to the hideaway islands of St. Lucia, Mustique, Bequia, and the Tobago Cays.

Whatever route you choose, you'll fly down to Miami or San Juan (or, in the case of some smaller ships, to St. Thomas, Martinique, or Santo Domingo) to meet the ship. As you are about to land, you might fly right over the ship, lit up like a Christmas tree and sending rays of brilliance over the bay; you'll feel a tremendous sense of anticipation.

From the moment you board, life revolves around the golden sun and aqua seas. Shipboard time is divided among sunning at poolside, sipping rum punches, and gazing through binoculars at islands that glide by the ship's rail. Days in port vary from island to island. Dock in San Juan, and you'll explore the streets of Old San Juan, where you'll buy hand-carved wooden *santos,* snap photos at the El Morro fortress, and look for bargains on gold jewelry. Dock in St. Thomas, and you'll gather together your traveler's checks for a whirling duty-free shopping spree. Dock in Mustique, and you can dine at the elegant Cotton House, and see where Princess Margaret and Mick Jagger built their homes.

Most cruises try to include a stop in a deserted cove for passengers to barbecue, snorkel, or bask on the silky sands that made the Caribbean famous. Excursions are planned to let you see the islands from every angle: from 50 feet underwater on scuba trips; from a horseback perch, as you ride along the beach; from air-conditioned buses that tour all around; or on your own, as you wander through bright-colored streets, venturing into busy markets and basket-filled crafts shops.

Caribbean nights are especially beautiful. Even horn-tooting capital ports soften in the moonlight. The sea turns to black satin, and the outline of island peaks looks soft, smooth, and otherworldly. Whether you're whooping it up in the nightclub, or just strolling round and round the decks, island evenings will fix themselves in your mind; the rustling palms, the light on the water, the breezes on tanned skin are sensations that stay vivid for a long time to come.

A Transatlantic Crossing

Crossings are not cruises. No rum-punch parties by the pool, no "San Juan Highlights" slide shows, no Baked Alaska parades in the dining room. Instead, you'll be reminded of shipboard scenes from *Brideshead Revisited*, as tuxedoed gentlemen and jeweled ladies nibble caviar while their ship slices through the Atlantic night.

Cunard's *Queen Elizabeth 2* is the only ocean liner providing regular transatlantic service today, taking you from New York to Southampton, England (or vice versa), in six days, May through November. And while you won't find a floating Versailles (crystal chandeliers and gold leaf are in short supply), there is a sense of Old World gentility that comes from shopping in the *QE2*'s branch of Harrods and from knowing that an English nanny is tending the babies on board, that the Golden Door spa is toning your muscles, and that Elizabeth Arden is waiting to varnish your nails.

A program slipped under your door each morning helps you plot your time: It could be leg lifts at the spa or a massage or an introductory computer course. There are movies and lectures by bona fide celebrities (Barbara Walters, Meryl Streep, and Art Buchwald have spoken on board), games of Trivial Pursuit, and a respectable library. When the weather cooperates, there are deck sports; at other times you can console yourselves with food or by settling into a couch or deck chair for an hour of staring out to sea.

Six days at sea may sound like a honeymoon eternity, especially when the Atlantic is acting up and it's too rough to venture outside. But stormy sailings are not the rule (play it safe by avoiding crossings in late autumn), and no voyage on the high seas would be complete without at least one sudden tilt of the ship and a troupe of fox-trotters sliding right off the dance floor.

One tradition, more than any other, lends a *QE2* crossing its own anachronistic charm. This is the class system. Unlike cruises, crossings have always had two price levels, with First Class passengers enjoying larger staterooms, more rarified dining, and access to some spaces lower-paying, Transatlantic Class passengers can't use. First Class is also *very* expensive, so you'll have to decide whether unlimited caviar, stewards at your beck and call, and deck chairs reserved for sweet little you are really worth it. But for couples with money to burn, there's really no grander way of running away to sea.

An Alaskan Adventure

Today's Alaska-bound visitors turn to cruise ships because they offer a decidedly un-Alaskan level of luxury. And in a state where infinite icefields and snow-glazed peaks can make road building impossible, cruising the Inside Passage makes great sightseeing sense. These floating hotels can bring you face to face with Alaska's glacial wonders, quirky pioneer towns, and the endless spread of waterside mountains that edge America's final frontier.

You'll sail from Vancouver, Seattle, or San Francisco, and after several days at sea, Columbia Glacier comes into view. From high white-striped mountains comes a huge sweep of ice—jagged, swirling, and curving to the deep blue of Prince William Sound. The ship floats silently while everyone oohs and aahs. When a chunk of ice breaks off the tip, the crew hauls it on deck and plops it in the swimming pool.

The ship steams down to Valdez for tours at the Alaska Pipeline Terminal, then sails for Seward. Named after the man who purchased Alaska for about two cents an acre, the town sits in the shadow of Mount Marathon, where beer-happy locals race to the summit every July 4. Seward shore excursions include a motorcoach tour to cosmopolitan Anchorage and a helicopter trip over Bear Glacier and the Harding Icefield—a lake of snow that's a thousand feet deep. You can browse through gift shops that sell native crafts, gold jewelry, and novelty moose-nugget gifts. Those thirsty for local color head to the Yukon Bar, where big bearded men trade raunchy jokes, and their waist-tall dogs leap up onto bar stools at the snap of a finger.

Excitement peaks in Juneau, once Alaska's foremost gold-rush town and now its capital; the city comes alive in summer months. A mass of camera-toting passengers heads straight through the historic district to the Red Dog Saloon, a re-created miners' hangout, complete with honky-tonk piano, moth-eaten moose heads, and sawdust on the floor. Juneau also boasts many of Alaska's best shore excursions. River raft trips, salmon bakes, gold mine tours, and wilderness lodge adventures are all popular. But the helicopter sightseeing trip to Mendenhall Glacier may be the most thrilling of all. You fly over row after row of monumental glacier teeth, finally landing on a spot where you can walk on the glacier and drink from its icy pools.

After Juneau, you'll cruise down to Ketchikan, where houses on Creek Street perch on stilts above the water. Totem poles stand tall in the nearby state park, and seaplanes are forever landing just off the ship's rail. Board a seaplane for a ride that lands on a secluded mountain lake, the pinnacle of piney serenity. Back on board, there'll be a last-night bash, everyone partying hard, determined to celebrate as the ship leaves Alaska's frontier charm for the cosmopolitan beauty of Vancouver.